The sustainability of development in Latin America and the Caribbean: challenges and opportunities

UNEP

Economic Commission
for Latin America and the
Caribbean

Regional Office for
Latin America and the
Caribbean

Santiago, Chile, July 2002

Libros de la CEPAL

68

The following persons contributed to the preparation of this document

ECLAC	UNEP Regional Office for Latin America and the Caribbean
Substantive coordination	
Alicia Bárcena Ibarra	Ricardo Sánchez Sosa
Authors	
Roberto Guimarães	Julia Carabias Lillo
Guillermo Acuña	Fernando Tudela Abad
	Enrique Provencio
	José Luis Samaniego Leyva
Consultants	
Antonio Elizalde	Manuel Rodríguez Becerra
Ramiro León	Ronald Vargas Brenes
Collaborators	
Jean Acquatella, Hugo Altomonte, Ernesto Espíndola, Gilberto Gallopín, José Javier Gómez García, Arthur Gray, Ricardo Jordan, Arturo León, Jorge Mattar, Carlos de Miguel, Niels Holm-Nielsen, Georgina Nuñez, María Angela Parra, Verónica Rengifo, Jorge Rodríguez, Marianne Schaper, Claudia Schattán, Miguel Villa, Ricardo Zapata	Raúl Brañes, Exequiel Ezcurra, Oscar Ramírez, Jorge Ronzón, Rossana Silva Repetto, Kaveh Zahedi

United Nations Environment Programme
Regional Office for Latin America and the Caribbean (UNEP)
Boulevard de los Virreyes 155, Lomas de Virreyes, CP 11000, Mexico City, Mexico
Tel. (52) 5 202 6394 - 5 202 4841 Fax (52) 5 202 0950
E-mail: unepnet@rolac.unep.mx
http://www.rolac.unep.mx

United Nations Publication
LC/G.2145/Rev.1-P
ISBN: 92-1-121357-6
Copyright © United Nations, July 2002. All rights reserved
Sales No. E.02.II.G.48
Printed in United Nations, Santiago, Chile

UN2
LC/G.2145/Rev.1-P

Contents

Tables, figures and boxes

Tables

Figures

Boxes

Foreword

The United Nations Conference on Environment and Development was held in Rio de Janeiro, Brazil, in June 1992. This conference, which has also come to be known as the "Earth Summit," marked the beginning of a new round of world conferences focusing on the analysis of development problems. This "new social cycle" of United Nations conferences was launched in response to the wishes of Member States and has led to a renewal of efforts first made 20 years ago to find solutions to the most pressing problems coming to the fore on the global stage. These conferences have also contributed to the ethical and political consolidation of a cooperation regime based on new international legal principles.

The Conference in Rio de Janeiro laid the groundwork for a new world consensus on sustainable development and on global conventions dealing with emerging issues such as biological diversity and climate change. In the course of this process, an awareness of the environmental aspects of development, which had traditionally been quite limited or entirely absent in the region, gradually percolated into the public and political spheres. The preparatory activities and the Conference itself involved many civil society organizations, bringing together more than 18,000 citizens from around the world.[1] This led to the creation of institutions and to the formulation of government strategies and policies for the promotion of sustainable development. It also prompted steps to address this issue within the spheres of education, culture and the media. More recently, the concept of sustainable

---

[1]   Bárcena (1999) analyses the importance of the involvement of civil society organizations in the Earth Summit and in other global conferences.

development has been incorporated into subregional cooperation agreements and into the practices of economic agents, particularly large business enterprises.[2]

The Earth Summit marked a major shift away from the approach that had previously been taken to the development of a system of international public law relating to global environmental problems. Up until that time, attention had focused on the oceans, the protection of species through restrictions on international trade, and nuclear threats. During this period it took an excessively long time for countries to sign and ratify international agreements —and consequently for those agreements to enter into force— and accession was not universal. By contrast, the instruments agreed upon at Rio de Janeiro were rapidly adopted and, where applicable, ratified by virtually all the countries. As a result, they have been implemented without delay and, what is more, have been incorporated into national legislation.[3]

Despite this progress, the principles of environmental protection and sustainable development are still viewed in many sectors as a constraint on economic and social development, which has limited governments' ability to control pollution and to halt the increasing environmental damage being done to critical ecosystems. Most of the explicit environmental policies now in effect, as well as the direct and indirect regulatory instruments in use in the region, are essentially reactive in nature. Prevention and incentive policies aimed at improving environmental quality as it relates to industrial competitiveness have received far less attention. Furthermore, environmental institutions are only just beginning to create the capabilities they need to achieve the goals set out in these agreements in terms of the formulation of effective cross-sectoral and subregional policies and to strengthen the international negotiating position of the countries. The consequences of this institutional frailty are particularly serious when the relevant environmental impacts are associated with the export structure and the economic strategies of countries and subregions.

Five years after the Earth Summit, a special session of the United Nations General Assembly was held to evaluate the progress achieved since 1992. This conference, which was popularly known as "Rio+5" (New York, 23 to 28 June 1997), was attended by representatives of some 180 countries, including 44 heads of State and Government. The participants in this meeting found that the progress made in implementing the Rio agreements had been quite modest. Furthermore, they noted that the advances that had been made

---

[2]   See ECLAC (2000a, chapter 13) for an analysis of the implications of the Earth Summit for environmental management in the region.
[3]   See UNEP (2001d and 2000) for an analysis of the evolution of environmental legislation in Latin America and the Caribbean in the 10-year period since the Earth Summit.

had more to do with capacity building than with actually halting worldwide environmental deterioration.

Ten years on from the Earth Summit, the Latin American and Caribbean region has taken no more than the first few steps along the path towards sustainable development. The region was enthusiastic in signing on to the commitments made at the Summit in 1992 and set in motion a number of initiatives to implement the Rio Declaration and Agenda 21, but not enough has yet been achieved. This process has been followed not only by national Governments, but also by many civil and business organizations, universities and research centres, as well as numerous local governments, which have become more and more involved in its implementation as time goes on. There is still, however, much to be done and many new challenges to meet, some of which did not exist at the time the Conference was held. One of the distinctive features that sets today's international context apart from those times is undoubtedly the consolidation of the globalization process, in which the region is now fully involved. In many circles, globalization is viewed as an inevitable process. Although it is true to say that its main driving force is technology and the expansion and integration of markets, it is no less true that globalization is not a force of nature, but rather the outcome of processes directed by human beings. This process therefore needs to be controlled and placed at the service of humanity. In order to accomplish this, it will have to be carefully managed —managed by sovereign countries at the national level, and through multilateral cooperation at the international level (Annan, 2000).

It is clear that existing patterns of production and consumption are socially, economically and environmentally unviable. The region is faced with the enormous challenge of devising strategies and setting priorities aimed at the formation of a global alliance and a renewed, enhanced commitment to the Rio consensus by rekindling the spirit of cooperation between developed and less developed societies. This spirit has been the subject of much rhetoric, but little action.

Pursuant to General Assembly resolution 55/199, the international community is preparing for a World Summit on Sustainable Development, to be held in Johannesburg, South Africa, in August and September 2002, 10 years on from the Earth Summit. This is a good opportunity to take stock, analyse what has taken place over the last decade, evaluate the progress made, think about what tasks lie ahead and explore new forms of cooperation that can speed the transition towards sustainable development.

In Latin America and the Caribbean, preparations for the World Summit began, as agreed by the General Assembly, with national evaluations of the progress made in applying Agenda 21 and the Rio Declaration. These assessments, which were then continued at the subregional level, culminated in the Regional Preparatory Conference of Latin America and the Caribbean for the World Summit on Sustainable Development, held in Rio de Janeiro on 23 and 24 October 2001.

This regionwide preparatory process has enjoyed the support of the Economic Commission for Latin America and the Caribbean and the United Nations Environment Programme, together with the collaboration of other specialized agencies and programmes of the United Nations system. One of the steps in this process was the preparation of an overview of the status of sustainable development efforts in Latin America and the Caribbean since the Earth Summit. The substance of this overview, which was submitted to the Governments of the region for their consideration, was largely drawn from national and subregional meetings. These meetings were unprecedented in processes of this type and served to enhance the countries' participation, as well as enabling them to identify the main stumbling blocks and the prospects for a future platform of action.[4] Civil society has been one of the major contributors to the process through its participation in national sustainable development councils, equivalent organizations and meetings held at subregional events, which have provided an opportunity for the region's main groupings to air their views.

This revised version of the above-mentioned overview is now being published in book form by the two organizations as a contribution to the region's ongoing efforts to identify the major obstacles to progress in this area, along with future prospects and challenges.

The Johannesburg Summit will provide the Latin American and Caribbean countries with an excellent opportunity to consolidate their achievements, strengthen their commitment to making regional contributions to global solutions and revitalize the hope that a conference of this nature can serve as the cornerstone of an alliance for sustainable development.

Klaus Töpfer   José Antonio Ocampo
Executive Director   Executive Secretary
UNEP   ECLAC
United Nations   Economic Commission for
Environment Programme   Latin America and the Caribbean

---

[4]   See (UNEP, 2000c), in particular Decision 17, where the Governments accept the offer made by UNEP and ECLAC to support the regional preparatory process for the World Summit on Sustainable Development (UNEP, 2000d), which provides a detailed account of the regional preparatory process for the World Summit on Sustainable Development to be implemented with the support of UNEP, ECLAC and other agencies within and outside the United Nations system.

Summary

The original aim of this study was to serve as an input for the Regional Preparatory Conference of Latin America and the Caribbean for the World Summit on Sustainable Development, which took place in Rio de Janeiro, Brazil, on 23 and 24 October 2001.

This document was produced by the United Nations Economic Commission for Latin America and the Caribbean (ECLAC) and the Regional Office for Latin America and the Caribbean of the United Nations Environment Programme (UNEP). In preparing the study, national preparatory activities and inputs from subregional meetings were taken into account. Those meetings, which were unprecedented in processes of this type, encouraged the countries to play a dynamic role in the preparations and enabled them to identify the main stumbling blocks to progress in this area, as well as the prospects for a future platform of action for sustainable development in the region. A major contribution to the process was also made by civil society through its participation in national sustainable development councils and in meetings held at subregional events, which provided an opportunity for the region's main groupings to air their views.

The first part of the document reports on regional economic performance, focusing in particular on economic growth and public finances. It also analyses the relationships and effects of capital flows, economic openness, trade and integration processes. The main trends in social development in the 1990s are then described, with consideration being given to topics such as regional employment, income and land distribution, public social spending and the social challenges to be met as the region works towards sustainable development.

Population dynamics and the challenge they pose to governments and societies are also examined, together with the relationship between population, on the one hand, and resources and carrying capacity on the other, regional migration and spatial trends in human settlements.

The environmental situation in the region is analysed from the point of view of natural ecosystems, water resources and, in particular, their availability in the region; pollution is considered in relation to its effects on air, water and land, and special attention is given to energy trends in the region and their relationship to global climate change. The socio-environmental vulnerability of the region is then discussed.

With regard to the institutional framework, the development of environmental and sustainable development policies are studied, and the stance adopted by the countries in the region in regard to global environmental problems and the multilateral regime of environmental accords is explored.

The second part of the document contains more specific proposals and suggests what kind of role the region might play in a global alliance, taking into account the progress that has been made and the remaining challenges, within the framework of the region's own agenda and the global agenda.

In the final section, proposals are made for future action, in relation to the opportunities and challenges facing the region in terms of sustainable development. These proposals take the individual characteristics of the countries concerned into account based on an analysis of issues such as the protection and sustainable use of natural ecosystems, biodiversity and access to genetic resources, vulnerability, water and energy management, urban issues and the need to strengthen the institutional underpinnings for a sustainable development process.

This document is not intended to provide an exhaustive evaluation of how Agenda 21 and the Rio Declaration have been implemented in Latin America and the Caribbean. Instead, it simply seeks to present an overview of the progress made towards sustainable development, particularly the most significant aspects, and an assessment of the challenges and opportunities that should be taken into account with a view to the adoption of future measures, after the Johannesburg Summit.

Introduction

Far-reaching changes were made in the international agenda in the early 1990s. The turning point in this process was marked by the United Nations Conference on Environment and Development (also known as the "Earth Summit" and the "Rio Summit"), which was held in Rio de Janeiro, Brazil, in 1992. This meeting laid the foundations for a new world view of sustainable development and of global conventions on emerging issues such as biodiversity and climate change. In the course of this process, an awareness of the environmental aspects of development, of which there had been little or no evidence in the region until that time, gradually percolated into the public and political spheres. A wide range of civil society organizations, bringing together more than 18,000 citizens from around the world, took part in the preparatory activities and the Conference itself.

These advances notwithstanding, in many sectors the principles of environmental protection and sustainable development are still seen as a constraint on economic and social development, and this has limited Governments' ability to control pollution and to halt the increasing environmental damage being done to critical ecosystems. Most of the explicit environmental policies now in effect, as well as the direct and indirect regulatory instruments in use in the region, are essentially reactive in nature. Prevention and incentive policies aimed at improving environmental quality as it relates to industrial competitiveness have received far less attention. Furthermore, environmental institutions are only just beginning to develop the capabilities they need to achieve the goals set out in these agreements through the formulation of effective cross-sectoral and subregional policies and to strengthen the international negotiating position of the countries.

Almost 10 years on from the Earth Summit, the Latin American and Caribbean region has taken no more than the first few steps along the path towards sustainable development. The region was enthusiastic in signing on to the commitments made at the Summit in 1992 and set in motion a number of initiatives to implement the Rio Declaration on Environment and Development and Agenda 21, but not enough has yet been achieved. This process has been followed not only by national Governments, but also by many civil and business organizations, universities and research centres, as well as numerous local governments, which have become more and more involved in its implementation as time goes on. There is still, however, much to be done and many new challenges to meet, some of which did not exist at the time the Conference was held.

The study entitled "The sustainability of development in Latin America and the Caribbean: challenges and opportunities" was prepared by ECLAC and the UNEP Regional Office for Latin America and the Caribbean for submission to the Governments participating in the Regional Preparatory Conference of Latin America and the Caribbean for the World Summit on Sustainable Development (Johannesburg, 2002), which was held in Rio de Janeiro on 23 and 24 October 2001. Drawing upon national processes and the results of subregional meetings, this study reviews the situation with respect to sustainable development in the region since the Rio Summit. The organization of subregional preparatory meetings, which had never been a feature of processes of this type before, encouraged the countries to become active participants and helped them both to identify the main types of problems that have been encountered and to outline a future platform of action. An important contribution to this process has also been made by civil society through such activities as participation in national sustainable development councils and in meetings held at subregional events which have provided an opportunity to learn more about the positions of the region's main groupings.

The nine chapters of this study provide an overview of the region's economic performance as well as tracing the main trends seen during the 1990s in its social development, population dynamics, environmental conditions and situation with respect to socio-environmental vulnerability. It also analyses changes in public policies on the environment and sustainable development, the international framework and the role of the region in a global alliance. It concludes with a series of proposals for future action.

In strictly *economic* terms, over the last decade the Latin American and Caribbean countries have undergone a process of change that has included sweeping economic reforms directed towards liberalizing trade, national financial markets and cross-border capital flows and giving private enterprise a central role in the production of goods and services and in the provision of public services and social benefits. In 1990, production activity in the region began to make a recovery , and many inflationary and destabilizing pressures gradually waned as the region emerged from the "lost decade" in its economic development process. The region's overall growth rates have, however, remained far lower than they were before the debt crisis. In addition, as a result of their close linkage to international capital cycles they exhibit a marked degree of volatility.

A review of the situation in the region reveals clear progress in the area of public finances, and this is reflected in substantially smaller deficits and more careful public debt management. Serious problems remain, however. Generally speaking, the tax burden is low and in many cases taxes are based on volatile income streams whose growth has tended to be slow. What is more, rates of tax evasion and avoidance are high. In addition, the weak fiscal structure existing in most of the countries is accompanied by fragile national financial systems and low national savings rates which have shown no increase since the 1980s. The region's main economic achievements have been in the areas of export growth, the revitalization of trade and investment within subregional integration schemes, and the conclusion of a large number of free trade agreements with other countries and regions. The weaknesses that remain are a consequence of the region's insufficient degree of export diversification, its small share of world trade, the many barriers to free trade that still exist, and the adverse effects that financial and macroeconomic volatility have on the growth of trading activity.

In the *social* sphere, during the 1990s the Latin American and Caribbean region witnessed a consolidation of the demographic transition and the progressive ageing of its population. Poverty was reduced in relative terms but job creation was sluggish and the level of inequality increased in a number of countries. On the other hand, progress was made in promoting gender equity and increased participation by women in the labour market. In addition, there was an upswing in social investment, and major reforms were implemented in social policies and sectors. It has become clear that the inability of the economic growth process to satisfy the social requirements of sustainability is due more to a *development style* —and the patterns of production and consumption that it engenders— than to annual growth rates as such. In other words, while it is true that the reactivation of growth seen over the last decade has fallen short of what is required to meet the growing needs of a still-expanding population, this should not distract attention from the structural aspects of socio-economic conditions in the region. What this situation indicates is that historical patterns of accumulation in Latin America and the Caribbean —i.e., the region's *styles* of development, in the sense of the term originally proposed by ECLAC— have not succeeded in changing the social asymmetries that manifest themselves, even during periods of rapid growth. What all this demonstrates once again, over and above short-term growth imperatives, is the urgent need to make effective structural changes in the region's existing development styles.

This overview of socio-economic development in Latin America and the Caribbean since the Rio Summit is followed by an analysis of major *environmental* trends in the region. One of the region's most notable environmental features is the fact that, although its land area amounts to a little over 2 billion hectares —no more than 15% of the total area of the planet— it has the greatest diversity of species and eco-regions in the world. Furthermore, Latin America and the Caribbean have around one third of the world's total endowment of renewable water resources, with South America alone accounting for nearly 30% of total world run-off.

Alongside this enormous potential, however, there are disturbing signs that pollution is growing worse as a result of the combination of economic and population growth and the intensification of certain types of production and consumption patterns. For the most part, the increase in air, soil and water pollution in the region and the consequent adverse health impacts are associated with urban sprawl and with agriculture. Because of the considerable pace of urban growth, a large proportion of the population is being affected by the deterioration of air quality and of coastal areas, pollution from hazardous solid waste and the contamination of water resources. What is more, since overcrowding and faulty infrastructure increase people's exposure to pollutants, the poorest strata of the population are usually affected the most by pollution.

Ironically, the health problems caused by the poor air quality and toxic substances associated with the development process are just as serious as the health problems that were once caused by underdevelopment, such as gastrointestinal ailments. A comparison of Latin America and the Caribbean with other regions shows that it is less densely populated, has more water resources and has an economic structure in which relatively "clean" sectors account for a large share of total activity. The high levels of pollution that exist despite these favourable features point to the existence of serious shortcomings in planning and other weaknesses in environmental management.

The 1990s were designated by the United Nations as the International Decade for Natural Disasters Reduction. During the decade efforts to increase and improve information, education and public awareness about natural disasters were redoubled. Prevention, early warning, and emergency response systems, as well as rehabilitation and reconstruction or repair services, were strengthened. Paradoxically, however, the incidence and intensity of natural disasters and the resulting damage have been increasing in recent years. Droughts, forest fires, floods, landslides, tropical storms, hurricanes, tornadoes, earthquakes and volcanic eruptions have been claiming a growing number of victims and have given rise to losses which seriously jeopardize the development of many communities, especially the poorest ones.

In the world as a whole, some 700,000 persons lost their lives between 1991 and 2000 as a result of natural disasters. Although this figure —while undoubtedly an underestimate— is lower than the figure for the preceding decade, the number of disasters, their intensity, the number of persons affected and the economic damage they caused greatly exceeded the levels recorded for the 1980s. Thus, while the average number of persons affected by natural disasters per year between 1981 and 1990 was 147 million, this figure rose to 211 million per year for the period from 1991 to 2000. The more serious nature of the disasters is particularly marked in the case of weather-related catastrophes and those caused by extreme hydrometeorological phenomena, which represent rather more than half the total number of disasters but account for over 90% of the victims and at least 85% of the total economic damage sustained. Furthermore, over 90% of the victims of weather-related disasters live in developing countries.

The region's physical environment is such that there is a particularly high risk of potentially disastrous natural phenomena. The Sierra Madre mountains, the neo-volcanic area in Mexico and Central America, the Central American isthmus and almost the entire length of the Andean range are very active tectonic zones which are the site of violent earthquakes and volcanic eruptions. In the tropics, the region is prone to tropical storms and hurricanes which occur seasonally in both the Atlantic and the Pacific. Droughts are occurring with increasing frequency even in humid and sub-humid ecosystems. Extensive areas of the Southern Cone suffer from severe flooding. Almost the entire region is periodically subject to the El Niño/Southern Oscillation, which, depending on the location of the areas affected, intensifies rainfall or increases the severity of droughts which heighten the risk of forest fires.

The region's vulnerability to these phenomena has been amply illustrated by the devastating effects of recent disasters in the Andean region (El Niño, 1997-1998), the Caribbean (Hurricane Georges), Central America (Hurricane Mitch) and Venezuela. There have also been more localized disasters which, taken together, have likewise caused heavy damage. The Caribbean is the subregion which has been most seriously affected by natural disasters. These islands are not only prone to volcanic activity, but, like most small island States in the world, are extremely vulnerable to recurrent climatic disasters. The twin-island State of Antigua and Barbuda, for example, has been struck by nine hurricanes in the last 10 years. In 1999, which was not a particularly unfavourable year, the Caribbean was hit by 12 tropical storms, 8 of which reached hurricane strength. Five were classed as Category 4 hurricanes on the Saffir-Simpson scale.

Damage assessments provide a clearer idea of the threat that natural disasters represent for development in the region as a whole. Economic damage from natural disasters in the last 30 years has been estimated by ECLAC at US$ 50,365 billion (in 1998 dollars). Since the information collected did not cover all of the natural disasters in the region, however, the real socio-economic impact is thought to have been much greater. In Central America, economic damage caused by natural disasters since 1972 amounts to an annual average of close to US$ 800 million, or 2% of subregional GDP. In Meso-America, hydrometeorological disasters claimed more than 20,000 lives between 1990 and 1999 and affected almost 4.5 million persons, in contrast to the 1,640-victim toll registered for this type of catastrophe in the subregion between 1980 and 1989. The devastating passage of Hurricane Mitch in Central America in 1998 was the main reason for this shift in the scale of disaster-related losses between the 1980s and the 1990s.

In the 1970s, the State entrusted its environmental management responsibilities to sectoral bodies, and, subsequently, to environmental entities headed by health officials with the rank of undersecretary or deputy minister; later, in the 1980s, these duties were assigned to urban development agencies. During the same period, the trend in the industrialized and highly urbanized countries was to attach environmental agencies to the urban development and housing sector. In some cases, environmental management was addressed from the perspective of planning, based on an intersectoral approach, and was assigned to high-level consultants with close ties to the executive branch, to councils, committees or offices linked to the ministry of planning or to presidential offices. The 1980s were a difficult period, owing to the structural adjustment processes brought about by the economic crisis in the region, which diminished the public sector's capacity to halt environmental degradation of critical ecosystems and control pollution.

In general, the highest environmental authority may be one of two types. In most cases, it is a ministry, but in others, it is a collegiate body. In the latter case, the tendency in most countries —given the multisectoral nature of environmental management— has been to place such a body at a high level within the government hierarchy and to include representatives from all areas of the Administration whose decisions impinge in one way or another on natural resources. In some cases, representatives of non-governmental organizations and of academic, production and other sectors also participate.

The Rio Summit ushered in changes in regulatory frameworks as well as in institutions. Some of the most significant legislative advances made in Latin America and the Caribbean in the past decade relate to the following issues: environmental impact assessment, land management, new offences and sanctions, accountability for environmental damage, scales of charges for pollution and other economic instruments, legal actions for environmental protection purposes, mechanisms for citizen participation and limitations on ownership rights for environmental reasons. Major reforms have also been made in sectoral laws governing the development, use and conservation of renewable and non-renewable natural resources, these reform processes have given rise to wide-ranging discussions in the countries concerned and some of them have met with resistance from both public agents and members of civil society.

Advances and setbacks have also been registered in efforts to mainstream environmental issues into sectoral policies. For the most part, countries are just beginning to take steps towards incorporating the concept of sustainable resource use and conservation of the environment in the different areas of production and services. Traditionally, scant regard has been given to environmental issues in macroeconomic and sectoral policies (relating to health, education, agriculture, mining and others), and this state of affairs is reflected in the numerous market failures which have been identified as some of the main underlying causes of environmental degradation. This is also true in sectors that use biological diversity directly or handle the elements on which it is based, such as agriculture, forestry, fisheries and water resources. In addition to the main environmental authority, a number of other government agencies often have mandates for the management of renewable natural resources (e.g., ministries responsible for fisheries, forestry or agriculture, and agencies that oversee water and energy resources), which, in many cases, overlap and give rise to inter-agency conflicts. With respect to economic and social policies, the overall assessment of events in the 1990s is a mixed one.

On the economic front, considerable advances have been made in correcting fiscal disequilibria, reducing inflation, speeding up the growth of exports, reviving regional integration processes or starting new ones, attracting substantial flows of foreign direct investment and restoring economic growth. Significant progress has also been made in the development of strong macroeconomic institutions and, albeit with some delay, new institutional challenges have been tackled in other fields, such as the regulation of financial services and public utilities and the promotion of competition. Public social spending has been increased and the proportion of persons living in poverty has diminished to some extent, although not to a sufficient degree. By contrast, economic and productivity growth during the same period have been disappointing. Unstable economic growth and the frequency of financial crises indicate that not all causes of instability have been eliminated and that some may even have become more disruptive.

In short, existing environmental regulatory agencies in Latin America and the Caribbean face the increasingly urgent challenge of having to design management instruments that are effective and economically efficient in achieving environmental goals. This task is all the more pressing because traditional regulatory systems have not responded appropriately to the environmental degradation affecting the region. Furthermore, because of the fiscal constraints faced by most countries in the region, environmental authorities have less scope for strengthening their capabilities through the use of larger budgetary allocations and must therefore explore other means of financing environmental management measures.

On the international level, changes in the negotiating agenda have been reflected in significant advances since the 1992 Conference in Rio. Since then, an unprecedented international environmental system, represented by a new generation of multilateral environmental agreements, has begun to take shape. The environmental dimension is recognized in the Rio Declaration as an aspect of development that should serve to orient economic and social growth since it has a direct bearing on the very foundations of production and consumption processes.

This new environmental and institutional era entails new imperatives for global environmental management and, consequently, for international cooperation. On the one hand, Governments are urged to play a more proactive role on the international stage in order to protect global public goods through innovative multilateral arrangements; on the other, the private sector is increasingly being called upon to play a leading role, especially under certain multilateral environmental agreements and their protocols, including the United Nations Framework Convention on Climate Change, the Kyoto Protocol, the Convention on Biological Diversity and the Cartagena Protocol on Biosafety.

The countries of Latin America have ratified at least ten legally binding multilateral agreements on the environment. The swift action taken in ratifying these instruments contrasts, however, with their limited degree of implementation, which is attributable to various factors. One of them is non-fulfilment by the developed countries of the fundamental commitments undertaken at the Earth Summit.

Countries in the region have played a leading role in negotiations relating to climate change and biological diversity, two of the most crucial environmental issues on the global agenda. The negotiations on the Kyoto Protocol —and more specifically on the clean development mechanism— provide a clear example of this role. The Governments of the region have been in the vanguard of international negotiations on the design of this mechanism, which can be a source of economic income for Latin America and the Caribbean for use in the adoption of measures for sustainable development.

Lastly, attention should be drawn to the future potential of an economic valuation of environmental services provided by natural ecosystems in the region. A number of activities have been initiated for this purpose; in Brazil, for example, a system has been established whereby the proceeds of the goods and services tax are allocated to municipalities which protect natural ecosystems that provide environmental services. Another interesting case is that of Costa Rica, where recognition is given to some of the environmental services provided by the forests and a mechanism has been established for paying owners for such services. Similarly, in Colombia and Guatemala, downstream users are charged for the use of water from river basins. These revenues are then used to finance conservation activities in the upper reaches of the river basin.

Although Latin America and the Caribbean eagerly adopted the agreements reached at the Rio Conference, the pace of their implementation declined as the decade drew on. Domestic structural constraints, distortions in the interpretation and application of agreements, the directions taken by various international negotiations and the worsening of global asymmetries, among other factors, have weakened the sustainable development agenda. Whereas the region has plainly undergone institutional and regulatory change, this has not been paralleled by either the vision or the reformatory and mobilizing potential of the agenda for sustainable development. Even though the foundations have been laid for this, Latin America and the Caribbean are still in the preliminary phases of a transition towards sustainable development.

The region's economic performance has not been strong enough to close the gaps that were already in evidence in 1992, and more significant achievements have been made at the macroeconomic level than in terms of well-being since then. Inequality and inequity have been perpetuated in most countries and have worsened in comparison with the developed world. Relative poverty has abated very little, and the number of persons who cannot even meet their basic needs has actually increased. As a result, the situation in the region is no more socially and economically sustainable than it was 10 years ago. Nor are there any convincing signs of progress towards environmental sustainability. Degradation continues at an alarming rate, albeit with significant differences depending on the specific process concerned. Ecosystems continue to falter under the impact of unsustainable production and consumption patterns and rates of urban expansion. The natural resource base continues to be affected by increasing demographic pressure, and environmental services are now called upon to absorb a heavier burden in terms of pollution. It is true, however, that some progress is starting to be made with respect to environmental protection and the sustainable use of resources thanks to the efforts of economic organizations which have taken up the challenge of using sustainable modes of production.

The advances achieved in terms of sustainable development cannot be ignored, but the overall assessment is a disturbing one and must be addressed as a major challenge for Latin America and the Caribbean. It is essential to build a vision for the future of the region and to determine the viability of a necessary and desirable development path, both for the individual countries and for the region as a whole. In the twenty-first century, biological diversity together with the diversity of cultures, knowledge and information can play a decisive role in promoting sustainable development in Latin America and the Caribbean.

In order to make the transition towards sustainable development, the region needs to initiate economic and social change, starting with a reorganization of its production structure which satisfies the threefold prerequisite of raising competitiveness, reducing social lags and halting the environmental degradation associated with current patterns of specialization. This will necessitate an increase in domestic saving, which has so far been insufficient to sustain the endogenous capital accumulation needed to reverse the poverty afflicting a high percentage of the population. It will also require an increase in social spending, especially on education and health, and the creation of good-quality jobs, with special attention to gender equity and to better social integration for young people in the region. Achieving appropriate levels of national saving can also help to reverse current processes of environmental degradation and the loss of natural and human capital, which are one of the main causes of declining production capacity.

If the reorganization of the production structure is to be properly directed, qualitative changes must be made in patterns of public, private and social investment so that they can be reoriented towards sustainable projects with high social returns. This is contingent on the existence of effective national systems for technological development and knowledge creation. Such systems must be capable of stimulating types of technical progress that are appropriate to the region, bearing in mind its vast natural-resource endowment and the high percentage of the labour force engaged in low-productivity activities. In the legal and institutional sphere, the region is faced with the task of adapting existing frameworks in order to facilitate the use of environmental management tools at different levels of government that will help to ensure the consistency of sectoral policies. The territorial specificity of environmental management calls for the establishment of close operational ties with local authorities through strategies that link the whole range of administrative structures to a wider range of management tools, including economic instruments.

The above considerations suggest that the rapid economic growth pursued by countries in the region on the basis of their current production and export patterns may not be feasible within a sustainable framework. Thus, the document concludes with a proposal concerning a set of priorities identified at the four subregional meetings held as a prelude to the Regional Preparatory Conference of Latin America and the Caribbean for the World Summit on Sustainable Development. These priorities should be established with reference to those processes that call for stronger joint action not only within the region but also between the community of nations and the global environmental system.

Part one

Sustainability in the region

Chapter I

Economic performance in the 1990s

During the 1990s, the countries of Latin America and the Caribbean went through a series of sweeping changes involving profound economic reforms whose main components were greater openness to trade and liberalization of domestic financial markets and international capital flows, with private enterprise taking a predominant role in the production of goods and services and in the provision of public services and social benefits. As production activity recovered from 1990 onward, and many of the pressures that had given rise to inflation and instability gradually eased, it seemed that economic development in the region had moved on from the "lost decade" of the 1980s. Economic growth rates for the region as a whole, however, continued to be significantly lower than those achieved in the decades prior to the debt crisis (see figure I.1).

Far-reaching changes also occurred during this period in the global situation, the most distinctive development being the consolidation of the globalization process. A heightening of United States supremacy, European progress in creating a bloc capable of playing a leading role in world affairs, rapid growth in China and the transformation of the countries in the old socialist bloc were major developments in this process. These changes were accompanied by the progressive emergence of global markets. While the highest degree of integration was seen in the financial markets, trade and investment flows also increased, as did the spread of technological developments originating, for the most part, in the developed countries (ECLAC, 2001a), particularly open-use information technologies and those designed for industrial and services applications.

Figure I.1
LATIN AMERICA AND THE CARIBBEAN: ECONOMIC GROWTH, 1951-2000
(Average annual GDP growth)

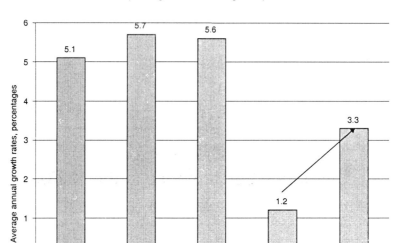

Source: ECLAC.

A. Economic growth in Latin America and the Caribbean

Figure I.2 compares the growth rates achieved by the Latin American countries in the period 1946-1980 with those of the 1990s. Only in Chile was growth substantially higher in the latter period than before the debt crisis, while the performance of Argentina, Bolivia and Uruguay was slightly better. These were the countries, however, that had seen the slowest growth in the earlier period. The other countries of South America were unable to restore growth to the previous level. In particular, Brazil, Ecuador and Venezuela, which expanded strongly in the period 1946-1980, saw much slower growth in the 1990s.

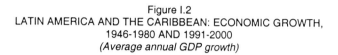

Figure I.2
LATIN AMERICA AND THE CARIBBEAN: ECONOMIC GROWTH,
1946-1980 AND 1991-2000
(Average annual GDP growth)

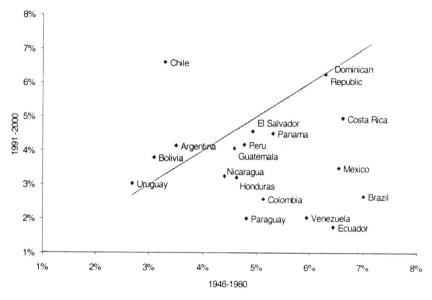

Source: ECLAC.

In the case of the Central American countries, the ending of armed conflicts and the replacement of authoritarian forms of government with more democratic ones has been a fundamental change that has allowed reconstruction of the social fabric to begin, creating a climate of confidence and more predictable conditions for investment and business with domestic and foreign capital. This is illustrated by the path of Central American GDP, which grew at an average annual rate of 4.3% in real terms over the period 1990-2000, a figure that is substantially higher than the 0.9% recorded in the 1980s. The Mexican economy, meanwhile, expanded at an annual average rate of 3.5% over the period, virtually double the average for the previous decade. From 1995 until the end of the decade growth was even stronger, averaging over 5% a year. Nonetheless, average annual GDP growth in the countries of that region was lower than in 1946-1980 (ECLAC, 2001a).

The economies of the English-speaking Caribbean are very open, being characterized, among other things, by their high degree of dependence on foreign trade: imports to cover their basic needs, and exports to provide income and employment. Tourism is the main source of revenue for many small island States. Although real growth rates in the subregion were high in the 1970s, rising oil prices and higher relative prices for manufactures began to affect the performance of most of its countries in the 1980s. By and large, the macroeconomic performance of small island members of the Organization of Eastern Caribbean States (OECS) has been better than that of the larger CARICOM countries, owing in part to prudent macroeconomic management and the preferential treatment they receive under trade accords such as the Cotonou Agreement (formerly known as the Lomé Convention) and CARICOM (León, 2001).

The Dominican Republic has shown the fastest growth since the mid-1990s, and is also the only country to have grown as vigorously over the decade as a whole as it did in 1945-1980. Cuba has been growing at a satisfactory rate since 1994, but the severity of the contraction the country experienced in the early years of the decade, following the collapse of the former socialist economies of Eastern Europe, means that economic activity is still below the levels of the late 1980s. The performance of Haiti, lastly, has been poor, largely because of the country's complex political situation.

B.   Public finances and inflation

Progress has unquestionably been made with public finances in the region. While budget deficits are much lower than before and public debt management is more cautious, however, serious problems remain. The tax burden is generally low, and in many cases the public finances are dependent on volatile, slow-growing revenue sources. Tax evasion and avoidance rates are high.

The weakness of most countries' tax structures is compounded by national saving rates that are as low now as they were in the 1980s, and by the persistent shortcomings of domestic financial systems (ECLAC, 2001b). Unless substantial progress is made in all these areas, the region's macroeconomic performance will not be soundly based, even though the record of the 1980s has been greatly improved upon.

In the early 1990s, a substantial increase in capital flows into the region combined with the implementation of structural economic reforms to facilitate the application and consolidation of anti-inflation programmes in a number of countries. As a result, average inflation has fallen very sharply, so that almost all of the region's countries now have single-digit rates.

C.   Capital flows and the instability of economic growth

As figure I.3 shows, economic growth in the 1990s was volatile and tended to follow the cycles of international capital flows (ECLAC, 2000b; ECLAC, 2001b). Net transfers of resources into the region resulted in a marked upsurge of economic activity in the first half of the decade. This upsurge, however, opened the way for an accumulation of large macroeconomic imbalances that were soon to be reflected in the vulnerability of the region's countries to "contagion" from external financial crises. Thus, the Mexican economy experienced a severe crisis in 1995, and this then spread to other countries in the subcontinent. Similarly, the emerging markets crisis that began in Asia in 1997 reversed the trend of GDP and foreign trade growth in the region in 1998. This crisis deepened the following year because of a fall in commodity prices (ECLAC, 2001b).

Figure I.3
THE EXTERNAL VULNERABILITY OF THE REGION
GDP GROWTH AND NET RESOURCE TRANSFERS, 1991-2000

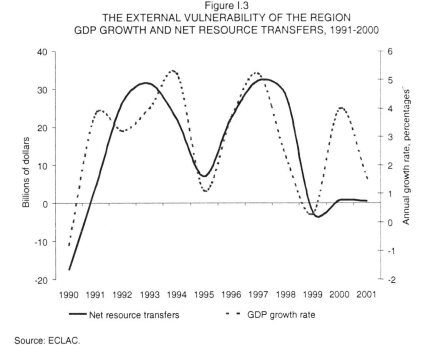

Source: ECLAC.

The recovery seen in 2000, which owed more to the strength of exports than to any new upsurge in external financing, was suddenly cut short at the end of that year by the deterioration in external conditions. As a result, 2001 is likely to be a disappointing year for the countries of the region, which are expected to grow by about 1.5%, less than half the 2000 level of 4%. During the current year, the region will feel the effects of lower world growth resulting mainly from slowdowns in the United States, Europe and the developing Asian countries and from the economic difficulties in Japan. This situation is compounded by internal factors, particularly the weakness of domestic demand and lending in a number of countries, electricity supply problems in Brazil and political difficulties in some States. The outlook could be even worse if the world economy continues on its present course.

D.   Economic openness, trade and integration

During the 1990s, the main advances in this area were a rise in exports, an upsurge of trade and investment within subregional integration schemes, and the signing of a large number of free trade agreements with other countries and regions. Unresolved weaknesses include a lack of export diversification, the region's low share of world trade, the numerous barriers to free trade that still exist and the adverse effects of financial and macroeconomic volatility on the dynamic of commercial transactions.

The evidence available shows that the region as a whole has not made significant progress in penetrating world markets. Latin America accounted for 5.6% of international trade in 1985 and 5.7% in 1998. As table I.1 shows, few countries have managed to increase their share of world trade flows over the period indicated (Katz and Stumpo, 2000). Of the 25 Latin American and Caribbean countries included in the table, only nine have gained world market share, while the relative positions of another four remain unchanged. Most (12 countries) have lost ground, some of them, such as Brazil and Venezuela, to a significant degree. This is directly related to three patterns of specialization that have been emerging in the region as a result of the industrial restructuring undertaken in response to international market developments.

The first pattern is characterized by dynamic growth in exports, primarily to the United States, of manufactures incorporating a large percentage of imported components. This is the pattern that predominates in Mexico and some Central American and Caribbean countries. It is found in conjunction with relatively large-scale domestic production networks in the case of non-maquila industries in Mexico, with traditional or diversifying agricultural exports in Central America, and with service export sectors (most particularly tourism) in the Caribbean.

Table I.1
LATIN AMERICA AND THE CARIBBEAN: WORLD MARKET SHARES, 1985-1998
(Percentages)

Country	1985	1998	Difference
Mexico	1.55	2.24	0.69
Argentina	0.37	0.51	0.14
Chile	0.23	0.32	0.09
Costa Rica	0.07	0.10	0.03
Guatemala	0.06	0.08	0.02
Honduras	0.05	0.07	0.02
Dominican Republic	0.08	0.10	0.02
El Salvador	0.04	0.05	0.01
Colombia	0.24	0.24	0.00
Paraguay	0.03	0.03	0.00
Nicaragua	0.02	0.02	0.00
Jamaica	0.04	0.04	0.00
Uruguay	0.07	0.06	-0.01
Cuba	0.03	0.02	-0.01
Guyana	0.02	0.01	-0.01
Suriname	0.02	0.01	-0.01
Bolivia	0.04	0.02	-0.02
Barbados	0.02	0.00	-0.02
Haiti	0.03	0.01	-0.02
Peru	0.17	0.12	-0.05
Panama	0.10	0.05	-0.05
Ecuador	0.17	0.11	-0.06
Trinidad and Tobago	0.10	0.04	-0.06
Venezuela	0.66	0.41	-0.25
Brazil	1.37	1.01	-0.36

Source: J. Katz and G. Stumpo, *Regímenes competitivos sectoriales, productividad y competitividad internacional*, Desarrollo productivo series, No. 103 (LC/L.1578-P), Santiago, Chile, July 2001. United Nations publication, Sales No. S.01.II.G.120.

The second pattern combines the predominance of natural resource-intensive primary or industrial exports to destinations outside the region with far more diversified intraregional trade. This is the model that prevails in the South American countries, and it is combined, in the case of Brazil, with some technology-intensive exports and, in this and other countries, with labour-intensive manufacturing exports and substantial industrial production for domestic markets.

There is also a third pattern of specialization, seen particularly in Panama and some small Caribbean Basin economies, which is characterized by a predominance of service exports (finance, tourism and transport).

The economic opening that began in the countries of the region in the early 1990s is linked to dynamic integration processes. The open regionalism strategy has made it possible to combine unilateral liberalization with negotiations in different forums to promote the liberalization of markets that are of interest to the region. In line with the tendencies towards regionalization seen in other parts of the world, in 1991 the Southern Common Market (MERCOSUR) was created,[1] and subregional integration has proceeded from there. Since the early 1990s, meanwhile, a customs union has gradually been consolidated in the Andean Group (now the Andean Community), although it is still imperfect, and Peru has played only a very limited part in the process. Lastly, tariff averages and dispersion have been reduced in the countries of Central America and Mexico as part of the macroeconomic reforms implemented since the 1980s. As in the case of the other schemes, Central American integration has made substantial progress in the Central American Common Market (CACM).

As table I.2 shows, exports within each regional agreement were very dynamic in the 1990s. Exports within MERCOSUR and within the Andean Community grew at average annual rates of over 20% between 1990 and 1997, so that their share of total exports rapidly increased. After falling sharply in 1999, these exports have once again shown a strong upward tendency in both subregions. The value of intra-Central American trade also rose strongly during the 1990s.

Imports grew even more rapidly than external sales, something that may help to explain the modest growth rates of the region's economies, as discussed earlier. Of course, it was to be expected that the determined trade liberalization measures undertaken in all the countries of the region would cause imports to surge for a time. There must be concern, however, about the continuing strength and persistence of import flows today, almost ten years after many of the region's trade barriers were removed.

There is evidence that in some of the region's countries this performance reflects a substantial rise in the income-elasticity of imports, a development that is probably due to the breakdown of important value added chains in local production processes. These chains will need to be rebuilt or replaced if the region wishes to return to the path of high and sustained economic growth.

---

[1] MERCOSUR was created by the Treaty of Asunción (Treaty Establishing a Common Market between the Argentine Republic, the Federal Republic of Brazil, the Republic of Paraguay and the Eastern Republic of Uruguay), signed in Asunción, Paraguay, on 26 March 1991. Bolivia and Chile are now associate members of the agreement.

Table I.2
LATIN AMERICA AND THE CARIBBEAN: EXPORT, IN TOTAL AND BY SUBREGIONAL INTEGRATION SCHEME, 1990-2000
(Millions of current dollars and percentages)

	1990	1994	1995	1996	1997	1998	1999	Jan-Sep 2000
LAIA								
1. Total exports [a]	112,694	167,192	204,170	229,164	255,390	251,345	264,235	230,916
Percentage of annual growth	10.6	36.8	22.1	12.2	11.4	-1.6	5.1	24.1
2. Exports to LAIA	12,302	28,168	35,552	38,449	45,484	43,231	34,391	30,500
Percentage annual growth	13.2	26.2	26.2	8.2	18.3	-5.0	-20.4	21.01
3. Percentage exports within LAIA (2:1)	10.9	16.8	17.4	16.8	17.8	17.2	13.0	13.2
Andean Community								
1. Total exports	31,751	33,706	39,134	44,375	46,609	38,896	43,211	44,085
Percentage annual growth	30.2	13.6	16.1	13.4	5.0	-16.5	11.1	41.0
2. Exports to Andean Community	1,324	3,472	4,859	4,698	5,621	5,411	3,940	3,777
Percentage annual growth	31.0	21.5	39.9	-3.3	19.7	-3.7	-27.2	35.2
3. Percentage exports within Community (2:1)	4.2	10.3	12.4	10.6	12.1	13.9	9.1	8.6
MERCOSUR								
1. Total exports	46,403	61,890	70,129	74,407	82,596	80,227	74,300	64,714
Percentage annual growth	-0.3	13.9	13.3	6.1	11.0	-2.9	-7.4	15.8
2. Exports to MERCOSUR	4,127	12,048	14,451	17,115	20,478	20,027	15,133	13,145
Percentage annual growth	7.3	17.8	20.0	18.4	19.7	-2.2	-24.4	17.9
3. Percentage exports within MERCOSUR (2:1)	8.9	19.5	20.6	23.0	24.8	25.0	20.4	20.3
Central American Common Market (CACM)								
1. Total exports	3,907	5,496	6,777	7,332	9,275	11,077	11,633	9,016
Percentage annual growth	9.2	7.2	23.3	8.2	26.5	19.4	5.0	5.7
2. Exports to CACM	624	1,228	1,451	1,553	1,863	2,242	2,333	1,925
Percentage annual growth	8.9	6.0	18.2	7.0	19.9	20.3	4.1	27.5
3. Percentage exports within CACM (2:1)	16.0	22.3	21.4	21.2	20.1	20.2	20.1	21.4

(continued)

Table I.2 (concluded)

	1990	1994	1995	1996	1997	1998	1999	Jan-Sep 2000
CARICOM								
1. Total exports	3,634	4,113	4,511	4,595	4,687	4,791	4,223	...
Percentage annual growth	11.6	3.1	9.7	1.9	2.0	2.2	-11.9	...
2. Exports to CARICOM	469	521	690	775	785	...	...	...
Percentage annual growth	2.9	2.6	32.4	12.3	1.2	...	...	...
3. Percentage exports within CARICOM (2:1)	12.9	12.7	15.3	16.9	16.7	...	...	....
Latin America and the Caribbean [b]								
1. Total exports	120,572	177,336	216,031	241,648	269,996	267,213	280,091	243,074
Percentage annual growth	6.5	32.6	21.8	11.9	11.7	-0.8	4.8	23.1
2. Exports to Latin America and the Caribbean	16,802	35,065	42,740	46,562	54,756	51,674	42,624	37,854
Percentage annual growth	8.2	20.1	21.9	8.9	17.6	-5.6	-17.5	21.9
3. Exports within region as percentage of total (2:1)	13.9	19.8	19.8	19.3	20.3	19.3	15.2	15.6

Source: ECLAC, International Trade and Development Finance Division, on the basis of BADECEL data and official sources.

[a] Includes Mexican maquila exports from 1992 onward.
[b] Includes LAIA, Barbados, Guyana, Jamaica, Panama and Trinidad and Tobago, MERCOSUR, Andean Community, CACM and CARICOM.

E.   Foreign direct investment

Deregulation and privatization in the Latin American economies meant that new investment opportunities opened up in sectors that used to be largely closed to private enterprise in general, and foreign companies in particular. The result has been a massive influx of firms, particularly in the areas of financial services, infrastructure and extraction activities. Foreign companies have also responded to the opportunities opened up by the different trade accords, particularly the North American Free Trade Agreement (NAFTA), the trade preferences granted by the United States to the countries of the Caribbean Basin, and the South American integration processes.

As a result, foreign direct investment (FDI) grew continuously throughout the 1990s. In absolute terms, net FDI inflows into the region rose from US$ 16.5 billion a year in the five-year period 1991-1995 to US$ 58.2 billion a year in the period 1995-2000 (see figure I.4).

Figure I.4
LATIN AMERICA AND THE CARIBBEAN: FOREIGN DIRECT INVESTMENT, 1991-2000

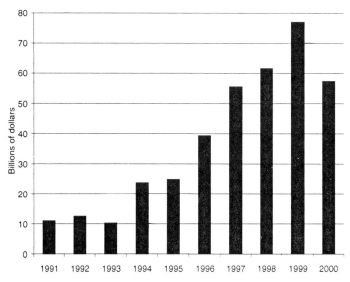

Source: ECLAC.

The main FDI flows are generated by the international expansion of transnational companies, which use them both to purchase existing assets and to create new ones, thereby increasing their presence and role in the emerging global market. It is estimated that half of all the FDI that arrived in the region in the 1990s was used to purchase existing assets. As a result of all this activity, transnational companies strengthened their strategic position in the countries of the region (ECLAC, 2000b).

F.   The impact of production transformation on sustainable development

The production transformation that took place in the region in the 1990s was directly linked with the dynamic of globalization. However, the external trade performance and industrial export dynamic analysed in the previous sections have not altered the tendency towards a structural shift in which services have increased their weight in the economies of Latin America, while the shares of primary and industrial production in the economic structure have continued to diminish.

These tendencies need to be evaluated in terms of their environmental implications and their effect on the sustainability of development. In the 1990s, the relative decline of primary and industrial production did not lead to a reduction in direct environmental pressure on the resource base, or to a lessening of ecological damage. In fact, although the share of total production accounted for by the primary sector has fallen, the agricultural frontier has continued to expand, albeit more slowly than in the past (see table I.3 and section 1 of chapter V), and the extraction of mineral and oil resources has continued to increase.

Table I.3
LATIN AMERICA AND THE CARIBBEAN: SELECTED ENVIRONMENTAL INDICATORS
(Cumulative percentage growth rates)

Indicator	1989/1980	1999/1990
Area of arable farmland	7.30	6.3[a]
Volume of agricultural output	26.80	28.3
Total fertilizer consumption	5.30	42.2[a]
Cattle holdings	7.40	0.8
Industrial uncut timber production	25.40	18.1[a]
Firewood and coal production	12.30	0.4[a]
Marine fishing production	17.9 (1985-1990)	-24.3[a]
Marine fish farming production	165.0 (1985-1990)	116.0
Mining output by volume, including oil	25.90	43.1
Mining output by volume, excluding oil	46.20	67.6
Carbon dioxide (CO_2) emissions	22.90	37.1
Carbon monoxide (CO) emissions	23.50	28.4
Reference data		
Cumulative percentage population growth	21.93	17.0[b]
Cumulative GDP growth	13.95	33.22

Source: Compiled on the basis of ECLAC, Statistical Yearbook for Latin America and the Caribbean (LC/G.2118-P), Santiago, Chile, February 2001. United Nations publication, Sales No. E.01.II.G.1; and United Nations Environment Programme (UNEP), "GEO. Estadísticas ambientales de América Latina y el Caribe", San José, Costa Rica, University of Costa Rica, 2001, forthcoming.

[a] 1998/1990.
[b] 2000/1990.

During the period 1980-1995, the volume of exports from sectors known to have an environmental impact, such as primary products and products from contaminating industries (paper and cellulose, for example, and aluminum) increased at least threefold in most of the countries. Cleaner production systems may mean that primary activities are causing less environmental damage per unit of output than in the past, but at the cost of continuing depletion of the resource base, especially in countries whose participation in external markets has been based on exports with a high natural resource content. In the case of some activities, the overexploitation of resources has already had direct effects on production, one example being the continuing decline in fish catches at sea, while reorientation towards alternative activities has not been without risks to fragile ecosystems either (see table I.3).

The traditional effects of primary activities, particularly changes in land use, are now becoming concentrated in smaller, more fragile areas of greater ecological importance, insofar as the ecosystems concerned are critical to the conservation of national, regional or world biological diversity. In other words, the main impact is now on areas that are more ecologically sensitive, and perhaps more vulnerable than before, chiefly because of global environmental problems. Furthermore, as the analysis in chapter IV will show, the rural population of the region will not decline significantly over the coming decades even if the trend towards urbanization continues, so the relationship between population and pressure on resources will continue at its current level.

In the secondary sector of the economy, there can be no doubt that structural changes now in progress have positive environmental features that are improving production quality. In most branches of this sector, better processes, quality requirements, environmental administration systems, certification mechanisms, staff training and other developments associated with technical change and globalization have operated in synergy with the consolidation of national environmental policies, better application of laws and standards, the application of new management instruments, increasing environmental awareness among businesses, greater social demands and other factors that are helping to reduce the environmental impact of industry.

This change is being seen chiefly in large companies, and particularly those that have ties to transnationals or are linked to them through industrial chains. Foreign direct investment can thus have positive implications for the environment, insofar as foreign firms in high-technology sectors tend to employ cleaner technologies in their production systems. The spread of these technologies to small and medium-sized enterprises (SMEs) is barely beginning, mainly because of the high costs involved, although many SMEs are now bringing in environmental quality practices as they modernize. There are gaps in the information on the subject which could be remedied if information systems were supplemented by better oversight methods.

This process is certainly having positive repercussions, but there are worrying tendencies that it has not yet influenced. For example, certain greenhouse gas emissions are now increasing more rapidly than before. The higher production that will be required over the coming decades, against a general background of increasing participation in the world economy and the need to increase employment, means that sustainable energy policies that can address these disturbing tendencies are called for more urgently than over (ECLAC/OLADE, 1999).

In the service sector, some very dynamic activities that are of great economic importance, particularly in certain subregions, are contributing to economic growth but are also adding to environmental pressures. This is the case with large-scale beach tourism, especially in the Caribbean. Meanwhile, the reorientation of certain service businesses, exemplified by the growth of ecotourism, has emerged as an opportunity to achieve more sustainable use of natural resources. The increasing diffusion of information services will probably provide a basis not just for improved communication and a better understanding of the issues involved, but also for more effective environmental administration systems.

If accurate, systematic knowledge of these tendencies and pressures and their interrelationship with economic processes is to be obtained, there is still a need to collect and systematize data, create operative measurement systems to ascertain the economic value of natural resources and environmental services, develop integrated economic and environmental accounting systems and improve natural resource accounting, as a basis for policy integration.

To sum up, the region is at a contradictory stage where the environment is concerned. Some economic and technological developments are beginning to improve matters, particularly in manufacturing and services, but also in some emerging activities in the primary sector. At the same time, pressures from old production and land-use processes are continuing to build up, there is still a need for rapid production growth, and existing problems are being compounded by emerging environmental tensions resulting from increased vulnerability to global environmental processes.

The imminence of the Word Summit on Sustainable Development, which is to be held in 2002, makes it particularly urgent for the region to adopt sustainable forms of production and consumption, and to improve the basis on which it participates in a globalized economy.

Chapter II

Major trends in social development in the 1990s

The main features of the social situation in Latin America and the Caribbean in the 1990s were the continuing demographic transition and gradual population ageing, inadequate job creation, a relative decline in poverty combined with rising inequality in a number of countries, progress towards greater gender equity and increased participation by women in the labour market, a recovery in social investment, and implementation of major reforms in social policies and sectors. It is clear that the inability of the economic growth process to satisfy the social requirements of sustainability is due more to a *development style* —the patterns of production and consumption that this process engenders— than to the level of growth as such (Guimarães, 2001a). In other words, while it is true that the recovery in growth seen over the last decade has fallen short of what is required to meet the growing needs of a still-expanding population, this should not distract attention from the structural aspects of the region's socio-economic situation. What this situation reveals is that historical patterns of accumulation in Latin America and the Caribbean, the region's *styles* of development, in the sense of the term originally proposed by ECLAC (Pinto, 1976), have not succeeded in changing the social asymmetries that manifest themselves even in periods of vigorous growth. What all this highlights once again, over and above short-term growth imperatives, is the urgent need to make permanent structural changes to current development styles.

As was pointed out in the previous chapter, the most salient economic development of the 1990s in Latin America and the Caribbean was the resumption of growth, against a background of greater concern about internal macroeconomic balances. This concern was reflected, in turn, by the steady decline of budget deficits and the stabilization of inflation at single-digit levels in most of the countries by the end of the decade. Nonetheless, average growth in the region still falls short not only of what is needed to close the gap with the more developed countries, but also of what ECLAC (2000c) has judged to be desirable and necessary if the serious problems of poverty that afflict it are to be overcome (6% a year). Another feature of the 1990s, at least in some countries, was that years of high growth alternated with periods of slower expansion and indeed of contraction, so that the record over the decade as a whole was one of great instability. This instability exacerbated the adverse employment effects of low average growth, so that job creation did not necessarily bear a linear relationship to changes in economic growth rates.

A.   Employment

Although the region returned to moderate levels of growth, successive crises caused employment to decline in many countries, so that the employment situation as the decade ended was not encouraging. In particular, open unemployment was on an upward trend (see figure II.1).

Among the countries of the Southern Cone, it was in Argentina and Brazil that unemployment rose the most between 1990 and 2000, with rates climbing from 7.4% to 15.1% and from 4.3% to 7.1%, respectively. In most of the countries, the negative trend of unemployment was heightened by the financial crisis. This was particularly noticeable in Chile, where the stagnation of GDP in 1999 resulted in the national unemployment rate rising from 6.4% in 1998 to 9.2% in 2000. There was a similar rise in Paraguay, from 6.6% in 1998 to 10.7% in 2000 (ECLAC, 2001c). Over the last two years of the decade, unemployment rose in most of the Andean countries. In Colombia, Ecuador and Venezuela, the countries most affected by the economic crisis, output fell by 5% or more in 1999, and as a result unemployment rates rose by three or four percentage points, so that in 2000 unemployment averaged 20.2% in Colombia, 14.1% in Ecuador and 14.0% in Venezuela. In Bolivia and Peru, the effects on unemployment were not so great, and rates ended the decade at approximately 7.6% and 8.5%, respectively. In Central America, the rate of formal job creation was too low to meet the demand from an economically active population that was still growing exceptionally quickly (by between 2.9% a year, in Panama, and 3.8%, in Honduras) during the 1990s. Not only did open unemployment in urban areas not fall up until 1997, but it carried on rising until the end of the decade (from 9.5% in 1990 to 10.8% in 2000).[1]

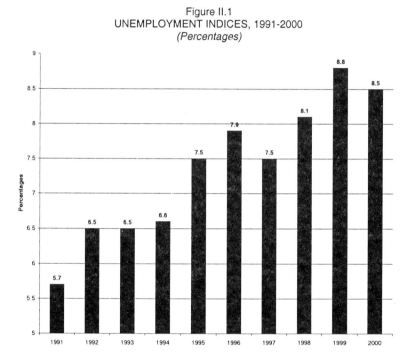

Figure II.1
UNEMPLOYMENT INDICES, 1991-2000
(Percentages)

Source: ECLAC, *Social Panorama of Latin America, 2000-2001* (LC/G.2128-P), Santiago, Chile, 2001. United Nations publication, Sales No. E.01.II.G.141.

Not only did the new style of growth in Latin America and the Caribbean produce little in the way of new employment, but the production system was restructured in a way that resulted in more intensive use of specialized labour and rising labour productivity in companies operating in the sectors most exposed to international competition. Furthermore, employment trends over the decade were strongly influenced by the relatively high rate of labour supply growth, averaging 2.6% a year in the aggregate and 3.3% in urban areas between 1990 and 1999, which was caused by the increase in the working-age

[1] These figures are simple averages of each country's unemployment rate. According to ECLAC estimates (ECLAC, 2000c), weighted averages for the economically active population show unemployment rising from 5.8% in 1990 to 8.5% in 2000.

population. Growth in the labour supply was also contributed to by the increase in total participation rates that resulted from rising female participation in the labour market. Between 1990 and 1999, average participation rates rose from 37.9% to 42% overall and from 39.5% to 43.7% in urban areas.

In most of the countries where the percentage of unemployment increased, the informal sector also increased its share of urban employment (Argentina, Brazil, Colombia, Mexico, Uruguay and Venezuela). This tendency was even seen in some countries where unemployment fell or remained stable (Bolivia, Costa Rica, the Dominican Republic and El Salvador). Countries where formal employment grew faster than the labour force and unemployment fell were the exception in the region (Chile and Panama). The informal sector was the one that created most jobs; in urban areas, employment growth in this sector averaged 4.2% a year, about three percentage points more than the growth rate of formal employment, so that the percentage of working people employed in low-productivity sectors rose across the region as a whole. In the 1990s, seven out of every ten jobs generated in Latin American cities were in the informal sector.

The recovery in economic growth was accompanied by increases in the average incomes of urban workers, which rose by between 1% and 6.5% a year. Wages also rose, although by less than employers' incomes. This disparity is one of the factors that explains the worsening of primary income distribution. Between 1990 and 1997, the average pay of urban wage earners in 10 countries rose by between 0.9% and 5.4% a year. Of the countries for which information is available, only Ecuador, Honduras, Mexico and Venezuela saw the average incomes of urban wage earners decline over the period. The improvements achieved, however, and particularly the rise in minimum wages, were not enough to restore real earnings to the levels attained prior to the early 1980s crisis, and only in Chile, Colombia, Costa Rica, Panama and Paraguay was the minimum wage higher in 1998 than in 1980. In the region as a whole, the minimum wage was 28% lower on average in 1998 than in 1980.

The increase in female labour market participation is worth noting, since it is a positive development that has been seen right across the region (ECLAC, 2001c). Women's share of the workforce rose from an average of 37% in 1991 to just over 41% in 1998. In a number of countries, this trend has been accompanied by a narrowing of the pay gap between the sexes, although this remains wide. As regards the challenge of increasing female participation in public decision-making, steady if limited progress was made in the 1990s.

B.   Loss of job security

Even as unemployment has risen, those in work have seen their position became increasingly insecure and unstable owing to the weakening of labour rights and of workers' organizations. As governments have deregulated labour markets, employers have moved towards short-term hiring (temporary, seasonal or part-time), the grounds on which contracts can be terminated have been extended, redundancy payments have been cut and the right to strike has been limited. The clearest indication of increasing job insecurity is the significant increase in the proportion of wage earners employed in temporary positions (ECLAC, 2000c; ECLAC, 2001c).

In Costa Rica, for example, which is one of the countries for which information is available, the proportion of the waged workforce employed on a non-permanent basis rose by more than eight percentage points between 1981 and 1997, from 1.1% to 9.5%. In El Salvador, this proportion had risen to 26.3% of wage earners by 1995. Meanwhile, subcontract producers in free trade zones (maquiladoras), which take advantage of proximity to the United States, are providing employment to low-skilled workers, particularly women, albeit under disadvantageous working conditions. Thus, maquiladoras benefit not only from tax advantages but also from low-cost labour and the lack of social benefits.

Another aspect of the situation is the large proportion of urban wage earners working without contracts. According to the information available, between 1990 and 1998 the percentages of wage earners without contracts increased by about 11 percentage points in Argentina (to 33%) and Brazil (to 46%), and by more than 7 points in Chile (to 22%). In Paraguay the figure was 64.9% in 1995. In 1996, the percentages of urban wage earners without contracts were still high, with rates of 41% in Peru and 31% in Colombia. The figure for Peru shows that the situation had deteriorated, with an increase of as much as 11 percentage points between 1989 and 1996 in the proportion of wage earners without employment contracts, from 30% to 41%. In Colombia, however, while the proportion of urban wage earners without contracts was still large in 1996 at 31%, it represented a fall of seven percentage points from an earlier level of 38%.

C.   Inequality in income distribution

Despite economic growth, lower inflation and higher public social spending in the 1990s, there was generally little change in the income distribution situation (ECLAC, 2001c). The reasons for the continuing concentration of income in the 1990s remain disputed. The most evident cause was the limited job creation capacity of the region's economies, which was due in part to inadequate growth and to an economic structure that was unfavourable to production sectors making intensive use of direct labour. The second cause would seem to be the continuing concentration of human capital, particularly education (those with university education benefited most from rising demand for labour). Poor distribution of income and opportunities was also a reflection of serious problems of social stratification and exclusion, which continue to be transmitted from generation to generation, and for which the current development model has provided no solution.

In relative terms, Uruguay is the only country in the Southern Cone where income distribution is more equitable now than in 1990. Nor did the Andean countries make major progress over the decade; only in Bolivia did income distribution in urban areas improve, while in Colombia, Ecuador and Venezuela it remained stable or worsened. In Venezuela, the country with the weakest economic performance, income concentration rose sharply. Developments in rural areas do not always coincide with those in urban areas. In Colombia, for example, rural income became significantly less concentrated in the period 1990-1997, while in Venezuela concentration increased in the countryside to an even more marked degree than in urban areas between 1990 and 1994.

The general trend in the Mexican and Central American economies was towards greater income concentration during the 1990s. The gap between average urban and rural incomes, which is a source of great inequity, barely narrowed over the decade. In Honduras, distribution improved slightly in both urban and rural areas, while in Mexico it did so in urban areas alone. In the context of an adverse distribution structure, average urban and rural incomes in Panama grew so strongly that poverty declined markedly, as will be seen further on.

The level of distributive inequality in the region, the highest in the world, condemns millions of people to extreme poverty and seriously limits the poverty-reducing effects of growth. This means that if Latin America and the Caribbean are to be able to achieve the development objective of a 50% reduction in poverty by 2015 laid down in the Millennium Declaration, they will need to reorient current growth patterns drastically so that growth can begin to have a significant and positive impact on the poor.

D.   Inequalities in land distribution

Where the distribution of assets —in this case, land— is concerned, the situation in Latin America and the Caribbean generally continues to be one of inequality so marked as to be incompatible with the objectives of greater equity and efficiency that sustainable development entails (ECLAC, 2001c).

Chile, Mexico and Paraguay are countries where land ownership is highly concentrated, with Gini indices that have stood above 0.90 for decades. Colombia, Costa Rica, El Salvador, Panama and Venezuela belong to a group of countries with intermediate concentration indices (between 0.79 and 0.9). Concentration is slightly lower in Argentina and Brazil, with Gini index values of about 0.8. The country where land ownership is most equitably distributed is Uruguay, whose Gini index fell from 0.8 in 1985 to 0.76 in 1994. In Honduras, the index stands at between 0.6 and 0.7.

Inequality in the access of the rural population to this basic asset is a source of social tension. In Paraguay, the most rural country in South America, land access problems and high levels of rural poverty gave rise to numerous conflicts during the 1990s. Similarly, the number of families involved in land occupations in Brazil grew from 8,000 to 63,000 between 1990 and 1997. In Chile, land demands from indigenous communities have increased in recent years.

Although awareness of the inequities suffered by indigenous and Afro-American cultures —of enormous importance in the countries of Meso-America— has been awakened by the conflicts in Chiapas, Mexico, as a result of which legislative changes are planned, the practical results in terms of higher incomes for these groups, most of which are vulnerable rural inhabitants, have been slight. To address this problem, governments have applied a variety of policies. In Costa Rica, it is estimated that almost 2 million hectares, or roughly a third of the country's total land area, have been redistributed through large-scale land title allocation, acquisition and settlement programmes. In El Salvador, large amounts of funding have been invested as part of the agrarian reform and the land-transfer programme that came out of the Peace Agreements. At present, 75.1% of land is owner-occupied, 18.4% is rented and 6.5% is held on some other basis. In Mexico, the 1991 constitutional reform legalized land sales and trading in agricultural rights, practices that had been informal up until then.

In the Andean countries, land access problems and the inability of campesinos and indigenous people to obtain access to credit, technology and appropriate markets for their traditional products have led large numbers of these to turn to illicit crop growing, a situation that has persisted owing to the profitability of these crops and the greater incomes they thus provide. Bolivia, Colombia and Peru account for virtually all of the world's coca leaf production. According to government figures for 1999, coca-related activities account for about 6.4% of total employment in Bolivia. The expansion of illicit crop growing, as in Colombia, parts of Amazonia, the Orinoco basin and low-lying plateaux, is having an adverse environmental impact, both because of the land and water resources it consumes and because of pesticide and other chemical input use. Surveys carried out among the governments of the region indicate that drug use is also a challenge for their social integration policies, as they consider —Bolivia is a case in point— that the groups worst affected by this are mainly to be found in the sectors of society that are the most socially vulnerable, such as the young (the so-called "street children").

E.   Relative decline in poverty

As a result of economic growth, poverty declined by 5.7 percentage points between 1990 and 1999 in the 19 countries of the region for which information is available (see table II.1). The fall in poverty was gradual, with large variations from country to country.

Table II.1
LATIN AMERICA: POVERTY AND INDIGENCE RATES, 1980-2000 [a]

| | Percentage of households | | | | | |
| | Poor [b] | | | Indigent [c] | | |
	Total	Urban	Rural	Total	Urban	Rural
1980	34.7	25.3	53.9	15.0	8.8	27.5
1990	41.0	35.0	58.2	17.7	12.0	34.1
1994	37.5	31.8	56.1	15.9	10.5	33.5
1997	35.5	29.7	54.0	14.4	9.5	30.3
1999	35.3	29.8	54.3	13.9	9.1	30.7

Source: ECLAC, on the basis of special tabulations of household surveys from the countries concerned.

[a] Estimate for 19 countries in the region.
[b] Percentage of households with incomes below the poverty line. Includes indigent households.
[c] Percentage of households with incomes below the indigence line.

Although almost 30% of Brazilian households are poor, this figure represents a large reduction (11.5 percentage points between 1990 and 1999), achieved thanks to effective channelling of monetary transfers from the public sector to poor households and to the ending of hyperinflation, which affected the lower-income population severely in the early part of the decade. Success in controlling hyperinflation also helped to bring down poverty in Argentina, but to a lesser degree, so that the poverty rate was still higher in 1997 than it had been in 1980. In Chile, poverty fell by 15.5 percentage points between 1990 and 1999 owing to exceptionally strong economic growth and, to a lesser degree, the positive effects of lower inflation. Uruguay is the only country where a decline in urban poverty between 1990 and 1999 (from 11.8% to 5.6%, the lowest rates in the entire Latin America and Caribbean region) was accompanied by the maintenance of relatively equitable income distribution.

In Colombia and Venezuela, by contrast, between 45% and 50% of households are poor. Poverty rates are also high in Bolivia and Ecuador, where 50% or more of all households are in this position. The reasons are to be found in the economic stagnation or recession these countries have experienced as a result of the crises of recent years, especially that of 1999, and the rise in open unemployment, in spite of success in controlling inflation and of public spending increases, which have counteracted the effects of recession. Progress has not been rapid or very evident, owing to rapid population growth, particularly in those countries with a higher incidence of poverty, and to falling incomes. Given these circumstances, it can be assumed that there will be an interruption to the downward trend of poverty in the Southern Cone countries. In the countries of the Andean region, the numbers living in poverty are believed to have increased.

In the Central American countries which already had the lowest poverty levels, namely Costa Rica and Panama, further substantial falls took place (from 23.7% to 18.2% and from 36.3% to 24.2%, respectively, between 1990 and 1999) as a result of specific anti-poverty policies and improved economic performance. Of the countries with high levels of poverty, Mexico achieved only a marginal improvement (from 39.3% to 38% between 1989 and 1998), as the severe financial crisis that the country suffered in late 1994 resulted in a major contraction in the middle of the decade. The poverty rate in El Salvador held steady at about 45% over the decade. In countries with very high poverty levels, there were no major improvements either. In Honduras, for example, the percentage of households that were poor fell only slightly, from 75.2% to 74.3%, between 1990 and 1999.

F.   Public social spending

By and large, the countries of the region have increased public social spending both per capita and as a proportion of GDP (ECLAC, 2000c; ECLAC, 2001c). In Latin America as a whole, it is estimated that public social spending rose from 10.4% to 13.1% of GDP, with more substantial increases in those countries whose per capita social spending was lower at the beginning of the decade (see figure II.2). Priority was given to investment in human capital (health and education), although social security was also boosted, albeit to a lesser degree, in that financing had to be provided for the pension system reforms that came to be applied throughout the region. Housing was the most neglected sector.

Figure II.2
LATIN AMERICA: SOCIAL SPENDING, BY SECTOR

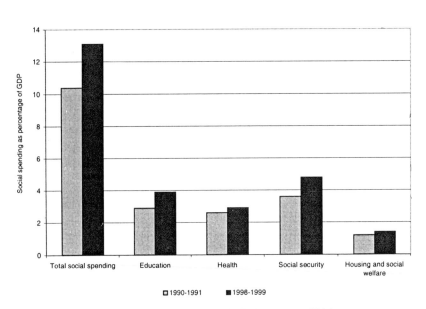

Source: ECLAC, database on social expenditure of the Social Development Division.

The Southern Cone countries whose public social spending increased most as a proportion of GDP between the periods 1990-1991 and 1998-1999 were Uruguay (6 percentage points) and Paraguay (4.4 points), while the increases seen in Argentina, Brazil and Chile were more modest (between 2.5 and 3 percentage points). In 1998-1999, social spending in Argentina (20.5%), Brazil (21%) and Uruguay (22.8%), as a proportion of GDP, was very close to and in some cases higher than that of a number of developed countries. Public social spending in Paraguay, although modest as a proportion of GDP (7.4%), showed remarkable growth over the decade, with per capita social expenditure increasing by a factor of two and a half between 1990-1991 and 1998-1999. In Chile and Uruguay, per capita spending virtually doubled. Rising per capita social spending in Argentina, Brazil, Chile and Uruguay was primarily due to economic growth, while in Paraguay it was due to the expansion of public spending in this area.

In the Andean subregion, the largest increase in social spending as a proportion of GDP in the period 1990-1999 was seen in Colombia, where it rose by 7 percentage points, followed by Bolivia with 3.7 points and Peru with 3.5 points. In per capita terms, comparison of social spending in the Andean countries at the beginning and end of the decade shows that it has now returned to pre-debt crisis levels. Per capita social spending grew particularly strongly in Bolivia, Colombia and Peru, more than doubling between 1990-1991 and 1998-1999. In Venezuela, by contrast, it fell by 7%. In Bolivia and Peru, rising per capita spending was the result of higher priority being given to the social sectors in the public budget, while the rise in Colombia can be attributed to the combined effects of higher economic growth, increased public spending and higher priority for social spending. In terms of per capita GDP, there are wide differences between the spending of each country and the regional average. In relation to their income levels, Bolivia and Colombia, along with other countries in the region, have high levels of social spending. In Peru and Venezuela, on the other hand, per capita social spending is below the regional average.

After falling sharply in the "lost decade", public social spending in the Central American countries and Mexico recovered more than proportionately in the 1990s. Countries in the subregion where social spending was already high included Costa Rica and Panama; the latter continued to increase it substantially, distancing itself further and further from the others. Countries whose levels of spending were intermediate (Mexico) and low (all the rest) made extraordinary efforts to increase it, the only exception being Honduras, where it ultimately declined both as a proportion of GDP (down by half a percentage point) and in absolute per capita terms (down by 5%). In per capita terms, very large increases were achieved by El Salvador (40% higher in 1998-1999 than in 1994-1995) and Guatemala (where it doubled). During the decade, a widening gap opened up between Panama, which in 1998-1999 devoted virtually a fifth of its GDP (US$ 642 per capita) to the social sectors, and El Salvador, with just 4.3% of GDP (US$ 82 per capita), and Nicaragua, with 10.8% (US$ 57 per capita).[2]

Of course, it is difficult to evaluate social progress simply on the basis of public spending in this area. Growing private-sector participation in the provision of education, health, social security and other social services makes the direct impact of public spending even more complex to measure. A proper evaluation of social progress would now require more careful analysis of vital quality of life indicators, something that is outside the scope of this report.

Note should also be taken of a facet of the situation that is analysed in another section of this paper. Demographic projections indicate that one of the historical characteristics of Latin America and the Caribbean, the high participation of younger groups in the age pyramid, will change radically over the coming decades, with older strata coming to predominate. If all the countries in the region are now faced with the need to carry out far-reaching reforms to their social security and pension systems because of the inability of governments to meet the costs involved, in two or three decades, depending on the country, the economically active population will be much smaller than the inactive population it will have to support. From the point of view of the social challenges facing the region, then, Latin American and Caribbean societies have very little time left in which to rectify current social security imbalances and prepare themselves to meet needs that will be even more pressing in financial terms than those they now have to deal with.

Another development in the 1990s was that particular attention began to be paid to the concept of vulnerability, and thus to the identification of vulnerable groups with a view to implementing social integration policies, insofar as this was feasible. One area in which there was progress was the integration of women into the economy and the advancement of gender equity in its different aspects. Particular attention was also paid to the marginalized young, owing to the increasing risk they faced of becoming involved in situations of violence and illegality as a result of the adverse labour market situation. Older adults began to be viewed as a population cohort of importance for future social policy, while the position of ethnic groups had to be reassessed, mainly because of the outbreak of conflict in Chiapas, Mexico. Anti-poverty programmes were generally focused on extremely poor groups, and the policies followed were compensatory ones that only rarely resulted in their being integrated into the formal economy.

---

[2] Nicaragua's per capita GDP is among the lowest in the region, however, so social expenditure of almost 13% of GDP represents a considerable financial effort.

Over and above the actual social situation in each country, social integration efforts have to take account of the way members of society perceive their own position. While the issue cannot be dealt with fully here, attention should be drawn to the importance being taken on by the growing gap between symbolic consumption and physical consumption (ECLAC, 2000c). While access to knowledge, images and symbols has risen over recent decades as educational levels, the number of televisions and radios and, recently, Internet access have increased, consumption of real goods has not grown at the same rate. Thus, the increase in access to knowledge, information and advertising is out of all proportion to the rise in access to higher incomes, greater well-being and higher consumption. The 1980s and early 1990s saw a significant jump in levels of violence and a growing perception of citizen insecurity, developments which may be regarded as mutually interacting symptoms of social disintegration.

G.   Social challenges for sustainability

As a general conclusion to this discussion of social developments in the countries of Latin America and the Caribbean over the last decade, and of the challenges that these pose for the sustainability of development in the region, it should be said that new winners and losers are emerging because of the pace of economic structuring. The structural heterogeneity that characterizes the region's production systems has increased, owing to a widening of the productivity gap between large firms at the forefront of the modernization process and the wide, varied range of unmodernized activities that account for the bulk of employment. This has not only created a material basis for greater social inequality, by accentuating domestic productivity and income gaps, but it has also affected growth potential by holding back the creation of links between different production sectors, the diffusion of technical progress and the knock-on effect of exports. The most serious of the region's shortcomings is linked with the phenomena described above, and is to be found in the areas dealt with by the Copenhagen World Summit for Social Development, as the severe social disadvantages accumulated over a long period, and further added to by the crisis of the 1980s, are being remedied only very slowly, particularly in three interrelated areas: the employment situation, the poverty rate, and social exclusion. As a result, the absolute number of people living in poverty in Latin America and the Caribbean, at 211 million, is now higher than ever.

The first factor that determines how rapidly poverty is reduced is the rate of economic growth and the success achieved in eliminating hyperinflation; the second is the determination with which social spending is increased and the concern, a growing one among the governments of the region, to see that it is allocated more efficiently. The fact is that the countries which made most progress in reducing poverty were the ones that managed to combine relatively high growth rates over a number of years with falling unemployment and rising participation rates in the poorest families. Lower inflation also provided the basis for real improvements in work incomes and, in some cases, pensions, and was conducive to investment continuity, which had positive repercussions on the labour market.

Macroeconomic balance, and the way this balance is achieved, are crucial for rapid, more equitable growth, the foundations of genuinely sustainable development. As well as lower inflation and a better fiscal balance, countries need to achieve current-account stability, a level of domestic saving that matches investment needs, an appropriate real exchange rate and a level of domestic expenditure that is compatible with sustainable use of production capacity. It also needs to be borne in mind that growth does not in itself guarantee better distribution. The crucial thing is for growth to be of high quality; in other words, it needs to be sustainable over time and to feed through into productive jobs and better wages.

One feature of growth in the region, as discussed in the previous chapter, is that it now depends very closely on the dynamism of activities linked to natural resources. If growth is to have a greater impact on employment, then, the links between these activities and those of the other production sectors need to be strengthened. Such links do not just result in intermediate demand for goods, services, and labour; they also stimulate quality improvements and the diffusion of technical progress and of better business and managerial practices. This comes about through the promotion of quality standards, the creation of technical training institutes and the provision of modern production support services, educational services and technical, financial and organizational support for small and medium-sized enterprises and microbusinesses.

Lastly, social policy reform attaches particular importance to more efficient resource management. If this is to be achieved, it seems indispensable for reforms to be accompanied by institutional changes that are oriented towards better standards of service for users, appropriate targeting and further decentralization, and that link resources to performance and service quality. If more effective progress is to be made towards compliance with the undertakings signed up to at the World Summit for Social Development, there needs to be an integrated economic and social policy approach so that measures to stimulate competitiveness and those that seek to improve social cohesion can support and complement each other. Although there may be conflicts between the two in the short term, public policy can avail itself of the many ways in which they complement each other, the key being macroeconomic management that is capable of stimulating high and stable growth so that competitiveness is enhanced and the employment impact of growth is strengthened. Investment in human resources and measures to stimulate production are the best ways of making progress with these tasks. Similarly, agricultural modernization can help to combat rural poverty, as long as public policies to provide access to land and regularize titles are in place, efforts are made to improve production infrastructure, and closer links are forged between agro-industry and small producers.

Chapter III

Demographic trends

An analysis of demographic trends in Latin America and the Caribbean over recent decades verifies the general validity of the demographic transition model, bearing in mind that modalities, degrees and rates of progress vary according to specific conditions in each country.

As is well known, the demographic transition is a long-term population transformation process relating to socio-economic development and consisting of two sequential phases. The first of these involves a quite rapid fall in mortality rates as a result of public-health improvements. The second more complex phase entails a sustained reduction in the overall fertility rate. This two-stage process generates rapid population growth which then slows down steadily. In addition, the initial broad base of the age pyramid shrinks in reflection of the steady population ageing that occurs in the final phase of the transition.

The demographic transition occurs in response to a variety of factors, including modernizing social changes in the economic, urbanization, culture, education and public-health domains. These changes are also reflected in the role of women in both family and society.

In most of the region's countries, the major decline in mortality rates took place in the middle of the twentieth century. Fertility has also been declining steadily, especially since the 1950s, and will continue to do so as we move into the twenty-first century.

The status of individual countries in the demographic transition during the 1990s can be expressed in the following four categories: (i) *incipient* (Bolivia, El Salvador, Guatemala, Honduras and Nicaragua), with persistent relatively high birth and mortality rates, resulting in natural growth rates of slightly over 2% per year; (ii) *moderate* (Paraguay), which displays a clearly falling mortality rate but a still relatively high birth rate, resulting in the region's highest rate of population growth; (iii) *full* (Brazil, Colombia, Ecuador, Peru, Venezuela, Costa Rica, Mexico and Panama), characterized by clearly falling birth rates and relatively low mortality rates, giving natural growth rates close to 2% per year; and (iv) *advanced* (Argentina, Chile and Uruguay), with low birth and mortality rates, and natural growth rates of close to 1% per year (ECLAC, 2001d).

Most of the region's population is in the intermediate phase of the demographic transition process, although different situations may exist within any given country. Differentiated sociodemographic patterns reflect acute social inequalities: the highest fertility and mortality rates persist in rural areas where socially disadvantaged peasant populations and ethnic groups tend to be concentrated (ECLAC, 2001d).

The region as a whole is still young, with nearly one-third of its inhabitants under 15 years of age. Regional population grew at an average of 1.9% per year during the 1990s, with a steadily slowing trend that could reduce the rate to 1% by 2025 (IDB/ECLAC/CELADE, 1996).

The overall effect of the various demographic transition processes unfolding across Latin America and the Caribbean leads to the regional projection shown in figure III.1, where total population is broken down by main age groups.

As a result of the region's varied passage through the demographic transition, population ageing is beginning to occur in some countries. In Argentina, Chile and Uruguay, adults over 60 years old now represent more than 10% of the population. So, in addition to the traditional problems of absorbing and channelling large numbers of young people trying to enter the labour market for the first time, the region is now facing the additional problem of a steadily ageing population, which will require complex adjustments in development institutions and strategies.

Figure III.1
LATIN AMERICA AND THE CARIBBEAN: POPULATION BY AGE GROUP, 1950-2045
(Millions)

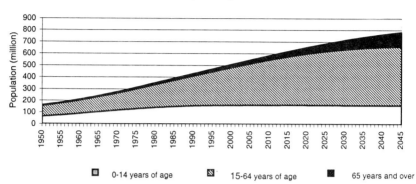

Source: Economic Commission for Latin America and the Caribbean, Population Division - Latin American and Caribbean Demographic Centre (CELADE), "Latin America: population by calendar years and single ages, 1995-2005", *Demographic Bulletin*, year 33, No. 66 (LC/G.2099-P), Santiago, Chile, July.

A.   Population and environmentally sustainable development

Conventional demographic analysis has thus far paid insufficient attention to environmentally sustainable development. The urban-rural divide is a key distinction in this context, and is considered elsewhere in this document. Here we analyse other demographic aspects of particular relevance to the prospects for sustainable development.

1.   Demographic transition as a challenge for governments and societies

In earlier decades, the specially rapid population growth of the initial phase of the demographic transition overwhelmed governments and societies in the region. Social needs have clearly grown faster than the means, especially financial ones, to address them. Between 1950 and 2000, the population of Latin America and the Caribbean tripled from 167 million to 519 million inhabitants. In that half-century the region faced the major task of providing infrastructure, food, services and jobs to accommodate an additional 350 million people —more than the total population of the entire American continent, including the United States and Canada, in 1950. Institutional service capacity, infrastructure building of various types, human resource formation, job creation —and the provision of social satisfiers in general— have been unable to keep pace with population growth. This has led to an expansion of the informal economy and increasingly precarious employment.

In such circumstances, it has been difficult for governments to assume extra responsibilities and take on new tasks, such as those relating to environmental management, which are seen as additional to their traditional ones.

The demographic transition means that the population of Latin America and the Caribbean is unlikely to double in this century. Nonetheless, although population growth rates are headed downwards, demographic growth still represents a major challenge for the region.

2.   The dependency ratio and the demographic bonus

At the household level, the region's economically active population has to sustain family members who are not of working age, particularly children. The dependency ratio is defined as the ratio of the dependent populations (those over 64 years of age or under 15), to the working-age population between 15 and 64. In nearly all countries this ratio is lower among urban populations than rural ones.

As the process of urbanization advances and the second phase of the demographic transition plays out in the region, the dependency ratio is expected to decline. Each working-age family member will carry a smaller burden in providing for children and old people. This favourable situation will then be reversed, as the final stage of the demographic transition leads to population ageing, and the relative weight of retired people increases. Over the next two decades, however, most of the region's countries will be able to enjoy a temporary fall in the dependency ratio —a phenomenon sometimes referred to as the "demographic bonus".

The demographic bonus could lead to an improvement in the quality of life, together with increased saving capacity and the chance to undertake expenditure and investment in previously neglected areas such as the environment. This is an opportunity that needs to be exploited to make up lost ground and pre-empt future needs in the field of the development sustainability. To gain a lasting advantage from the demographic bonus, saving conditions need to be improved and institutions and public policies adapted, in order to address more effectively the needs arising from a very different future population structure than what the region has known in recent decades.

3. The population/resources ratio. Carrying capacity

Without reference to outdated Malthusian predictions, it should be understood that the region's extraordinary population growth has put greater pressure on natural resources, both renewable and non-renewable, through complex, mostly indirect mechanisms. Pressure on resources is generally mediated by economics, production and technology, which modulate it and do not always remain in proportion to demographics, and the pressure on resources has often exceeded the carrying capacity of important regional ecosystems. "Population pressure" cannot really be blamed as the main cause of the region's environmental deterioration, but there is no doubt that it has helped to aggravate the problem.

Despite the indirect and mediated nature of the population-environment nexus, population density has often been used as an indicator related to the carrying capacity of a piece of territory generally defined by administrative criteria to exploit aggregate census information.

Latin America and the Caribbean is a region with low average population density: 252 inhabitants/1,000 hectares in 2000, or under one quarter of the average population density in Asia. Subregional differences are very marked, however. While population density in some Central American and Caribbean countries exceeds two inhabitants per hectare, no southern cone country attains a density of even 0.2 inhabitants/hectare.

Several more precise and more representative analytical instruments and indicators have been proposed. Firstly, it has been recommended that the spatial limits of political-administrative entities be overcome by defining eco-regions or bio-regions, using both ecological and social criteria.

Attempts have also been made to construct the ecological footprint of a given human settlement, defined as the territory which bears the impact of the settlement in terms of the traces of its metabolic functions of exchanging mass and energy through economic processes. Satisfying urban food demand, for example, means a proliferation of productive processes in places and ecosystems that are often far from the settlement that generates the demand. The globalization process makes the job of specifying ecological footprints extremely complicated.

In the same vein, product life-cycle approaches have been developed, which take into account all of the various phases of the productive process, from raw material extraction to final disposal of the product and treatment of the resultant waste material, wherever that may occur.

An eco-systemic approach has been used to specify, where possible, permissible *thresholds* for component extraction and the absorption of various amounts of different types of pollutant, in order to preserve the functioning and stability of bio-physical systems.

As they are developed, these and other analytical efforts will make it possible to define and materialize the carrying capacity concept, as a key criterion for sustainable development. However, to date, the countries of the region have not yet agreed approaches and methodologies for standardizing information, comparing results and achieving synergies between the various analytical efforts undertaken.

4.   Mobility of regional population: migrations

Population mobility is the aspect of demography that is most sensitive to changes in the socio-economic conditions of development. The most dynamic sector of the population moves within national borders and beyond, in response to attraction or expulsion forces. This section focuses on international migrations.

At the start of the twenty-first century, about 150 million people, or just under 3% of the world's population, are estimated to be living outside their countries of origin. This figure, which is rising, does not include people who migrate without documents (IOM-United Nations, 2000) or those who move temporarily.

In Latin America and the Caribbean, over 17 million people are living outside their country of birth, which means that at least one in every 10 migrants worldwide comes from our region. Half of this contingent emigrated in the 1990s, particularly to the United States, which is the main destination country for various migratory flows. In addition, there is also an incipient increase in migration to Europe.

Although globalization does not embrace the free movement of people, its exerts a powerful influence on world migratory dynamics, and this is reflected in our region. Most people who migrate do so by overcoming barriers that generate multiple tensions, and in circumstances that affect their security and quality of life. The decision to migrate is generally taken against a backdrop of poverty, involving unemployment or underemployment, low pay or generally little chance of social mobility.

The figure below shows the pattern of migration from Latin America and the Caribbean to the main destination outside the region, the United States.

Figure III. 2
UNITED STATES: DISTRIBUTION OF IMMIGRANTS FROM LATIN AMERICA AND THE
CARIBBEAN, BY SUBREGION OF ORIGIN, 1971-1998
(Percentages)

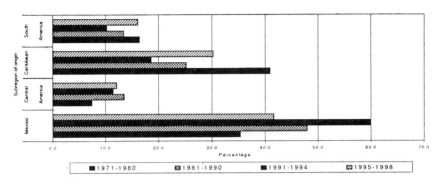

Source: Data figures provided by the United States Immigration and Naturalization Service (INS), 2000.

For the region, emigration represents a chance of employment and the generation of remittances, but it also involves a permanent reduction in skilled human capital. Already weak science and technology institutions are severely undermined by emigration which compromises their future still further.

Migration between the countries of the region has deep historical roots and occurs mainly between nations sharing common borders, where it is associated with the coordination of labour markets and circumstantial factors. Intraregional migration was particularly intense during the 1970s, in the wake of sociopolitical disturbances in a number of countries. This trend slowed down in the 1990s, when the cumulative total of intraregional migrants amounted to just 2.2 million people (Villa and Martínez, 2000).

Data on intraregional migratory patterns is not only out of date but also restricted to people moving residence. Until 1990 nearly two-thirds of all regional migrants were concentrated in Argentina and Venezuela, but this pattern has since changed, with both countries now reporting extra-regional emigration. Emigration from the Andean countries has been particularly heavy in recent years, to destinations both within and outside the region.

The serious sociopolitical disruptions in Central America in the 1970s and 1980s —added to traditional structural shortcomings in development— caused the number of Nicaraguan and Salvadoran migrants in Costa Rica to increase substantially between 1973 and 1984.

During the same period, Mexico took in a large number of immigrants from Guatemala and El Salvador. The same can be said of Belize —with smaller figures but even greater effects in the economic, social and cultural domains (Villa and Martínez, 2000). The evidence suggests that Costa Rica has maintained its status as a migrant destination within the Central American isthmus in recent years, while Mexico and Belize have become staging posts for Central American migrants on their way north.

Intra-Caribbean migration involves intensive circulation, as people migrate and then return by stages, in a process of moving to a destination outside the region. The major expansion of tourist activities in some countries, combined with fewer job opportunities in others, has increased intra-Caribbean mobility. Just over half of all immigration in 1990 came from the subregion itself (Mills, 1997), with Trinidad and Tobago, United States Virgin Islands and Barbados among countries registering the largest immigrant presence.

Women and highly-skilled people have been increasingly involved in recent intraregional migration, and evidence suggests that migration by highly skilled workers has remained strong during the 1990s. The territorial restructuring of the region's economies is generating new patterns of temporary migration, in response to the hiring plans of large corporations, economic openness and subregional integration initiatives.

5.   Migration and remittances

One of the clearest benefits of international migration for developing countries is the money that emigrants send back to their relations and communities of origin (see Villa, 2001). Regular or occasional contributions that emigrants save and remit in individual amounts have become a leading macroeconomic variable in many zones, and even for some countries of the region, particularly in Mexico, Central America and the Caribbean. In some cases this amounts to a genuine "migration industry". Many such remittances are informal, so difficult to track and measure; they also incur exorbitant transfer costs arising from commissions or unfavourable exchange rates. An approximate and conservative estimate suggests that total remittances to the region grew from about US$ 5.2 billion to some US$ 18 billion per year between 1990 and 2000. Their distribution and significance in relation to the main macroeconomic variables can be judged from table III.1.

Table III.1
LATIN AMERICA AND THE CARIBBEAN: MAIN REMITTANCE RECEIVING COUNTRIES,
1990-2000

	Remittances			Remittances/GDP (%)		Remittances/exports (%)	
	Millions of dollars		Average annual variation				
	1990	2000 *	1990-2000 (%)	1990	2000 *	1990	2000 *
Latin America and the Caribbean	5,168 b	18,000	13.3	0.4	0.9	3.6	4.4
Mexico	2,492	7,000	10.9	0.9	1.2	9.5	3.8
El Salvador	358	1,800	17.5	7.5	13.9	70.7	51.6
Dominican Republic	315	1,600	17.7	4.5	8.1	17.2	17.8
Brazil	527	1,200	8.6	0.1	0.2	1.7	1.9
Ecuador	50	1,100	36.2	0.5	8.1	1.8	18.8
Colombia	488	800	5.1	1.0	1.0	7.2	5.1
Peru	87	800	24.8	0.3	1.5	2.6	9.3
Jamaica	136	700	17.8	2.1	10.6	12.3	41.8 c
Cuba	...	720	...	...	2.9	...	15.0
Guatemala	107	600	18.9	1.4	3.1	9.2	16.0
Other d	409	1,680	15.2	...	...	...	...

Source: ECLAC, on the basis of figures from the International Monetary Fund. National estimates in the case of Cuba.

a Estimates, based on 1999 data.
b In the absence of official figures, this total includes estimates of US$ 300 million for Cuba and US$ 200 million for Haiti.
c Figure refers to 1999.
d Mainly Haiti, Honduras and Nicaragua.

The remittances sent to Mexico, Central America and the Caribbean account for three-quarters of the regional total. With about US$ 7 billion per year, Mexico is the region's largest recipient country and second-largest in the world after India.

In smaller economies such as El Salvador, the Dominican Republic, Ecuador and Jamaica, remittances received have a much greater domestic impact, as they represent between 8% and 14% of GDP. In El Salvador and Jamaica, remittances are equivalent to 52% and 42% of total exports, respectively, and exert pressures on both the exchange rate and interest rates. Several other Central American and Caribbean countries also receive substantial amounts. One quarter of the remittances received by Nicaragua are estimated to come from Costa Rica; while those received by Cuba (just over US$ 700 million per year) basically represent family support from the Cuban community resident in the United States.

In South America, the amount and macroeconomic impact of remittances are greatest in Ecuador, while large amounts are also received in Brazil, Colombia and Peru, albeit with substantially less relative impact. In Brazil and Peru a fraction comes from emigrants living in Japan, who are descendants of former Japanese immigrants into those countries.

In Central America and Mexico, remittances are mainly used to improve food consumption. According to surveys carried out in the late 1980s by ECLAC, between 82% and 85% of family remittances in El Salvador, Guatemala and Nicaragua were destined for this purpose. Expenditure on children's health and education was another priority, with between 4% and 8% of total remittances being used in this way. Investment in home improvement and real-estate purchase accounted for between 5% and 6% of the total; financial savings and productive investment —which generate production and employment— were quite marginal (ECLAC, 2001d). Weak local business abilities, compounded by limited access to credit, restrict possibilities still further. There is an urgent need to facilitate and foster a productive use of remittances to generate employment and incomes, since this represents a potentially self-sustaining mechanism for overcoming poverty and furthering local development.

6.   Spatial trends in population settlement

There is only incipient understanding of the spatial distribution of population in the region as a whole, together with its recent evolution and trends. Knowledge about the pattern of population distribution in terms of major ecosystems or biomass is even more rudimentary.

In Latin America and the Caribbean, the basic features of the spatial pattern of population settlement were established in the colonial era, and there has been remarkable continuity since that time. The colonial settlement structure formed the basis for successive waves of densification, accompanied by opening up or expansion towards frontier areas. The latter is responsible for the major changes in spatial patterns that have taken place in recent decades. New areas have been colonized in connection with specific investments and the development of transport infrastructure: river and railroad networks and, more recently, through the expansion and consolidation of primary and secondary highway networks. It has proved impossible to break the link between deforestation and colonization in the humid tropics and the development of transport infrastructure.

In the 1960s and 1970s, many of the region's countries pursued State-organized colonization policies, frequently responding to national security criteria, and extensive frontier areas were occupied in this way. During the same period, many States, aided by international funding agencies, undertook major infrastructural works such as the construction of large-scale hydroelectric dams. These megaprojects had direct and indirect impacts on land occupation.

In the "lost decade" of the 1980s, these initiatives were drastically curtailed, after which the very concept of "megaproject" entered in crisis, following analysis of the environmental and social impact of past experiences.

In the past decade, induced colonization processes have been replaced by land occupation and population dynamics governed essentially by economic factors, such as the investment of private capital to exploit natural resources, energy sources and infrastructure building.

The resultant structure of land occupation in Latin America and the Caribbean consists of nuclei and zones of population concentration, such as the Caribbean islands, the neo-volcanic axis of the central portion of Mexico, and the south east of that country, the Pacific coast of Central America, the western side of most of the Andes, spreading towards the *altiplano* in its central portion, and spokes of population expansion radiating out from port hubs on South America's Atlantic coast (ECLAC, 2001d).

Chapter IV

The environmental situation in the region

A.   Natural ecosystems

1.   Natural land ecosystems

Latin America and the Caribbean has a land area of a little over 2 billion hectares —no more than 15% of the total land area of the planet— yet it has the biggest variety of natural species and eco-regions in the world.

The value of natural land ecosystems goes far beyond their direct economic value. The services they provide are indispensable for mankind's survival on this planet: they stabilize the climate and the atmosphere; they regulate the hydric cycle and mesoclimatic humidy; they are a source of timber, wildlife and pharmaceutical products, as well as having many other uses, and they are increasingly valuable in terms of tourism.

Unfortunately, a proper sense of the value of natural environmental services has not spread to all citizens or governments of this planet and made them aware of the urgent need to take action to check and reverse the serious impact on natural ecosystems that society has been causing for several decades past.

The lack of planning in the use of natural resources and the lack of suitable technologies and policies to ensure their preservation have led to severe deterioration of the environment in the region, which has been reflected in loss of biodiversity, soil degradation, reduction of the availability of fresh water, changes in river beds through silting, and reduction of their water quality through pollution and sedimentation.

Latin America and the Caribbean are privileged to be one of the regions with the greatest abundance of natural resources in the planet, but this also involves an enormous responsibility to the rest of the world. We must therefore give the highest priority on our action agenda to the conservation, sustainable use and restoration of the plant cover of our region.

(a)   Diversity of eco-regions and natural species

Latin America and the Caribbean has examples of all the different types of biomes that exist in the world, except for the coldest ones such as tundras and taigas.

It is difficult to use a single classification system to cover the entire variety of ecosystems in the region. Each country has its own classification system, which makes comparisons very difficult. Without any intention of replacing any of them, and for purely practical reasons, in this study we have used the classification of biomes of the World Wide Fund for Nature (WWF), to which the FAO (United Nations Food and Agriculture Organization) refers in its reports (see box IV.1).

Box IV.1
BIOMES OF LATIN AMERICA AND THE CARIBBEAN[a]

1. Tropical and subtropical moist broadleaf forests. This includes lowland humid tropical forests (up to 600 metres above sea level),[b] upland tropical forests (between 600 and 1200 metres above sea level) and tropical cloud forests (between 1200 and 2000 metres above sea level, approximately). The most important and extensive of these forests are in Amazonia. Much smaller in area, but nevertheless important, are the Massif of Guyana, Suriname and French Guiana; the tropical forests of Venezuela; those of the Atlantic coast of Brazil; those of the coasts of Ecuador, Colombia and Panama, known as Darién-Ecuador-Chocó; those of the Atlantic coasts of Nicaragua, Honduras and Guatemala; and those in southern Mexico, especially Lacandona and Chimalpas (original area = 920.4 million hectares, or 44% of the region).[c]

(continued)

Box IV.1 (continued)

2. Tropical and subtropical dry broadleaf forests. The most important of these, because of their size, are those of the Chaco, in northern Argentina, western Paraguay and southwestern Bolivia; those of the Chiquitano area in eastern Bolivia to the borders of Amazonia; those of the Atlantic coast of Brazil, between the Cerrado and the Caatinga; those of the Caribbean regions of Venezuela and Colombia; those of northern Peru and southwestern Ecuador; those of the Pacific coast of Mexico and part of the Pacific coast of Central America; those of Yucatán and Veracruz in Mexico; and those of the Caribbean countries themselves (original area = 177.8 million hectares, or 8.5% of the region).[b] In the nearctic realm, this biome is found in Mexico in the Sonora and Sinaloa region. It occupied an area of 5 million hectares, 0.2% of the region (original area = 5.1 million hectares, or 0.2% of the region).[c]

3. Temperate broadleaf and mixed forests. These are found in the southern (Pacific) coast of Chile, and are known as the Magellanic and Valdivia forests (original area = 39.5 million hectares, 1.95% of the region).[c]

4. Mediterranean forests, woodland and scrub. These are located in the central part of Chile, and are unique of their kind (original area = 14.8 million hectares, 0.7% of the region).[c]

5. Tropical and subtropical coniferous forests. These are located in the cordilleras and sierras of Central America, Mexico, Cuba and the Bahamas. Their distribution varies at different altitudes (original area = 32.2 million hectares, 1.5% of the region).[b] In the nearctic realm, they are found in the eastern and western Sierra Madre ranges of Mexico (original area = 28.8 million hectares, 1.4% of the region).[c]

6. Temperate coniferous forests. These correspond to the nearctic realm in Mexico. They form a small part of the Mediterranean-climate biome in northern Baja California, at San Pedro Mártir and Sierra Juárez (original area = 0.4 million hectares, 0.02% of the region).[c]

7. Tropical and subtropical grassland, savannah and shrubland. The most important examples of these are north of Amazonia in Venezuela and Colombia, in the area known as the llanos, and also south of Amazonia, in the area known as the Cerrado of Brazil. Other notable areas are the savannah of Uruguay, called the "pampa", which occupies practically the whole of that country's territory, and the humid Chaco of northern Argentina and Paraguay (original area = 341.1 million hectares, 16.3% of the region).[c]

8. Flooded grassland and savannah. The most important of these areas is the Pantanal area (Bolivia - Brazil - Paraguay), which occupies over 17 million hectares and is the largest in the world. It is flooded every year between December and June. Other similar areas are those of the Orinoco, the Paraná in Argentina, and those of Cuba, as well as other smaller areas (original area = 32.3 million hectares, 1.5% of the region).[c]

(continued)

Box IV.2 (concluded)

9. Montane grassland and shrubland. These areas are very special because they are located mainly in the upper part of the Andes range and are known as *punas* (the drier ones) or wetlands (wetter and more limited areas). The vegetation is dominated by herbaceous plants and those typical of alpine areas. These areas are found at altitudes over 3,000 metres above sea level, up to the snow line. They are also found in the cordilleras of Venezuela and of Mérida (Colombia). In Mexico they are known as *zacatonales* and are found in the highest parts of the eastern and western Sierra Madre range (original area = 81.1 million hectares, 3.8% of the region).[c]

10. Temperate grassland, savannah and shrubland. These are located in Argentina, from Patagonia to the Chaco and Mesopotamia. They are ecosystems in which grasses predominate, and are known as pampas or, in Patagonia, steppes (original area = 164.3 million hectares, 7.7% of the region).[c]

11. Desert and xeric shrubland These are the ecosystems of the driest parts of the region. Among the driest and most extensive are those of southern Peru, the Sechura sandy desert and coastal dunes (14 million hectares), and in northern Chile the Atacama desert, with very sparse vegetation except for sporadic oases known as *lomas*. The least dry areas of this type, covered with shrubland, are in the Caatinga on the Atlantic coast of Brazil, on the Caribbean coasts of Colombia and Venezuela (Guajira-Barranquilla) and on the coast of Venezuela (original area = 117.6 million hectares, 5.8% of the region).[c]

The biomes of the nearctic realm are found in Mexico. They occupy 40% of the country and represent 5.8% of the region (117.6 million hectares). They are the deserts of Sonora and Chihuahua and the central area of the country (original area = 117.6 million hectares, 5.8% of the region).[c]

12. Mangrove swamps. These are of enormous importance because of their regulatory function between the fresh water that flows into the sea from inland areas and the salt water of the sea. They are key ecosystems in which many marine species carry out their reproduction. They are located all along the coasts of the region, from Mexico to Brazil and Peru and the whole of the Caribbean. Only Uruguay, Argentina and Chile do not have mangrove swamps. They are found on both coasts, although the Atlantic and the Caribbean account for 70% of these ecosystems (original area = 11.6 million hectares, 0.5% of the region).[c]

The most northerly mangrove swamps are those of Mexico, in southern Baja California, which belong to the nearctic realm (original area = 0.5 million hectares, 0.02% of the region).[c]

[a] Metres above sea level.
[b] The WWF (World Wide Fund for Nature) classification is used here. See (http://wwf.org.wildworld/).
[c] This refers to the area of the territory of Latin America and the Caribbean which was occupied by these biomes before human intervention.

The region comes under two bio-geographical realms, the nearctic and the neotropical. Most of it (64%) is in the neotropical realm (from the Tropic of Cancer in Mexico to Patagonia). The nearctic part is only in northern Mexico. As may be seen from figure IV.1, 44% of the original area of the region corresponds to tropical moist broadleaf forest, where the biggest variety of species is concentrated.

Figure IV.1
AREAS OF BIOMES

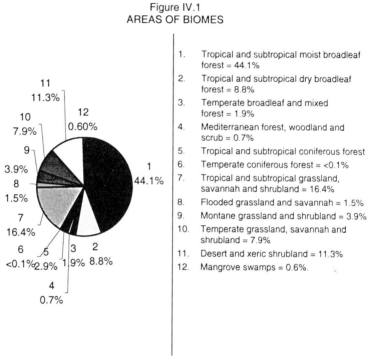

1. Tropical and subtropical moist broadleaf forest = 44.1%
2. Tropical and subtropical dry broadleaf forest = 8.8%
3. Temperate broadleaf and mixed forest = 1.9%
4. Mediterranean forest, woodland and scrub = 0.7%
5. Tropical and subtropical coniferous forest
6. Temperate coniferous forest = <0.1%
7. Tropical and subtropical grassland, savannah and shrubland = 16.4%
8. Flooded grassland and savannah = 1.5%
9. Montane grassland and shrubland = 3.9%
10. Temperate grassland, savannah and shrubland = 7.9%
11. Desert and xeric shrubland = 11.3%
12. Mangrove swamps = 0.6%.

Source: Prepared by the author on the basis of the classification of the World Wide Fund for Nature (WWF): (http://www.ww.org/wildworld/).

Indeed, Latin America and the Caribbean is the region with the greatest diversity of species in the world, and six of its countries are considered to be megadiverse: Brazil, Colombia, Ecuador, Mexico, Peru and Venezuela. The region's importance lies not only in the number of species it has, but also in the number of endemic species: that is to say, species that belong only to a particular habitat and have not spread to other areas because of natural, geographical, climatic or behaviour-related barriers.

The existence of so many endemic species in the region, which are found only there and nowhere else, represents a great responsibility for their care and protection, since their disappearance here would mean their extinction in the whole planet. Moreover, these endemic species may also be of value on account of the products that may be derived from them. This gives the region some advantages over other areas, but it also makes it vulnerable if it does not have biosecurity mechanisms that guarantee that any benefits will be distributed within the region itself. Figure IV.2 shows the total number of species of the main groups of vertebrates and higher plants which exist in the megadiverse countries of the region.

Figure IV.2
BIODIVERSITY IN MEGADIVERSE COUNTRIES OF LATIN AMERICA AND THE
CARIBBEAN

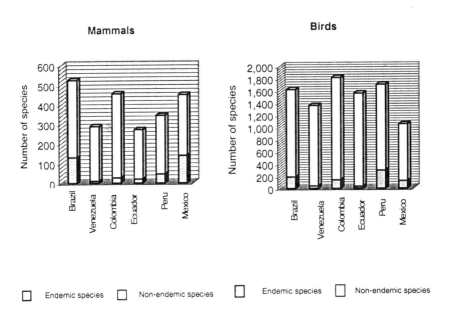

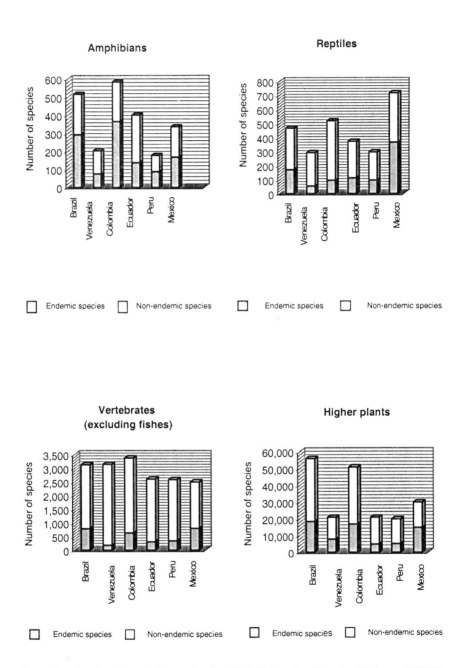

Source: Rusel Mittermeier and others, *Megadiversidad*, Mexico City, Cementos Mexicanos (CEMEX), 1997.

(b)   Use of plant cover

The plant cover of Latin America and the Caribbean, including both wooded and non-wooded ecosystems, was estimated in 1990 to amount to 1,250 million hectares, or 63% of the total land area of the region (FAO, 1995a). Of this area, in 1995 the FAO estimated that there were 940 million hectares of forests (with 10% tree cover), the rest being non-wooded biomes. This makes the region eminently suitable for forestry (see table IV.1), although the most dynamic primary sector activities are agriculture and stock-raising.

In the light of the above table and FAO data on the area devoted in 1995 to crops and permanent grazing land, the approximate situation with regard to land use in Latin America and the Caribbean is as follows: agriculture occupies nearly 160 million hectares (8% of the land area of the region); stock-raising activities occupy 601 million hectares (30%); forests and woodland cover 941 million hectares (46%),[1] while another 15% (292 million hectares) of the land area of the region corresponds to other types of non-forest plant cover (FAO, 1995a). These data should be viewed with caution because of the different criteria used in their calculation, since they involve figures from different years and the dividing line between the different categories used is not always clear. Thus, for example, part of the stock-raising is carried out in natural ecosystems with or without tree cover. Nevertheless, the data are useful as an approximation.

(i)   Use of land for agriculture

Between 1989 and 1999, the area cultivated for agriculture grew by 7.3% (from 149 million to 160 million hectares). According to the FAO, the total number of head of cattle in the region in 1999 was 350 million: 8% more than in 1989. Brazil alone had 45% of the total for the region, followed by Argentina with 15% and Mexico with 10%. The approximate area occupied by these cattle is of the order of 601 million hectares, but this does not mean in all cases the complete transformation of the plant cover, as happens in the tropical moist forests, since the natural vegetation is used in the case of the savannahs, grassland and shrubland (FAO, 2000a).

---

[1]   The 1995 data on forest coverage (FAO, 1999) are used because they employ the same definition of forests as the 1990 data. In the FAO report *Forest Resources Assessment 2000* (FAO, 2001a), there was a change in the methodology for defining forests which make it impossible to compare the data with previous periods.

Table IV.1
LATIN AMERICA AND THE CARIBBEAN (33 COUNTRIES): AREA OF FORESTS AND OTHER WOODED AREAS
(Thousands of hectares)

Country	Land area [b]	Population density (inhabitants/ km²),1999 [b]	Forests and other wooded areas, 1990 [a] Total	Other wooded areas, 1990 [a]	Total forested area, 1995 [c]	Total forested area 2000 [b] Total	Plantations
Central America and Mexico	**241,942**		**160,150**	**89,863**	**75,018**	**73,029**	**729.0**
Belize	2,280	10.3	2,117	119	1,962	1,348	3.0
Costa Rica	5,106	77.0	1,569	113	1,248	1,968	178.0
El Salvador	2,072	297.0	890	763	105	121	14.0
Guatemala	10,843	102.3	9,465	5,212	3,841	2,850	133.0
Honduras	11,189	56.4	6,054	1,446	4,115	5,383	48.0
Mexico	190,869	51.0	129,057	80,362	55,387	55,205	267.0
Nicaragua	12,140	40.7	7,732	1,705	5,560	3,278	46.0
Panama	7,443	37.8	3,266	143	2,800	2,876	40.0
Caribbean	**21,505**		**6,168**	**2,396**	**4,025**	**5,319**	**557.0**
Antigua and Barbuda	44	152.3	26	16	9	9	
Bahamas	1,001	30.1	186	0	158	842	...
Barbados	43	625.6	5	5	0	2	0.0
Cuba	10,982	101.6	3,262	1,302	1,842	2,348	482.0
Dominica	75	94.7	50	6	46	46	0.1
Dominican Republic	4,838	172.9	1,530	446	1,582	1,376	30.0
Grenada	34	273.5	11	5	4	5	0.0
Haiti	2,756	293.4	139	108	21	88	20.0
Jamaica	1,083	236.4	653	399	175	325	9.0
Saint Kitts and Nevis	36	108.3	24	11	11	4	
Saint Vincent and the Grenadines	39	289.7	12	1	11	6	
Saint Lucia	61	249.2	34	29	5	9	1.0
Trinidad and Tobago	513	251.3	236	68	161	259	15.0
South America	**1,744,709**		**1,084,541**	**199,609**	**862,604**	**877,692**	**10,456.0**
Argentina	273,669	13.4	50,936	16,500	33,942	34,648	926.0
Bolivia	108,438	7.5	57,977	8,632	48,310	53,068	46.0
Brazil	845,651	19.9	671,921	105,914	551,139	543,905	4,982.0
Colombia	103,871	40.0	63,231	9,041	52,988	49,601	141.0
Chile	74,881	20.1	16,583	8,550	7,892	15,536	2,017.0
Ecuador	27,684	44.8	15,576	3,569	11,137	10,557	167.0
Guyana	21,498	4.3	18,755	331	18,577	16,879	12.0

(continued)

Table IV.1 (concluded)

Country	Land area [b]	Population density (inhabitants/km²),1999 [b]	Forests and other wooded areas, 1990 [a]		Total forested area, 1995 [c]	Total forested area 2000 [b]	
			Total	Other wooded areas, 1990 [a]		Total	Plantations
Paraguay	39,730	13.5	19,256	6,388	11,527	23,372	27.0
Peru	128,000	19.7	84,844	16,754	67,562	65,215	640.0
Suriname	15,600	2.7	15,093	317	14,721	14,113	13.0
Uruguay	17,481	19.0	933	120	814	1,292	622.0
Venezuela	88,206	26.9	69,436	23,493	43,995	49,506	863.0
Total (Latin America and the Caribbean)	2,008,156		1,250,859	291,868	941,647	956,040	11,742.0

Source: [a] Food and Agriculture Organization of the United Nations (FAO), *Forest Resources Assessment 1990, 1995, Global Synthesis*; [b] Food and Agriculture Organization of the United Nations (FAO), *State of the World's Forests, 1999*; [c] Food and Agriculture Organization of the United Nations (FAO), *Forest Resources Assessment, 2000, 2001*.

(ii)   Use of natural ecosystems for logging and non-logging purposes

The forested area reported by the FAO for Latin America and the Caribbean in the year 2000 amounts to 956 million hectares, of which 11.7 million hectares are plantations (FAO, 2001a) (see table IV.1). The United Nations Environment Programme (UNEP) reports that the region has 721.8 million hectares of closed forest (i.e., with 40% tree coverage). The region has the largest extension of closed forest in the world (32% of the whole), while Europe and Asia have 21%, Australia and the Pacific 16.8%, Africa 9.25%, and the United States and Canada 30% (UNEP, 2001c).

In spite of the great potential of Latin America and the Caribbean, however, the region only produces 140 million m³ of industrial roundwood and 30 million m³ of sawnwood per year (see table IV.2), which represent only 9.4% and 7.2%, respectively, of world production. In contrast, Asia produces 18.8% of the world output of roundwood, Europe 24.8%, and Canada and the United States 39.6%. Production in the region in very inefficient, and the average yields per hectare are very low. In addition, not enough has been done to increase the value added to the lumber that is produced, and this production activity's linkages to international markets are insufficient.

In the last three to five years, the growth of tropical forest products has slackened, and it is expected that it will be the paper and paperboard market which will grow most rapidly in the next few years, at the rate of 2.4% per year.

In short, the use being made of the region's forestry resources is far below potential. Data are not available on the exact area being used for this purpose in the region, but it is estimated that at the world level half of the forested area is available for logging (FAO, 1999).[2]

Table IV.2
LATIN AMERICA AND THE CARIBBEAN (33 COUNTRIES): OUTPUT OF
FOREST PRODUCTS
(Thousands of cubic metres)

Country	Firewood and charcoal	Industrial roundwood	Sawn wood	Wood panels	Wood pulp	Paper and paperboard
Central America and Mexico	**51,227**	**9,682**	**4,286**	**763**	**521**	**3,182**
Belize	126	62	20	0	0	0
Costa Rica	3,440	1,651	780	74	10	20
El Salvador	6,809	211	70	0	0	56
Guatemala	13,328	795	355	43	0	31
Honduras	6,038	664	326	14	0	0
Mexico	16,731	5,914	2,543	606	511	3,047
Nicaragua	3,786	267	155	5	0	0
Panama	969	118	37	21	0	28
Caribbean	**10,156**	**1,055**	**176**	**149**	**52**	**78**
Antigua and Barbuda	0	0	0	0	0	0
Bahamas	0	117	1	0	0	0
Barbados	0	5	0	0	0	0
Cuba	2,541	611	130	149	52	57
Dominica	0	0	0	0	0	0
Dominican Republic	976	6	0	0	0	21
Grenada	0	0	0	0	0	0
Haiti	6,305	239	14	0	0	0
Jamaica	312	43	12	0	0	0

(continued)

[2] In the case of Latin America and the Caribbean, the FAO has made considerable efforts to systematize the information from the countries in order to gain a better idea of the area of forests and the use being made of them. In a recent publication it summarizes the reports for each of the Central American countries and will shortly do the same for South America (FAO, 2000a). A global analysis needs to be made of the area potentially available for forestry purposes in each country and the area which is currently being used. Such information is only available for a few countries: for example, Mexico has 59 million hectares with tree cover, of which 21 million hectares has forestry potential, but only 9 million are actually being used.

Table IV.2 (concluded)

Country	Firewood and charcoal	Industrial roundwood	Sawn wood	Wood panels	Wood pulp	Paper and paperboard
Saint Kitts and Nevis	0	0	0	0	0	0
Saint Vincent and the Grenadines	0	0	0	0	0	0
Saint Lucia	0	0	0	0	0	0
Trinidad and Tobago	22	34	19	0	0	0
South America	**192,936**	**129,830**	**28,321**	**6,036**	**9,719**	**9,335**
Argentina	4,498	6,220	1,000	590	822	1,108
Bolivia	1,419	892	176	2	0	2
Brazil	135,652	84,711	19,091	3,558	6,225	5,885
Colombia	18,062	2,703	644	176	307	676
Chile	9,984	21,387	3,802	844	2,123	597
Ecuador	5,474	5,514	1,886	380	0	86
Guyana	21	468	101	100	0	0
Paraguay	6,524	3,877	400	96	0	13
Peru	7,315	1,546	693	83	48	140
Suriname	19	103	29	7	0	7
Uruguay	3,050	1,043	269	6	29	86
Venezuela	918	1,366	230	194	165	735
Total, Latin America and the Caribbean	**254,319**	**140,567**	**32,783**	**6,948**	**10,292**	**12,595**

Source: Adapted by United Nations Environment Programme (UNEP) from Food and Agriculture Organization of the United Nations (FAO), *State of the World's Forests, 1999*, Rome, 1999.

Nor is it accurately known which of the forestry operations are being carried out on a sustainable basis, or what area they involve. Generally speaking, however, it can be considered that only a small part are being operated in this way, even though most of the countries are involved in international initiatives to develop sustainability criteria and indicators (Intergovernmental Group on Forests, Centre for International Forestry Research, International Tropical Timber Organization, etc.).

Major efforts have been made in the field of the certification of timber, which involves evaluation of the production process, but this continues to be a highly controversial issue which it has not been possible to institutionalize at the world or national levels. The danger with these certification processes is that they could be abused for the purpose of unfair economic competition. They do, however, have the great virtue of being means for making forestry a more orderly activity and keeping checks on its sustainability. For the moment, 90% of the certified forests are temperate forests in the developed countries. The Forestry Stewardship Council (FSC) is one of the international certification bodies.[3]

Early in 2001, the World Bank and the WWF signed an agreement to certify 200 million hectares in the world.

Forestry plantations have increased substantially in the last two decades, but even so almost all timber comes from native forests, except in Chile, where 84% of timber is obtained from plantations (see table IV.1).

Argentina, Brazil, Costa Rica, Cuba, Peru and Uruguay have initiated major programmes to promote plantations through different kinds of subsidies. If these trends are maintained, it is estimated that by 2010, 40% of timber will be obtained from plantations (FAO, 1999). Some of these subsidies may ultimately undermine the sustainability of the forests to which they apply.

Another great challenge in the region is controlling the illegal cutting of wood. While the extent of this illegal cutting is not known exactly, it is estimated that it amounts to double the legal cutting.

Furthermore, the consumption of firewood and charcoal continues to be very high in the region, especially among rural families, and the amount of wood cut for this purpose is almost double the amount cut for roundwood, although the growth rate of this form of woodcutting has gone down in the last decade (see table IV.2). Practically all the wood used for this purpose is cut at random, since there are no plantations for this type of use. Brazil consumes 53% of the region's firewood, while Mexico and Guatemala account for 59% of the firewood cut in Central America and Mexico.

The under-utilization of forestry potential is not only due to insufficient use of the total area suitable for forestry and inefficient management, but also to poor integration of large and small enterprises processing lumber and non-lumber products, to limitations on the use of potential environmental goods and services or the development of tourism to capitalize on the existing woods and forests, and to the low prices of non-lumber products.

This situation has got worse because sectoral development strategies and policies have been based almost exclusively on the commercial value of forests, woodland and areas with natural vegetation

---

[3]   The FSC has 311 members from 50 countries and has certified over 15 million hectares of forests in the world. Only a very small part of this production is sold as labeled goods to end-users. Most of the output ends up being used in regular, non-labeled products (FSC, 1999).

in terms of the production of lumber or their conversion for agricultural and stock-raising purposes.

Generally speaking, natural ecosystems provide the local population with important resources for various uses. The price of this raw material is usually very low, however, and does not make as much of a contribution to the local economy as it should, thus giving rise to intensive over-exploitation of these natural resources to obtain some gains, small though they may be. This is a clear example of how market prices do not reflect the value of environmental services or the importance of species.

In contrast, however, this biodiversity is more and more intensively exploited by enterprises which have developed specialized technologies for identifying different applications of these genetic qualities in agriculture and health. The lack of a clear and fair regulatory framework at the national and multinational levels means that there is no guarantee that the benefits from these products will be fairly divided among the real owners of the natural resources in question.[4]

Forest ecosystems in general also provide a large number of products in the form of food, building materials, fibres, medicines, etc. which do not enter the national market but are fundamentally for self-consumption and are generally not recorded in any way.

(c)   Deterioration of natural land ecosystems

(i)   Deforestation

Although this is a self-evident fact, it is nevertheless worth repeating that the growing population of the region and the backward conditions in which the majority of the population live give rise to serious pressures on natural ecosystems. Over decades, this has caused heavy impacts which must be taken into account in order to take suitable measures before these ecosystems disappear altogether. Deforestation has been closely linked with settlement policy, through the opening of roads, the relocation of human communities and the expansion of agricultural land (Gligo, 2001).

---

[4]   It is estimated that nearly US$ 40 billion is obtained from species of the humid tropics, through the sale of prescription and non-prescription drugs containing active ingredients derived from forest plants. Nearly 80% of 50 pharmaceutical products sold in the United States comes from natural forest products. Of the 3,000 species of plants which have been identified as having anti-cancer properties by the National Cancer Institute of that country, 70% come from the tropical forests.

The main cause of deforestation in Latin America and the Caribbean has been the use of land for agricultural activities. The region is now devoting almost half of its natural ecosystems to agriculture and stock-raising.

The risk run by natural ecosystems is that if they do not supply products that generate income and employment for the local inhabitants and they cease to be economically profitable, the use of the land in question is changed and it is devoted to agricultural activities.

Moreover, as regards the use of forest resources, few of the region's forests are managed in a sustainable manner. Since the nineteenth century, the approach has tended to be one of "mining" the forests by extracting all the species of commercial value from them and then abandoning them or changing the land use, once it no longer has immediate economic value. Furthermore, the promotion of commercial forest plantations in recent decades has meant that they have taken the place of large areas of highly varied and fragile native forests in the region.

The promotion of private or governmental megaprojects has also played a very significant role in the deforestation of enormous areas of vegetation, especially in the tropics. The most significant examples of this are in Mexico (Chontalpa, Tenosique, Uxpanapa) and Brazil (Rondônia), with the conversion of tropical areas to stock-raising in the 1970s and 1980s.

Road-building and mining operations rarely include environmental impact studies, and the impact of new roads is not limited to their direct effects but also includes the secondary effects of the disorderly occupation of the areas around them.

Cutting firewood and making charcoal also have a considerable impact, depending on the ecosystems involved, which is all the more serious in the driest areas, where vegetation grows slowly and the areas with plant cover are few in number or highly fragmented.

Forest fires have also been an important factor in the loss of plant cover in the region. They had never before had such a serious impact as in 1997 and 1998, however, when the most devastating fires in recent world history took place.

These disasters are mostly due to the use of fire in agricultural activities: the burning off of vegetation or the use of slash-and-burn methods for the elimination of agricultural wastes in cultivated fields or to speed the growth of grass for grazing. When these agricultural burning activities get out of control and coincide with periods of extreme drought, real catastrophes can ensue, such as those witnessed in 1982-1983 and 1997-1998.

Because of these processes, the original area of the region with plant cover has been reduced to 1,250 million hectares, or 63% of the total land area of the region.

According to the FAO, the loss of forest cover between 1980 and 1990 was 7.4 million hectares per year, while between 1990 and 1995 it was 5.8 million hectares per year (see table IV.3). This means that in 5 years the region lost 29 million hectares of forest: much more than Africa (18.7 million hectares) or Asia (14.5 million hectares) (FAO, 1995b, 1999). Of this total amount of deforestation, 95% corresponds to the tropics (UNEP, 2000a).[5]

The deforestation in Central America and Mexico is much greater than in South America in terms of severity, although the areas involved are smaller in absolute values. In Mexico alone, deforestation affects over 500,000 hectares annually. Because of the small areas of forests which remain in some countries, the loss of 151,000 hectares in Nicaragua, 41,000 hectares in Costa Rica and 4,000 hectares in El Salvador gives rates of deforestation which are among the highest in the world: 2.5%, 3% and 3.3% respectively. The rate of deforestation in Costa Rica has gone down now, but in past decades the major part of that country's territory was deforested (see table IV.3).

The degree of deforestation is very high in the Caribbean, too. In this case, the area deforested (only 56,000 hectares) is very small compared with the total area of Latin America and the Caribbean, but it represents an enormous risk because of the sparseness and fragility of the vegetation that still exists in the islands. The rates of deforestation are 7.2% in Jamaica (the second highest in the world after Lebanon), 3.4% in Haiti and 3.6% in Saint Lucia. Furthermore, the areas involved are of high biological value, with a large number of endemic species, and provide indispensable environmental services, such as availability of fresh water and protection of the coastline. Haiti has already lost 98% of its original forests, and only 5% of its plant cover remains, including other types of non-forest vegetation (see table IV.3).

---

[5]   FAO data are not used in this case because in the corresponding FAO report (FAO, 2001b) there was a change of methodology which does not permit comparison with earlier periods.

The situation in South America is different, since the average annual rate of deforestation is 0.5%. The country which loses the largest area each year in absolute terms is Brazil, but the highest rates of deforestation are observed in Bolivia, Ecuador and Paraguay (see table IV.3).

Table IV.3
LATIN AMERICA AND THE CARIBBEAN (33 COUNTRIES): ANNUAL CHANGES
IN FORESTED AREAS

Country	Annual deforestation			
	1981-1990 [a]		1990-1995 [b]	
	Thousands of hectares	Percentage	Thousands of hectares	Percentage
Central America and Mexico	**1,117.0**	**1.8**	**959.0**	**2.1**
Belize	5.0	0.2	7.0	0.3
Costa Rica	49.6	2.9	41.0	3.0
El Salvador	3.1	2.2	4.0	3.3
Guatemala	81.3	1.7	82.0	2.0
Honduras	111.6	2.1	102.0	2.3
Mexico	678.0	1.3	508.0	0.9
Nicaragua	124.0	1.9	151.0	2.5
Panama	64.4	1.9	64.0	2.1
Caribbean	**89.8**	**2.8**	**73.0**	**1.6**
Antigua and Barbuda	<0.5	0.2	0.0	0.0
Bahamas	4.5	2.1	4.0	2.6
Barbados			0.0	0.0
Cuba	17.3	1.0	24.0	1.2
Dominica	0.3	0.7	0.0	0.0
Dominican Republic	35.1	2.8	26.0	1.6
Grenada	-0.2	-4.3	0.0	0.0
Haiti	1.5	4.8	0.0	3.4
Jamaica	26.8	7.2	16.0	7.2
Saint Kitts and Nevis	0.0	-0.2	0.0	0.0
Saint Vincent and the Grenadines	0.3	2.1	0.0	0.0
Saint Lucia	0.3	5.2	0.0	3.6
Trinidad and Tobago	3.7	2.1	3.0	1.5

(continued)

Table IV.3 (concluded)

Country	Annual deforestation			
	1981-1990 [a]		1990-1995 [b]	
	Thousands of hectares	Percentage	Thousands of hectares	Percentage
South America	**6,204.0**	**1.0**	**4,772.0**	**0.9**
Argentina			89.0	0.3
Bolivia	6,24.7	1.2	581.0	1.2
Brazil	3,670.9	0.6	2,554.0	0.5
Colombia	367.0	0.7	262.0	0.5
Chile			29.0	0.4
Ecuador	238.0	1.8	189.0	1.6
Guyana	18.0	0.1	9.0	---
Paraguay	402.5	2.7	327.0	2.6
Peru	271.2	0.4	217.0	0.3
Suriname	12.7	0.1	12.0	0.1
Uruguay			---	---
Venezuela	599.0	1.2	503.0	1.1
Total, Latin America and the Caribbean	**7,410.8**		**5,804.0**	

Source: [a] Food and Agriculture Organization of the United Nations (FAO), "Evaluación de los recursos forestales 1990. Países tropicales", *Estudio FAO Montes*, No. 112, Rome, *1995;* [b] Food and Agriculture Organization of the United Nations (FAO), *State of the World's Forests, 1999*, Rome, 1999.

(ii)   The impact in priority areas

Although Latin America and the Caribbean has suffered severe deforestation, it continues to be the region with the greatest plant cover and biodiversity in the world; it is also the region that has the biggest area of closed forest in the world (32%), according to the analysis made by UNEP (UNEP, 2001c).

This great wealth is concentrated in areas which are called priority natural land ecosystems and are described in greater detail below (Mittermeier, 1999; WWF, 2000).

They are priority systems because they contain a great variety of species, including many endemic species. They also provide extremely important environmental services, such as the production and regulation of fresh water and the absorption of CO_2, and offer great potential for development because they contain many species already known to be valuable and many others which have still to be explored.

Some of these areas have undergone very intense changes and are in great danger of disappearing (such as the Atlantic Forest, or Mata Atlántica, and the plant cover of the Caribbean), while others are quite well conserved (such as Amazonia, the Pantanal, and the deserts and xeric shrubland) but could be irreversibly damaged by the existing threats unless plans are made to apply environmentally-oriented policies for their use.

All these areas are unique in ecological terms, since they concentrate the greatest biodiversity of the region and hence offer the greatest potential for sustainable development. This makes it essential to adopt specific priority policies to secure true sustainable development in the region in keeping with the conservation of these ecosystems. Information from a variety of sources has been drawn upon in preparing the following descriptions of a number of priority natural land ecosystems (Mittermeier and others, 1999; WWF, 2000).

The tropical Andes

This area contains the greatest diversity of higher plants in the whole of Latin America and the Caribbean, with a large number of endemic species. Only 20% of the original area remains.

This area has been inhabited for thousands of years, and it has a current population of six million. It is the area of origin of a number of cultivated species, including potatoes.

The most environmentally affected areas are the densely populated inter-Andean valleys which are the site of cities such as Bogotá, Quito, La Paz and Arequipa.

These areas have been severely altered by mechanized agriculture (for example, in the River Cauca area), seasonal burning for agriculture, mining, the over-exploitation of firewood, and the introduction by cattle farmers of exotic grasses which compete with the native species. Plantations of coca and opium poppies have taken the place of large areas of native forests, and the measures taken to combat these illicit crops through fumigation are affecting the flora and fauna of the areas, especially the amphibians.

There are also various hydroelectric dams in these areas which have involved the flooding of large extensions of land, and there is also one of the largest oilfields in the world, whose exploitation is expected to give rise to growing pressures on the environment in the next few years.

The areas which have suffered least alteration are in Venezuela, in the Western Cordillera of Colombia, and on the eastern slopes of the Andes in Bolivia and Peru.

Amazonia

This is the most diverse zone of all the taxa listed in Latin America and the Caribbean. It is estimated that it contains 50% of the world's biodiversity, and is in a good state of conservation. The environmental services it provides are essential for the stability of the planet. It contains 20% of the world's fresh water and is a very important sink for absorption of CO_2 from the atmosphere. It represents 30% of the world's humid tropical forests.

The deforestation which is taking place in Amazonia is directly linked with the development of infrastructure and colonization. Up to the late 1960s, clearing did not appear to have affected more than 2%, but the rate of deforestation speeded up in the mid-1970s, and the World Bank reports the loss of 59 million hectares between 1975 and 1988 (10% of the area) (World Bank, 1996), although the Institute for Space Research of Brazil claims that the loss was only 25 million hectares over the same period. The best-conserved areas are in southwestern Amazonia (Bolivia, Brazil and Peru). The Guyana-Suriname-French Guiana massif is almost intact; although it forms a different ecological unit it is also considered part of Amazonia (Amazonian Cooperation Treaty, not signed by French Guiana). The population density of these countries is the lowest of Latin America and the Caribbean (4.3, 2.7 and 2.0 inhabitants per square kilometre, respectively), and there are few threats to the environment.

Meso-America

The diversity and number of endemic species of this zone are very high because it contains elements of both the nearctic and neotropical realms. Only 20% of the original vegetation remains.

The zone has 127 million inhabitants, almost half of whom live in rural areas.

Some areas of the zone are subject to strong population pressures: for example, population growth is 7% per year in Lacandona (Mexico) and between 8% and 10% per year in Petén.

The rate of deforestation —an average of 2.1% per year— is among the highest in the world (see table IV.3). The original plant cover has mostly been replaced to permit the cultivation of coffee, bananas, coconuts and maize and above all stock-raising.

This zone has also been an area of constant resettlement and migration of population groups due to political, economic (slumps in the prices of agricultural products, especially coffee) or natural problems (droughts, floods).

The area which has suffered the greatest changes is El Salvador, where only 5% of the original forest coverage remains and only 0.25% is under protection. The population density of this country (297 inhabitants per km^2) is the highest in Central America.

The Caribbean

This is a region which is very fragile and vulnerable, but is of great importance in the world because of its biodiversity and the number of endemic species per unit of area. Only 10% of the original area still has plant cover.

This is far and away the area of Latin America and the Caribbean with the highest population density: Barbados has 626 inhabitants per km^2, Grenada 273, and Haiti 293.

There have been severe impacts on the environment in this region ever since the arrival of Europeans. All possible land was cleared for the cultivation of sugar cane, for which there was great world demand, but now the main crops are coffee, cocoa and tobacco.

The introduction of exotic species was also a problem. Mongooses were brought in to control rodents and serpents, but also caused severe damage to the native vertebrate fauna, especially reptiles and amphibians. Rats, goats, donkeys, monkeys and other exotic species were also introduced and competed aggressively with the local fauna, driving it out.

In recent times it has been the tourist industry which has most affected coastal landscapes.

Darién - Chocó - Western Ecuador

The Darién and Chocó zone is in a better state than western Ecuador, where only 2% of the original area of plant cover is left. Altogether, 24% of the original zone is left.

The destruction has speeded up because of population growth in this coastal area. Thus, the population rose from 4.4 million inhabitants in 1960 to 11.5 million in 1995, and the agricultural area and lumbering have likewise increased.

Road construction to extend the Pan-American Highway is another menace, as well as various mining concessions and, in the Chocó, some hydroelectric plants.

The Atlantic Forest (Mata Atlántica)

This is the zone of Latin America and the Caribbean which has suffered the greatest changes: only 7.5% of the original area remains. It was the first region of Brazil to be colonized, and it is now the most densely populated, containing the states of São Paulo (the most heavily populated in Brazil), Rio de Janeiro and Bahía, and it has the most important industrial pole in the country. There are extensive areas of sugar cane and coffee plantations in this zone. The forests of Minas Gerais and São Paulo have served as a source of charcoal, for which purpose 50% of their area was cut down and subsequently replaced with eucalyptus plantations.

The Paraguay and Argentina zone has lost all but 3.4% of its original area, and in Misiones (Argentina) 94% of the original plant cover has now disappeared, leaving only 360,000 hectares.

The Cerrado region (Brazil)

Eighty per cent of the original area of this region, in which evidence has been found of the presence of human beings at least 11,000 years ago, has now been completely changed. It had remained relatively unchanged, however, until the mid-1950s, when the capital of Brazil was moved to Brasilia, in the middle of the state of Goiás.

Brasilia, which is in the middle of the Cerrado, has given rise to intense industrial and agricultural activity and road construction. Indeed, during the 1970s this area was considered to be the solution to the need for food and relocation of the population which was causing pressures on Amazonia, where the development projects attempted had failed. Agricultural megaprojects for the production of maize, soya and rice through irrigation were promoted in this area. In order to make up for the infertile and acid soils, massive applications of agricultural chemicals were made, and grass was introduced for the raising of cattle. Most of the agricultural and stock-raising production of the country comes from this region.

The Central region of Chile

This region is notable for its native woods and forests, which are unique of their kind in the world, rather than for its diversity of species. Thirty per cent of the original area remains.

This is the most heavily populated area of Chile and has undergone severe changes in the past due to the non-sustainable exploitation of slow-growing trees and the replacement of plant cover for the introduction of livestock.

In the 1970s, an intensive and aggressive programme of private forest plantations was promoted, with very advantageous State subsidies, and these plantations (two million hectares of pine and eucalyptus) took the place of almost 25% of the original native forests.

Forest fires have also been an important factor in the deterioration of the native forests.

The Pantanal

In addition to its great biodiversity and large number of endemic species, this ecosystem is very important because it acts as a regulator of the flooding caused by the River Paraguay.

The expansion of agriculture and stock-raising, gold mining and charcoal-burning have reduced and affected some of its areas, but large tracts of the Pantanal still remain almost in their original state.

Deserts

There are three deserts in Latin America and the Caribbean which are specially important on account of their biodiversity, large number of endemic species, extensive area and degree of conservation. Two of them are in the nearctic part of Mexico (the deserts of Sonora and Chihuahua), and the other is in Chile and Peru (the Atacama-Sechura desert).

The Sonora and Chihuahua deserts are the most biologically diverse in the world. They are notable for containing over 500 species of cacti (out of the 1,500 known species), many of them endemic. Originally, they occupied nearly 40% (approximately 800 million hectares) of the territory of Mexico.

Human settlements in the Chihuahua and Atacama —Sechura deserts have been increasing, and with them the pressure for changes in land use. The diversion of water for irrigated agriculture, extensive cattle-raising, the over-exploitation of commercial tree species and the felling of trees for firewood and charcoal are among the causes of the deterioration of these regions. Even so, the remaining areas of the three deserts are still quite extensive and well conserved.

Mangrove swamps

These coastal ecosystems of the tropical and subtropical part of the region are extremely important because of the ecological services they generate. They are regulatory areas between fresh water and sea water, and their vegetation protects the coasts and is the habitat for the reproduction of many marine species.

In spite of their ecological importance, however, these ecosystems have been destroyed by the presence of human settlements established for agriculture, tourism and the extraction of firewood and timber. They have also been seriously damaged by the pollution of rivers with industrial chemical wastes and agricultural chemicals, petroleum extraction activities, the building of highways, and diversion of fresh water flows.

In some regions, the development of intensive aquaculture activities, especially shrimp farms, has altered very large areas, as in the case of Ecuador.

There are few reliable estimates of the degree of deforestation, but it is generally accepted that between 25% and 100% of this vegetation has been destroyed, depending on the country in question. In Mexico, the destruction is estimated at 60%, in Ecuador 70%, and in the Caribbean, over 35% (Yañez-Arancibia and Lara-Domínguez, 1999). The protection of these areas is thus an urgent necessity.

The Patagonian steppe

This is the only example of cold temperate/subpolar steppe in South America. The alterations in this ecosystem are due to changes in land use for agriculture and stock-raising and the use of fire to promote the renewal of grass. There are large desertified and eroded areas.

(d)   Progress towards sustainable use and conservation of natural land ecosystems

The progress made in gaining a fuller understanding of the way natural ecosystems work, based on both the traditional wisdom of indigenous communities and scientific knowledge, has made it possible to put forward alternative forms of use of these ecosystems which raise their productivity and make possible their conservation. Fortunately, there are already many examples which have already proved successful or are still under way and which show the viability of sustainable rural development.

A brief description is given below of some examples of projects or programmes designed to comply with the main aims of sustainability:

- Protecting and conserving natural ecosystems and their biodiversity;
- Using natural resources in a sustainable and equitable manner in order to improve the living conditions of the population;
- Restoring damaged priority areas.

(i) Protecting and conserving natural ecosystems and their biodiversity

Protected natural areas

The main element in the conservation of biodiversity *in situ* all over the world has been protected natural areas. Practically all the countries of the region have systems of protected natural areas.

UNEP estimates that 6.6% of the territory of the region is in the category of strictly protected areas (UNEP, 2000a). Other sources only take into account the protected forest areas, which only include ecosystems with tree cover. It is reported that the region has 97 million hectares of protected wooded areas, out of a total of 938 million hectares: i.e., only 10.3% of the total wooded area is under some form of protection (World Conservation Monitoring Centre, 2000).

There are however true protected areas in the region which are of great biological importance and are furthering sustainable regional development, although many of them have been kept as mere reserves of paper. Various efforts have been made in recent decades to strengthen the protected natural areas, including the Latin American Technical Cooperation Network on National Parks, Other Protected Areas and Wildlife; the cooperation among the Andean and Meso-American countries; border reserves; and the programmes being carried out by leading non-governmental international organizations, such as the WWF, Conservation International, The Nature Conservancy, etc.

Unfortunately, not all these initiatives have fully achieved their objectives. The shortage of economic resources, the inadequacy of the existing legal and institutional frameworks, and the lack of management instruments favouring sustainable development in these areas prevent their deterioration from being completely halted.

Biological corridors

Another complementary strategy for the protection of biodiversity and the corresponding ecosystems is the establishment of biological corridors designed to join together protected natural areas or form solid blocks of previously fragmented plant cover and promote sustainable management programmes in them. The corridors could even act as areas of restoration between fragmented areas in order to advance towards the recovery of the original ecosystems.

The most important and advanced example in the region is the Meso-American Biological Corridor.

Box IV.2

THE MESO-AMERICAN BIOLOGICAL CORRIDOR

The MBC is based on an integrative concept designed to pool the efforts of eight countries in the region to consolidate a sustainable development process. This corridor extends from southern Mexico, passing through Guatemala, Belize, El Salvador, Honduras, Nicaragua, Costa Rica and Panama, and is considered as a "bridge of life" which allows species from the north and south to migrate and reproduce in various extensive areas of the region. Thanks to the strategy endorsed by these eight countries, the resources in the woods, rivers, lakes, dams, mangrove forests and seas of this area can be conserved as natural riches and used in a sustainable manner.

The MBC programme is based on a concept which interlinks natural ecosystems, indigenous communities, population groups and cultivated land across eight countries, integrating environmental and economic objectives for the benefit of the whole population. It links conservation with production, the protection of natural areas with the sustainable use of natural resources, public and private management, scientific knowledge with traditional knowledge, decision-making with participation by the general public, and production efficiency with efforts to combat poverty. The challenges posed by this common strategy for the conservation of biodiversity and ecosystems include the harmonization of systems for the protection of natural areas, the joint management of transboundary ecosystems and the promotion of a territorially-based form of ecological management that will permit the linkage of protected areas with other important zones.

(continued)

Box IV.2 (concluded)

The programme is currently being carried out through a series of national projects specifically dealing with the Corridor and financed —since their aim is to contribute to the conservation and sustainable use of global biodiversity— by Global Environment Facility (GEF) projects executed by the World Bank; there are also regional coordination initiatives through a GEF project executed by the United Nations Development Fund (UNDP) and the United Nations Environment Programme (UNEP), as well as other actions financed by various international bodies. These initiatives are all fundamentally based on support for the original concept of the "Corridor" as an effort integrate protected areas in Meso-America.

Source: R. Vargas, "Anotaciones para promover una reflexión subregional mesoamericana sobre el desarrollo sostenible" (consultant's report), Mexico City, Grupo Ad Hoc/United Nations Environment Programme (UNEP), July 2001.

Territories transferred to ethnic minorities

The legal transfer of land to ethnic minorities (indigenous reservations and collective properties of black communities) is a strategy for conservation and sustainable use which has been applied in the Andean subregion and offers great potential for the future. Such indigenous reservations and collective properties of black communities amount to approximately 39,206,000 hectares (Rodríguez, 2001).

The major part of the indigenous reservations are in the Amazon basin, while the whole of the properties of black communities are on the Pacific side (Colombia), and a smaller proportion of the indigenous reservations (in terms of their area) are in the Andean region. The territories of the indigenous communities thus include a significant part of the ecosystems which are of great value because of their biodiversity (Rodríguez, 2001).

(ii)   Sustainable use of natural ecosystems

In many projects, plant cover has been the subject of an integral approach involving multiple forms of management. The use of land through territorial planning processes which make it possible to lay down guidelines for the use of ecosystems in the most suitable way has gained currency in all the countries: not as much as it should, but nevertheless with considerable success in some cases, which has made it possible to learn lessons and extrapolate experience.

The concept and practice of territorial planning is being updated with the aim of overcoming the serious limitations from which it has suffered in the past. Venezuela has one of the longest traditions in this respect. In Colombia, a territorial planning process aimed at the conservation of ecosystems classified as strategic because of their ecological value and their impact on production was completed in June 2000, while Bolivia has begun a process aimed at the same objective, based on the agro-ecological zoning carried out in most of that country's territory (Rodríguez, 2001).

Sustainable use of forest ecosystems for the production of timber

The FAO has promoted forest planning for many years, with the aim of securing the sustainable use of forest ecosystems for timber production.

Over the last decade, unprecedented progress has been made in this respect through the improvement of silviculture, the adoption of environmentally friendly timber extraction practices, modifications in the forest ownership structure, the growing tendency to promote forest planning at the local level, and greater participation by the private sector (see box IV.3).

Box IV.3
FOREST PLANNING: TWO SUCCESSFUL EXAMPLES

Guatemala: In 1994 the Guatemalan Parliament adopted a law empowering local communities to apply for forestry concessions in the buffer zones of the Mayan biosphere reserve: a protected area in northern Guatemala. The communities must legally register their organization or association, apply to use a particular zone, prepare a forest management plan covering a period of 30 or 40 years, and also prepare a plan of operations covering a period of one year. All these documents must be submitted to the National Council on Protected Areas (CONAP, in Spanish). The technicians of CONAP help in the preparation of the forest management plans, and an NGO advises the community on technical and legal aspects. The community organization undertakes to pay CONAP 1% of the income generated by the forest, signs contracts with private companies for the extraction of timber and non-timber resources, and supervises the management of the forest. So far, the use of a total of around 92,000 hectares has been granted to local communities under these local concessions.

Mexico: Project for the Conservation and Sustainable Management of Forest Resources in Mexico (PROCYMAF, in Spanish).

(continued)

Box IV.3 (concluded)

The general objective of PROCYMAF is to promote schemes for: (i) improving the use and conservation of natural resources by communities and ejidos possessing forests and ii) increase the options of those owners for earning income through the sustainable use of their forest resources. The programme is aimed at the following types of potential producers: producers who sell standing timber; producers of unprocessed forest products, and producers with processing and marketing capacity.

Real facilities for dissemination, consultation and social participation have been created at the regional level for the discussion and analysis of the various problems faced by communities with regard to the utilization, marketing and conservation of natural resources and evaluation of the potential for the use of community-owned natural resources.

The programme has also been successful in strengthening the technical capacity of the communities and bringing them into the Producers' Information System on Non-timber Forest Products, so that they can explore new options for earning income from the integral and sustainable use of their resources.

Source: United Nations Food and Agriculture Organization (FAO), *State of the World's Forests, 1999,* Rome, 1999, and Ministry of the Environment and Natural Resources (SEMARNAP), Proyecto de Conservación y Manejo Sustentable de Recursos Forestales en México (PROCYMAF), *Balance de tres años de ejecución,* Mexico City, 2000.

Utilization of wildlife

Many efforts have been made to diversify the use of ecosystems and not base such use solely on the extraction of timber. If rural communities gain benefits from the use of these resources and receive fair and competitive remuneration from their sale, this will help to ensure their conservation and reduce the amount of changes in land use.

Making possible the sustainable utilization of wildlife is one of the most effective ways of ensuring its conservation, since the economic benefits resulting from its management encourage those who possess such resources to make an effort to preserve them. The sustainable utilization of wildlife resources within their own habitat also reduces dependence on conventional agricultural or stock-raising practices which, in certain ecological contexts, can be harmful to the environment.

A coordinated cooperation strategy is still needed, however, to overcome some of the main obstacles connected with the lack of markets for sustainably produced natural products. There is also a need for fair regulations which will ensure that the benefits derived from the use of wild species are fairly shared among the population owning those natural resources.

Sustainable and organic agriculture

Organic agricultural production, using more environmentally friendly techniques, was developed centuries ago and has now been taken up once more in agro-ecological studies.

Agro-ecology has already put forward various technologies which are widely and successfully used in the region and have shown that they are compatible with increased and sustainable production. Certification methods have also been developed to guarantee that goods really are produced using sustainable techniques.

With regard to organic production and other forms of certification, the range of products for which there is demand and supply in the region is very wide, covering agricultural, stock-raising and forestry products and industrial products such as juices, oils and textiles, etc. The production of these goods offers substantial economic opportunities for the region in general, since these products can be sold at a higher price and strong growth of the market for them is expected.

Ecotourism and other non-traditional forms of tourism

Unlike traditional tourism, these alternative forms are aimed more at the observation and understanding of nature. Ecotourism has grown fast in recent years and is likely to continue to do so in the future, since the World Tourism Organization estimates that at the world level these non-traditional forms of tourism will grow much faster than traditional tourism, whose growth rate is estimated at between 2% and 4% per year.

Efforts along these lines have been made in many regions, as for example in the case of the Mayan Route, which covers an area of nearly 500,000 km^2 between Belize, Guatemala, El Salvador, Honduras and the Mexican states of Campeche, Chiapas, Quintana Roo, Tabasco and Yucatán.

In addition, the Central American countries (excluding Panama) have adopted a system of certification of the sustainability of tourism whereby the enterprises wishing to be certified must comply with a number of requirements in such areas as quality of service, protection of the environment, commitment to natural, historical, present-day and local traditional resources and their capacity to relate their clients or tourists with these policies. This system of certification will help to regulate tourism activities and their impact on the environment, thus increasing the credibility and attractiveness of the region to the rest of the world and hence favouring greater commitment to the environment by the entrepreneurs of the region (Vargas, 2001).

(iii)   Restoration

Considerable efforts have been made in the region for decades past to restore degraded areas, especially through reforestation. Unfortunately, the lack of an approach based on scientific considerations and aimed at recovering natural ecosystems has led in recent decades to the planting of millions of trees which did not grow up satisfactorily.

In many countries these programmes have been aimed at increasing employment rather than really recovering degraded areas. This has been changing, however, and there are increasing numbers of examples of reforestation programmes aimed at planting native species in the areas it is desired to restore, with the participation of the local inhabitants.

Box IV.4
FINANCE FOR THE CONSERVATION OF RENEWABLE RESOURCES

There is a wide variety of national, international, public and private sources of finance for the conservation and sustainable use of natural resources.

Among these sources are the more than 30 national environment funds operating in the region, which together handle over US$ 150 million in resources and have a combined annual operating budget of over US$ 70 million for activities in the areas of the conservation and sustainable use of natural resources. The environment funds of Latin America and the Caribbean, as institutional donors, have the advantage of having representatives of all sectors of society on their governing councils, and in most cases have solid and well-balanced relations with the governments of their respective countries. Environment funds have a profound knowledge of the social and environmental conditions of their countries and, because of their independent status, ensure the continuity of conservation efforts through changing political cycles. In the fields of training, learning and strengthening of institutions, the environment funds have set up a network (www.redlac.org) to serve as a community for strengthening facilities, cooperation and learning.

It is also worth noting that in the Latin American and Caribbean region 24 countries are participating in the Small Donations Programme of the Global Environment Facility executed by the United Nations Development Programme (UNDP), which has financed 779 grassroots and NGO projects for a total of US$ 13.4 million. This programme is based on the principle of the cooperation of civil society, the government and the private sector in environment funds and maintains close cooperation with the funds in order to ensure democratic and transparent access of the local communities to international financial resources.

(continued)

Box IV.4 (continued)

Between 1990 and 1997, 3,489 conservation projects were financed by the 65 sources of finance which answered a World Bank survey. The total investment for the conservation of biodiversity recorded by the survey was US\$ 3.26 billion. Of this global figure, 54.7% was invested in South America, 34.8% in Central America and Mexico, 5.5% in the Caribbean and 5.1% in programmes for the Latin American and Caribbean region as a whole. An analysis of finance by countries revealed that Brazil received the largest part of the funds, followed by Mexico. Altogether, these two countries received 45.5% of the country finance. After Brazil and Mexico comes a group of countries which includes Venezuela, most of the Central American countries, Argentina, Bolivia, Colombia, Ecuador and Peru, with 44.8% of the remainder of the country finance. The remaining 28 countries together received only 9.7% of the investment in the region at the country level. The Caribbean countries were mostly in the lowest part of the investment spectrum, with only 4.5% altogether. When this analysis is controlled for the size of the countries, however (dollars/km^2), the results change significantly. In this case, the countries which received most investment per km^2 were Venezuela, all the Central American countries, Ecuador, the Dominican Republic, Haiti and Jamaica, while the Southern Cone countries (Argentina, Chile and Uruguay), Cuba and French Guiana now came in the lower part of the scale. It is somewhat surprising to note that both Colombia and Peru also came in the low part of the scale, even though they are countries with megadiversity.

Conservation of biodiversity within the context of the main projects for the management of natural resources and protected areas accounts for over 70% of the finance. Policy projects account for 8.4%, while projects for extension activities, ecosystem management, sustainable enterprises, training and research only receive between 1.4% and 5% each out of the total amount invested. Support for land acquisition and *ex situ* conservation is insignificant. The small number of projects for land acquisition may be due to the fact that the majority of the organizations (particularly multilateral and bilateral institutions) cannot finance this type of activity.

Only 32% of the projects in the data base (which totals US\$ 1,2 billion) could be classified as belonging to the ecoregional level. On the basis of this subseries of data, the five ecoregions with the greatest investment are the Matorral Central in Mexico, the humid forests of Petén-Veracruz, the humid forests of the Central American Atlantic region, the humid forests of the Atlantic region of the Isthmus, and the llanos. There are 28 ecoregions which have level I priority according to the WWF classification, but they received less than US\$ 1 million in finance during the period studied.

Of the finance allocated at the ecoregional level, 66% went to the tropical forest and subtropical broadleaf forest ecoregions. Grasslands, savannahs and shrubland and xerophilic formations received around 15% each of the finance allocated at the ecoregional level, while the mangrove forests, coniferous forests and temperate broadleaf forest ecosystems received the smallest amount of investment.

(continued)

Box IV.4 (concluded)

Although there can be no doubt that the conservation of biodiversity has made great strides over the last two decades, this progress has proved to be insufficient in the light of the increase and evolution of the threats to biodiversity. A key element for achieving effective conservation is the strategic and efficient investment of financial resources. As this study shows —and if it is acknowledged that one of the main objectives of conservation in the region is to ensure proper representation of all the ecosystems and suitable finance for the priority ecoregions and other important areas— then the investment for the conservation of biodiversity in the Latin American and Caribbean region cannot yet be said to have been fully strategic. If the wealth of biodiversity of the region is to be conserved for future generations, it is essential that the donors supporting conservation and those responsible for implementing projects within the countries should coordinate their efforts in order to ensure that these objectives are fulfilled and that there are improvements in the collection and distribution of information. As a first step towards these goals, the World Bank, the United States Agency for International Development (USAID) and the Biodiversity Support Programme are to publish this data series. It is hoped that conservationists throughout the region will see this analysis and its publication as a stimulus for attaining better communication with and between donors and implementors (taken from Castro and Locker, 2000).

Source: Adapted by the United Nations Environment Programme (UNEP) from G. Castro and I. Locker, *Mapping Conservation Investments: An Assessment of Biodiversity Funding in Latin America and the Caribbean*, Washington, D.C., 2000.

2.   Marine and coastal ecosystems

Coastal and marine areas have represented not only a source of living and non-living resources for mankind, but also a means of communication: probably for this reason, coastal areas have been a favourite location for the establishment of human settlements. Most of the world's population lives in coastal areas, and there is a permanent tendency for it to concentrate in them. Latin America and the Caribbean are no exception to this, since some 60% of their population are settled in these areas.

(a)   Large marine ecosystems

The coastal and marine area of Latin America and the Caribbean is divided into 10 Large Marine Ecosystems (LMEs), which, according to the International Union for Conservation of Nature and Natural Resources (IUCN), the United States National Oceanic and Atmospheric Administration and the UNESCO Intergovernmental Oceanographic Commission (IOC), are regions which extend from the coastal area proper, including estuaries and some parts of river basins, up to the offshore continental shelf, their other borders being defined by the systems of currents. The ten LMEs in question are:

1.   The California Current
2.   The Gulf of California
3.   The Gulf of Mexico
4.   The Central American Pacific
5.   The Caribbean Sea
6.   The Humboldt Current
7.   The Patagonian continental shelf
8.   The South Brazil continental shelf
9.   The East Brazil continental shelf
10.   The North Brazil continental shelf

The conditions prevailing in these LMEs range from the subtropical region in the northern hemisphere to the temperate region in the southern hemisphere, so that they include a large variety of ecosystems, such as: macroalgae forests (kelp forests), mangrove forests, rocky reefs, sea grass, coral reefs, deltas, estuaries, coastal lagoons, salt marshes, sandy beaches, coastal dunes, pebble beaches, cliffs, and even underwater trenches with hot water springs, among many other types.

The apparent immensity of our seas has caused us to indulge in constant and growing abuse of them, and even when they are as rich and varied as those of the Latin American and Caribbean region we have managed to cause significant slumps in their levels of production, whether through over-exploitation, pollution, and/or physical alteration.

The Latin American and Caribbean region comprises the southern part of the nearctic zone and the whole of the neotropical zone, and the geomorphology of its coasts and winds, together with the patterns of currents, have made possible the development of seven highly productive zones known as upwelling zones (Monreal-Gómez and others, 1999), which are located along the region's 64,000 kilometres of coastline and its 16 million km^2 of maritime territory (UNEP, 2000b). In addition to these upwelling zones, there are also other areas which are very important for the productivity of the coastal and marine zones and which correspond to the mouths of great river basins such as those of the Amazon, Orinoco and Grijalva-Usumacinta, among others. Deltas, coastal lagoons and creeks can form in these river mouths and are highly productive systems which also act as areas for the reproduction, development and feeding of many species, including 70% of those which are of commercial importance.

Associated with these ecosystems are the mangrove forests, which, as well as being highly productive, also protect the coastline and are great consumers of the nutrients brought down by the rivers, thus reducing the eutrophication problems of the water column.

Mangrove forests cover between 40,000 and 60,000 km^2 in the Latin American and Caribbean region, their greatest degree of development being along the equatorial coasts; only the three southernmost countries (Argentina, Chile and Uruguay) do not have mangrove forests (Yáñez-Arancibia, 1994).

The most highly developed mangrove forests are in northern Ecuador, on the Pacific coast of Colombia, Panama, and southern Costa Rica. The best tropical conditions on the Atlantic coast are found from the area south of the Gulf of Paria (Venezuela) to São Luiz (Brazil). Brazil is one of the three countries with the greatest area of mangrove forests, together with Australia and Indonesia. Although they cover a large area, the mangrove forests of Latin America and the Caribbean only include 11 species out of the 54 which exist in the world (Tomlinson, 1986).

In the Caribbean subregion, the most important coastal and marine ecosystems are the coral reefs, which are comparable to the tropical rain forests because of their high productivity and biodiversity. Along the coasts of Mexico, Belize, Guatemala and Honduras is the Meso-American Caribbean Reef System, which is over 700 km long and is the second largest barrier reef in the world. The ecosystems which make it up include both coral barrier reefs and coastal lagoons and mangrove forests; they are currently in a good state of conservation, but it is estimated that 60% of the coral reefs in the Caribbean are in danger of suffering negative impacts (GESAMP, 2001). The reef system provides a habitat for many highly endangered species such as manatees (between 300 and 700 individuals), river and swamp crocodiles, tortoiseshell and white turtles, and over 60 species of corals, among many other organisms.

Another ecosystem which coexists with the coral reefs and mangrove forests is the sea grass areas: these systems usually occur in shallow waters with low wave energy and are very productive areas which are of decisive importance for some fisheries, such as the shrimp fisheries in the Gulf of Mexico.

(b)   Economic activities

Fishing

The most important fisheries in the region in terms of volume are in the Pacific Ocean, associated with the upwelling zones mentioned earlier, such as the Humboldt Current in Peru and Chile and the California Current off the west coast of the Baja California peninsula. In the Atlantic, rich fishing waters are associated with the continental shelf of Argentina and Uruguay and the Falkland Islands.

The sea fishery production of the area fell dramatically from 21 million tons in 1995 to around 11.6 million tons in 1998 (UNEP, 2000b and 2001a). The 1998 figure represented 13.6% of the world sea fishery catch (FAO, 2000b). Almost the whole of the catch (10.1 million tons) was obtained in South America.

Peru and Chile are among the 12 main fishing nations in the world, while Mexico is among the top 20. The slump in the fishery production of those countries in 1998 was due fundamentally to adverse climatic factors (El Niño), in conjunction with the overfishing observed during the last ten years, when many South American countries doubled or trebled their catches (UNEP, 2000b), causing a sustained fall in the biomass of the main fishery resources. Peruvian anchoveta went down by 78% and Chilean jurel by 44%. The fishery catches of these countries recovered in 1999, however, when the climatic situation returned to normal, registering increases of some 50% in spite of the low prices of their products on the market (FAO, 2000b).

In Mexico, fishery production grew by 4.3% in 1999 compared with the previous year (758,576 tons), thanks to the increases in the catches of sardines, tuna, shrimps and algae, although these catches are still far below those registered in 1997 (FAO, 2000b).

The outbreaks of disease and adverse meteorological phenomena in 1998 and 1999 caused a slump of over 80% in the output of shrimp farms in Ecuador and Peru (a drop from 100,000 to 16,000 tons).

The possibilities of growth of sea fishing are only marginal in the region (FAO, 2000b); such growth is expected to be limited to other areas such as the central/western Pacific and the Indian Ocean.

There are warning signs in the region. Population growth in coastal areas is putting pressure on fishery resources by causing unsustainable levels of exploitation, which represents a dangerous situation not only for the marine resources but also for the integrity of the oceans themselves. Unfortunately, there are no systematic indicators in the region of the state of health of the resources and ecosystems which would serve to guide action aimed at securing the recovery of overexploited marine populations and their environment (except for some isolated proposals in Argentina, Chile, Peru and Mexico). It is urgently necessary to formulate such a set of indicators to guide action: that is to say, to lay down rules for securing the sustainability of fishing operations.

According to the FAO, between 25% and 27% of the marine populations are currently under- or moderately exploited, between 47% and 50% are fully exploited, between 15% and 18% are overexploited and have no chance of growing, and between 9% and 10% are exhausted or in the process of recovery (FAO, 2000b). In other words, there is only marginal room for the growth of sea fisheries, and this room is not only limited spatially but is also limited to between only 25% and 27% of world fishery resources. In Mexico, the National Fishery Charter indicated in the year 2000 that the possible room for the growth of fishing in that country was 19%.

Tourism

Tourism is one of the most important activities of the countries of the region, especially in the Caribbean, and in some of them it is the main activity. Mass tourism —whether land-based (enjoyment of the beaches) or marine (cruise ships)— is a serious threat to the environment. One of its first effects is physical alteration of the habitat: for example, swamps are drained or mangrove forests are cut down to build infrastructure, and there are even cases where reefs have been destroyed to obtain building materials or to win land from the sea for the construction of support installations such as jetties, restaurants, etc. The tourism industry also needs inputs and services, and this has sometimes caused the destruction of coral reefs through the discharge of domestic sewage. All these impacts can be avoided, however, through planning, regulation and good strategies for the integral management of coastal areas.

Petroleum extraction

Petroleum extraction activity in the marine and coastal zone is highly localized, but it is a fundamental part of the economy in the countries where it takes place. In Mexico, for example, 70% of the petroleum reserves are under the sea bed. Likewise, petroleum extraction in Brazil, Venezuela and Trinidad and Tobago is carried on mainly on the continental shelf. There have been considerable advances in technology designed to reduce the effects of petroleum prospection and extraction work, but this nevertheless continues to be a high-risk activity and there are continual accidents in this respect, such as the recent collapse of the biggest oil rig in the world in Brazil and the sinking of a cargo ship off the Galápagos Islands.

(c)   Human settlements and land-based sources of pollution

Another serious problem causing deterioration of the Latin American and Caribbean seas is pollution from land-based sources. According to reported data, it is estimated that in Latin America as a whole only 2% of all liquid wastes is given any form of treatment (UNEP, 2000b). It is noted in particular that the quality of coastal waters has deteriorated due to the direct discharge of untreated municipal waste waters, while in the case of the Caribbean between 80% and 90% of the waste water is discharged into the sea without any kind of treatment (UNEP, 2000a). This is the biggest problem in the region, since the organic burdens being discharged into the bodies of water are not oxidized and eliminated because they considerably exceed the capacity of the host sites, thus causing anoxia or eutrophication of the systems in question, as well as serious public health problems.

(d)   Zones of special interest for conservation

Finally, it may be noted that the WWF has defined 15 marine ecoregions in Latin America and the Caribbean which call for special care in order to ensure their conservation. These major zones, which are the sites of particular groups of species, communities, dynamics and environmental conditions and require preferential attention because of their ecological value, are the following:

1. The California Current (United States and Mexico)
2. The Cortés Sea (Mexico)
3. The mangrove forests of Mexico
4. The mangrove forests of Central America
5. The Panama/Colombia/Ecuador sea basin
6. The mangrove forests of the Panama sea basin
7. The Galapagos Islands (Ecuador)
8. The Humboldt Current (Peru and Chile)
9. The Patagonian marine ecosystem (Argentina)
10. The northeast coast of Brazil
11. The mangrove forests of the Amazon and Orinoco
12. The coastal swamps of Venezuela, Trinidad and Tobago, Guyana, Suriname, French Guiana and Brazil
13. The southern Caribbean (Panama, Colombia, Venezuela, Trinidad and Tobago and the Netherlands Antilles

14.   The marine ecosystem of the Greater Antilles, Jamaica, Cuba, Haiti, Dominican Republic, Cayman Islands, the Bahamas, the United States, and the Turks and Caicos Islands

15.   The Meso-American reef system (Mexico, Belize, Guatemala and Honduras)

Among the main factors affecting these and other ecosystems in the region are: discharges of waste water by towns and industries, physical alteration due to urban expansion and the construction of port and industrial infrastructure, runoffs from agricultural areas, an increase in the burden of sediments due to deforestation, over-exploitation of fisheries and the use of destructive fishing methods, and alteration of hydrological patterns due to the damming of rivers.

It is important to note that 70% of all negative effects on the coastal and marine areas are due to land-based activities (UNEP, 1995), often hundreds of kilometres away from the coast. As long as strategies for the integral management of river basins and coastal areas are not developed, it will be very difficult to avoid these forms of impact.

B.   Water resources

1.   Water resources and their availability in the region

Latin America and the Caribbean is the region of the world which, on average, has the greatest availability of water resources. Although it has only a little over 15% of the land area and 8.5% of the population of the world, the region has about one-third of the total world supply of renewable water resources. South America alone has nearly 30% of total world runoff, calculated at 42,650 km^3 (WRI, 2001).

Table IV.4 shows the area, population, water resources and potential availability of water of the various regions of the world.

As may be seen from this table, the potential water availability per km^2 in South America is double the world average and is unparalleled in any other region. Brazil alone has nearly 40% of the region's water resources.

Table IV.4
RENEWABLE WATER RESOURCES AND AVAILABILITY OF WATER, BY CONTINENTS

Continent	Area (millions of km²)	Population (millions of inhabitants)	Water resources, km³/year				Potential availability of water 1,000m³/year	
			Average	Maximum	Minimum	Cv [a]	per km²	per capita
Europe	10.46	685.0	2,900	3,410	2,254	0.08	277	4.23
North America	24.3	453.0	7,890	8,917	6,895	0.06	324	17.4
Africa	30.1	708.0	4,050	5,082	3,073	0.10	134	5.72
Asia	43.5	3,445.0	13,510	15,008	11,800	0.06	311	3.92
South America	17.9	315.0	12,030	14,350	10,320	0.07	672	38.2
Australia and Oceania	8.95	28.7	2,404	2,880	1,891	0.10	269	83.7
World	135.0	5,633.0	42,785	44,751	39,775	0.02	317	7.60

Source: Igor Shiklomanov (coord.), "World Water Resources at the Beginning of the 21st Century", Paris, International Hydrological Programme, United Nations Educational, Scientific and Cultural Organization (UNESCO), unpublished, 1999.

[a] Coefficient of variation.

In Latin America and the Caribbean, only Barbados, Haiti and Peru suffer from water stress,[6] although there are various areas of other countries which are in this situation (northeast and northwest Mexico, areas of the Pacific coast of Central and South America, some areas of the Andean altiplano, and extensive areas of Patagonia).

Whereas in other regions of the world the population clearly perceive water shortage to be the main limitation on their development processes and have generated a special culture in this respect, in Latin America and the Caribbean there is only an incipient awareness of the need for rational management of water resources because of their relative scarcity.

---

[6] An area is considered to be suffering from water stress when its water availability does not exceed the threshold level of 1,700 m³ per person per year. Water stress is considered "very severe" or "critical" when water availability is less than 1,000 m³ per person per year.

Box IV.5
WATER RESOURCES OF THE REGION

Several of the greatest river basins of the world are located in the region: the Amazon, Orinoco, Paraná, Tocantins, São Francisco, Grijalva-Usumacinta, etc. The Amazon system, in particular, is the most important river system in the world, both because of the area covered by its basin (rather more than 6 million km^2) and the volume of its average discharge (175,000 m^3/second: over four times greater than that of the river Zaïre, which occupies second place).

The water resources of the region are unevenly distributed both in space and in time. Although the average annual rainfall in the region would appear to indicate a great abundance of water resources compared with other regions, Latin America and the Caribbean also has large arid or semi-arid areas. Almost 6% of the area of the region consists of deserts. The region thus displays the two world extremes of humidity and aridity: whereas the Colombian chocó receives over 9,000 mm of rainfall per year, some areas of the Chihuahua or Atacama deserts do not register any appreciable precipitation at all.

The Caribbean Island States, for their part, have much less rainfall than that of similar countries in other parts of the world, such as the Pacific or the Indian Ocean.

There are often big differences in the availability of water within a single country, because of the great internal diversity of climate. In Argentina, for example, 85% of the country's water resources are located in the River Plate basin, which occupies only 30% of the national territory. The arid and semi-arid zones of that country, which represent not less than 11% of its territory, have only 1% of the country's water resources.

Source: F. Tudela and others, *Disponibilidad de agua en América Latina y el Caribe*, Mexico City, El Colegio de México, 2001 (forthcoming).

As far as the sustainability of development is concerned, it is not only the absolute level of availability of water per inhabitant which is important, but also, and above all, the rate of change of that indicator, which is going down markedly in most of the countries of the region. It is also important to analyse the proportion of this resource used in relation to the total amount available. In the 1990s, the Dominican Republic extracted 40% of its annual availability of water for agricultural, industrial or municipal purposes. This same indicator amounted to 19% in the case of Mexico and 14% in Cuba. These countries, together with Barbados, Haiti, Peru and some other countries already mentioned, would be the first in the region to suffer the effects of water shortage as an imminent threat to the sustainability of their development processes.

In South America, the levels of extraction are in all cases less than 10% of the available supply: Argentina, with a level of extraction of 8%, is the country which comes closest to this threshold level (WRI, 2001).

(a)   Exploitation of aquifers

Ground water is a very important resource for many countries of the region. In many cases, however, the present level of utilization of this resource is not sustainable, because more water is being extracted from the aquifers than is restored to them. This over-exploitation of the resource makes it necessary to gradually increase the depth of the wells until the limit of sustainability is reached because of higher costs, exhaustion of the water deposits, or unsuitable quality of the water found at greater depths.

The information available at the regional level is scarce and is often not up to date, so that it is difficult to gain an integral view of the problem. The situation is particularly serious in arid and semi-arid areas. In Mexico, the over-exploitation of ground water, which is very frequent in the northern and central areas of the country, amounts to between 5 and 6 km^3 per year. At the present time, as many as 17% of the main aquifers of the country are already seriously over-exploited.

(b)   Water demand and extraction

In all the countries of the world there is a rapid increase in the demand for water and the amounts extracted to satisfy it. This demand has increased particularly fast in the last 40 years. In the course of the twentieth century, world extraction of water has increased by a factor of six and now amounts to nearly 4,000 km^2 per year, or one-fifth of the normal flow of the world's rivers. The pressure on world water resources is increasing twice as fast as population growth. The greatest and fastest-growing demand is from the agricultural sector, which accounts for 70% of the total extraction, or some 2,800 km^3 per year. Table IV.5 shows the evolution of water use (extraction and consumption), by continents.

As a function of its availability, the extraction and consumption of water has increased in Latin America and the Caribbean much faster than the world average. In the course of the twentieth century, total water extraction in Meso-America rose from 12.8 km^3 in 1900 to 127 km^3 in 1995: i.e., it increased tenfold. The same thing happened in the case of South America, where water extraction increased from 15.1 km^3 to 167 km^3.[7]

---

[7]   Meso-America is considered as being equivalent to natural-economic region 8 (southern North America) (Shiklomanov, 1999).

Table IV.5
PAST EVOLUTION AND FUTURE PROJECTIONS OF WATER USE,
BY CONTINENTS
(km² per year)

Continent	Past evolution								Projections		
	1900	1940	1950	1960	1970	1980	1990	1995	2000	2010	2025
Europe	37.5	96.1	136.0	226.0	325.0	449.0	482	455.0	463.0	535.0	559.0
	13.8	38.1	50.5	88.9	122.0	177.0	198	189.0	197.0	234.0	256.0
North America	69.6	221.0	287.0	410.0	555.0	676.0	653	686.0	705.0	744.0	786.0
	29.2	83.8	104.0	138.0	181.0	221.0	221	237.0	243.0	255.0	269.0
Africa	40.7	49.2	55.8	89.2	123.0	166.0	203	219.0	235.0	275.0	337.0
	27.5	32.9	37.8	61.3	87.0	124.0	150	160.0	170.0	191.0	220.0
Asia	414.0	682.0	843.0	1,163.0	1,417.0	1,742.0	2,114.0	2,231.0	2,357.0	2,628.0	3,254.0
	249.0	437.0	540.0	751.0	890.0	1,084.0	1,315.0	1,381.0	1,458.0	1,593.0	1,876.0
South America	15.1	32.6	49.3	65.6	87.0	117.0	152	167.0	182.0	213.0	260.0
	10.8	22.3	31.7	39.6	51.1	66.7	81.9	89.4	96.0	106.0	120.0
Australia and Oceania	1.6	6.83	10.4	14.5	19.9	23.5	28.5	30.4	32.5	35.7	39.5
	0.58	3.30	5.04	7.16	10.3	12.7	16.4	17.5	18.7	20.4	22.3
Total (rounded)	579.0	1,088.0	1,382.0	1,968.0	2,526.0	3,175.0	3,633.0	3,788.0	3,973.0	4,431.0	5,235.0
	331.0	617.0	768.0	1,086.0	1,341.0	1,686.0	1,982.0	2,074.0	2,182.0	2,399.0	2,764.0

Source: Igor Shiklomanov (coord.), "World Water Resources at the Beginning of the 21st Century", Paris, International Hydrological Programme, United Nations Educational, Scientific and Cultural Organization (UNESCO), unpublished, 1999.

Note: First row for each continent: extraction of water; Second row: consumption of water.

It is expected that in the first quarter of the twenty-first century total water extraction will increase by 21% in Meso-America, which will face several supply crises, and 43% in South America (Shiklomanov, 1999, table 11). Even where there is no crisis on account of scarcity, the generalized problems of pollution will complicate the outlook as regards the sustainability of development in the region and make necessary a thorough revision of public policies on water resources (Tudela, 2001).

(c)   Water use

The limited nature of water resources gives rise to growing conflicts between existing users and potential new uses. Sometimes the flow of surface or ground water supplying a settlement is threatened by competition from agricultural users. Discharges of waste water at some point in a river basin may affect the quality of the water and cause problems for its use downstream. There are more and more conflicts over water use which may even affect national security, and there are often many political, economic and social pressures on water management.

River systems, lakes, aquifers and coastal waters may extend over territories subject to the sovereignty of two or more nations. In these cases, it is necessary to seek a form of transnational management based on formal and equitable cooperation.

When classifying water use, a distinction is usually drawn between agricultural, industrial and municipal use. Generally speaking, in recent decades there has been an increase in industrial and municipal use and also in the storage of water, so that the relative weight of the agricultural use of water has gone down, although it continues to be the main type of use in the great majority of countries.

Half a century ago, the use of water for agricultural purposes accounted for 95% of total consumption in South America. At present, agricultural use of water for irrigation continues to account for between 69% and 75% of total water consumption, but it is expected that this figure will go down to 67% by the year 2025.

There are currently marked differences between subregions and countries in the forms of water use (WRI, 2001). Thus, in Meso-America and the Caribbean, countries like Costa Rica, Haiti, Honduras, Jamaica, Mexico, Nicaragua and the Dominican Republic use over three-quarters of the total amount of water extracted for irrigation, while in contrast Cuba, El Salvador and Panama use a large part of the water extracted for municipal consumption (49%, 34% and 28% of the total amount extracted, respectively).

In South America, agricultural use of water exceeds three-quarters of the total amounts extracted in Argentina, Chile, Ecuador, Guyana, Paraguay, Peru, Suriname and Uruguay, while the countries which make the greatest use of water for municipal purposes are Colombia (59%), Venezuela (44%), Bolivia (32%) and Brazil (21%). As a proportion of total extraction, it is expected that municipal and industrial use will grow most rapidly in the future.

(d) Irrigation

The region currently has 18.6 million hectares of irrigated land. The advance of irrigation may be analysed by examining the evolution of the area irrigated, as a percentage of the total cultivated area. In Meso-America and the Caribbean this indicator stood at 19% in 1997: a figure similar to the world average (18%). In South America, however, the irrigated area was only 9% of the total cultivated area, although there are marked differences from country to country: some countries, such as Bolivia or Brazil, have low percentages of irrigated land (5% and 4%, respectively), while others, such as Chile and Peru, have high proportions

(55% and 42%, respectively), and still others, such as Costa Rica and Mexico, are in an intermediate position (25% and 24%, respectively). With regard to its further expansion, irrigation is now facing growing difficulties, and some irrigated areas are now suffering from serious problems of salinization which bring their sustainability into question.

At the same time, irrigation is a prerequisite for the introduction of some technology packages that include the intensive use of agricultural chemicals such as fertilizers and pesticides, which are important diffuse sources of pollution.

(e)   Disposal of liquid wastes; pollution of watercourses and aquifers

Only a small fraction of the effluents from human settlements and industries receive some form of treatment before their final disposal. The percentage of the total liquid wastes given some form of treatment varies considerably: 100% in Barbados (PAHO-WHO, 2000); 22% in Mexico; 21.3% in Nicaragua; 16.7% in Chile; 10% in Argentina and Venezuela, and less than 9% in Colombia. The figures are difficult to interpret, however, especially on a comparative basis.

Firstly, it should be recalled that not all liquid wastes are collected through a conventional sewerage system. In Chile, for example, only 89% of the liquid wastes are collected, and the percentage is even lower in many other countries. Second, the figures are usually based on the existence of some kind of treatment plant, but the existing plants are often out of service or do not function properly because of maintenance problems. Third, the category "liquid wastes given some form of treatment" (almost always primary treatment) does not permit meaningful comparison, because of the differing quality of the effluents emerging from the cleansing process and the different environmental conditions of the watercourses which receive them.

In addition to the pollution from the discharge of municipal liquid wastes there is the pollution caused by industrial and mining effluents and diffuses pollution from the use of agricultural chemicals in irrigated areas. All these processes not only compromise the quality of surface water but also have an irreversible effect on the availability of aquifers. The deterioration of the region's water resources through pollution is one of the most serious burdens that the present generations are bequeathing to the coming generations. The financial cost of a large-scale operation to recover the bodies of water affected by decades of abuse as recipients of liquid wastes is incalculable. Indeed, in the case of aquifers such a rescue operation would not even be possible. Cleansing their polluted water and soil will long be beyond the economic reach of the region's societies.

Both in the region and at the global level, these problems of water quality have been taking on growing importance in recent years and also interlink with quantitative considerations: even though there may be more than enough water resources in general, what is lacking now is water of high enough quality for given purposes. There is no overall view with regard to the quality of ground or surface waters in Latin America and the Caribbean. We do know, however, that the pollution of the region's water resources is a time bomb which can lead to artificial shortages. Water pollution limits our access to the existing water resources, is a threat to public health, reduces biodiversity, and compromises the stability of the region's ecosystems.

2.   Water management in the region

The institutional structures adopted by the countries of Latin America and the Caribbean to manage their water resources are very heterogeneous. This is partly due to variations in the scale and complexity of management problems across a region where there are large differences in the main interests and conflicts arising from water supply and demand in the various countries, some of which are federal States and others unitary, with all the differences that this implies. Different national traditions and capabilities, and the effects of external influences in shaping administrative systems, are another factor. Recently, almost all the countries have undertaken reforms to the institutional structures that manage water resources (Jouravlev, 2001).

State organization in the region's countries has been essentially sectoral. Different sectors specialize in activities connected with the use of water resources for specific ends rather than approaching the issue comprehensively, which limits the scope for optimizing exploitation, minimizing water-related conflicts and dealing with issues that affect all those using water or a particular basin. The production of hydroelectric energy, the supply of drinking water and sanitation, irrigation or other particular uses have been and continue to be the sole aim of each of the individual organizations involved, which have always operated independently, interacting only through very limited coordination systems, or none. Depending on the country, the hydroelectricity, irrigation or drinking water and sanitation supply sectors have overwhelmingly dominated the development of water resources and, in many cases, their management. In many countries, these very marked sectoral interests have become even more entrenched as a result of privatization.

There may now be said to be general agreement in the region that the sectoral, fragmented approaches of the past, where the management of water resources is concerned, are leading to growing conflict, inefficiency and deterioration of these resources (Solanes and Getches, 1998). A paradigm shift is gradually taking place, with fragmentation by user sectors giving way to a more integrated approach. This process has been manifested in a profound organizational shift in the State systems responsible for water management and use. The driving force behind this change is recognition of the basic fact that sectoral bodies cannot perform the functions of administering and allocating water appropriately and resolving conflicts among competing uses, as their role in these circumstances is that of both judge and judged. In addition, their dependence on particular user groups undermines their authority.

Hydrological logic suggests that the most appropriate basic geographical unit for the management of water resources is the river basin. Although the region's countries are interested in implementing multiple water use management models at the river basin level, efforts to introduce these systems have been hindered by various difficulties. Many of the bodies set up have disappeared or have failed to make progress with integrated water management because of inter-institutional rivalries, conflicts with regional authorities, lack of the necessary funding, coordination and legal basis and confusion about their roles, which creates the potential for competition with other authorities and sectors, or because they have had a complex relationship of administrative or financial dependence.

The issue came back to the fore in the 1990s, at a time when the countries of the region were seeking to achieve sustainable development goals by reconciling economic growth with equity and environmental sustainability. As a result of this interest, recently passed water laws and many proposals for amending existing laws have embodied, for the first time, an explicit intention to administer water on a multiple-use basis at the river basin level. This is due, among other factors:

(i) to the intensification of conflicts deriving from water use, ultimately caused by ever-increasing demand, growing pollution problems, the effects of extreme natural phenomena and a perception that the deterioration of catchment basins and underground water replenishment areas is worsening;

(ii) to decentralization and privatization, which have brought many new actors (such as water users, local governments, the private sector, indigenous populations and non-governmental organizations) into the water management system, and faced it with new challenges; and

(iii) to the concentration and geographical differentiation of problems and conflicts connected with water management and use, which do not occur uniformly across a country but differ greatly, both in nature and in seriousness, from one basin to another.

It is worth drawing attention to the main advances made recently in creating bodies responsible for administering cross-border basins in the countries of Latin America and the Caribbean, examples being the basin of the rivers Catamayo-Chira and Puyango-Tumbes, shared by Ecuador and Peru, and the basin and coastal zone of the river San Juan, shared between Costa Rica and Nicaragua.

C. Urbanization and the environment

The Latin America and Caribbean region is the most highly urbanized in the entire developing world. In 2000, 74% of the Latin American and Caribbean population was urban, a total of more than 390 million people, while the rural population was less than 160 million. The degree of urbanization in the region is on a par with that found in most industrialized countries. The percentage of the population living in urban settlements is expected to stabilize at around 81% by 2020 (ECLAC-CELADE, 1999). The tendency of the urban-rural population ratio in the region can be appreciated from table IV.6, which shows the degree of urbanization in different countries.

The differences among countries and subregions in this respect are striking. At one extreme are countries at an advanced stage of urbanization, such as Argentina, Chile, Uruguay and Venezuela, whose urban population in 2000 accounted for 86%, 87%, 90%, and 93%, respectively, of the total. At the other extreme are very rural countries, such as the Central American countries and Paraguay, where the urban population makes up less than 60% of the total. The level of urbanization in the Andean subregion, meanwhile, is very close to the average for the region as a whole. The value of aggregating and comparing regional, subregional or national figures is questionable, however, given the variety of census criteria used by the countries to draw the line between the urban and rural populations.[8]

---

[8] The criteria used to determine the urban-rural threshold for the latest censuses in the region are described in ECLAC-CELADE (1999), Definitions used for urban and rural populations in censuses conducted by Latin American countries since 1960. In some cases the thresholds used are not based on size or population but are administrative, economic, etc., in nature.

Table IV.6
LATIN AMERICA AND THE CARIBBEAN (24 COUNTRIES): URBAN
POPULATION AS PERCENTAGE OF TOTAL, 1970-2000

Countries by stage of urbanization	Year										
	1970	1975	1980	1985	1990	1995	2000	2005	2010	2015	2020
Advanced urbanization											
Argentina	78.4	80.7	83.0	84.9	86.9	88.3	89.6	90.6	91.4	92.0	92.5
Bahamas	71.8	73.4	75.1	79.7	83.6	86.5	88.5	90.0	90.9	91.5	92.0
Chile	73.0	76.0	79.0	81.1	82.8	84.4	85.7	86.9	87.9	88.8	89.6
Uruguay	82.0	82.9	86.1	89.2	90.5	91.7	92.6	93.1	93.7	93.9	94.0
Venezuela	71.8	75.4	78.9	81.6	83.9	85.8	87.4	88.8	89.9	90.8	91.5
High urbanization											
Brazil	55.6	61.4	67.3	71.0	74.7	77.5	79.9	81.7	83.1	84.2	85.0
Colombia	57.7	61.8	64.4	67.0	69.4	71.7	74.5	76.6	78.4	80.0	81.4
Cuba	60.1	64.1	68.0	71.6	74.8	77.6	79.9	81.9	83.4	84.7	85.7
Mexico	58.9	62.3	65.5	68.6	71.4	73.4	75.4	77.2	78.8	80.2	81.3
Peru	58.1	61.9	64.2	66.3	68.7	71.2	72.3	73.5	74.6	75.5	76.3
Trinidad and Tobago	63.0	63.0	63.1	66.2	69.1	71.7	74.1	76.1	77.8	79.3	80.7
Moderate urbanization											
Barbados	37.1	38.6	40.2	42.5	44.8	47.3	50.0	52.8	55.6	58.4	61.1
Bolivia	36.2	40.5	45.4	50.5	55.6	60.4	64.6	68.2	71.0	73.1	74.8
Ecuador	39.5	41.8	47.1	51.3	55.4	59.2	62.7	65.8	68.5	70.7	72.5
El Salvador	39.0	41.5	44.1	47.0	49.8	52.5	55.2	57.8	60.3	62.6	64.7
Jamaica	41.5	44.1	46.8	49.2	51.5	53.7	56.1	58.5	61.0	63.5	65.9
Nicaragua	46.8	48.8	50.1	51.4	52.5	53.9	55.3	56.7	58.1	59.4	60.6
Panama	47.6	48.7	49.7	51.7	53.8	55.7	57.6	59.5	61.2	62.9	64.5
Paraguay	37.1	39.0	41.6	44.9	48.6	52.4	56.1	59.6	62.9	65.7	68.2
Dominican Republic	39.7	44.7	49.9	52.3	53.7	57.1	60.2	62.9	65.3	67.4	69.1
Incipient urbanization											
Costa Rica	38.8	41.3	43.1	44.8	46.7	48.5	50.4	52.3	54.2	56.1	57.9
Guatemala	36.2	36.7	37.2	37.5	38.0	38.6	39.4	39.9	40.5	41.2	41.8
Haiti	19.7	22.2	24.5	27.2	30.5	34.3	38.1	41.8	45.3	48.4	51.3
Honduras	29.0	32.0	35.0	37.7	40.8	44.4	48.2	52.1	55.9	59.5	62.7

Source: Adapted from ECLAC, Population Division - Latin American and Caribbean Demographic Centre (CELADE), current population projections. For the Caribbean, United Nations, *Population Growth, Structure and Distribution: The Concise Report* (ST/ESA/SER.A/181), New York, 2000. United Nations publication, Sales No. E.99.XIII.15.

In all events, if analysed in accordance with international parameters, urbanization has been particularly dynamic in the region; in the period 1970-2000, its urban population grew by 240%, while its rural population increased by barely 6.5%. Since 1985, in fact, the rural population of the region appears to have stagnated in absolute terms. This fact is enough in itself to refute simplistic interpretations that seek to establish a direct local relationship between demographic pressure and environmental deterioration. While the rural population of Latin America has virtually stabilized in absolute terms, the deterioration of ecosystems in the region's rural areas has continued owing to the workings of complex mechanisms that cannot be explained away simply by the pressure of increasing numbers on scarce resources.

The way society in the region has evolved in terms of the urban-rural polarity has major implications for the type of environmental problems that affect the sustainability of its development. On the one hand, urbanization creates jobs, increases educational opportunities, creates scope for higher levels of citizen organization and participation, accelerates social mobility, makes it easier for the State to attend to the problems of extreme poverty, stimulates economic and cultural modernization and speeds up the demographic transition. On the other hand, it is generating more and more acute problems of overcrowding, of air, water and soil pollution and of insecure and makeshift living conditions, among others, that threaten the quality of life of city dwellers. The tremendous growth of urbanization has put specifically urban environmental problems higher and higher up the national and regional agendas.

The environmental and social problems of the region's urban areas derive not so much from the scale of settlement as from the speed of change and growth. In Latin America over recent decades, major urban settlements that have grown at over 5% a year have been unable to contain the spread of makeshift settlement and to maintain an acceptable urban services infrastructure.

Over the last few decades, Latin America and the Caribbean have gained a great deal of experience with large urban centres, metropolitan areas, conurbations and megalopolises. Although Latin America and the Caribbean contain just 8.4% of the world population, the region accounts for some 15% of all human beings living in settlements of more than a million inhabitants.

Table IV.7
PEOPLE LIVING IN CITIES OF OVER A MILLION INHABITANTS

	1950	1970	1990	2015
Africa	3	16	59	225
Latin America and the Caribbean	17	57	118	225
Asia	58	168	359	903
Europe	73	116	141	156
North America	40	78	105	148

Source: United Nations, *World Population Prospects: 1994 Revision*, New York, 1995.

Of the world's 25 largest cities, five are in the region:

Table IV.8
THE LARGEST CITIES IN LATIN AMERICA, 1995
(Millions of inhabitants)

São Paulo	16.4	(+2.01%/ year)
Mexico City	15.6	(+0.73%/ year)
Buenos Aires	11.0	(+0.68%/ year)
Rio de Janeiro	9.9	(+0.77%/ year)
Lima	7.5	(+2.81%/ year)

Source: United Nations, *World Population Prospects: 1994 Revision*, New York, 1995.

Over the last decade, tendencies that had already begun to emerge in earlier periods have become firmly established. Rural-urban migration to the largest city is ceasing to be the main determinant of rising urbanization. Internal migratory flows are being redistributed right around the urban structure, and the cities growing most dynamically as a result are medium-sized ones, whose functions are being modified in the context of regional development (Jordán and Simioni, 1998). Urban-urban migration is taking on new importance. The supremacy of the countries' capital or main cities in different aspects of national life, and their top-heaviness in this respect, have declined as a result; in the 1990s, none of these cities was able to sustain the remarkable dynamism of previous decades. The "metropolitan explosion" has reached its limit in the region.

In Latin America and the Caribbean, urbanization has been a major force for economic growth, modernization and improvements in the well-being of the population. Nonetheless, as UNEP has pointed out, the urban environment, along with the depletion and destruction of natural resources, is the main problem facing the region in this sphere of development (UNEP, 2000a). Poverty is one factor that has had a close association with local urban environmental problems throughout the period analysed.

Since the early 1980s, in fact, most of the poor in Latin America and the Caribbean have been in urban areas, by contrast with Asia and Africa, whose poor populations are still mainly rural. Between 1980 and 1990, the region experienced an absolute rise of over 60 million in the number of urban poor. Although the incidence of poverty fell in relative terms during the 1990s, and in absolute terms from 1994 onward, in

1997 the urban poor still numbered 125.8 million (35% of households) (ECLAC, 1999a).

The causes underlying the unsustainability of urban development have been the rise in the urban population, combined with situations characteristic of underdevelopment and inappropriate urban policies, including informal urbanization, socio-spatial segmentation, unregulated land markets, infrastructure deficiencies and approaches to the development of transport systems that have favoured private transport. As regards the public policies adopted to deal with the problems described, for the last 30 years the instruments needed to control the growth of cities have been lacking in Latin America and the Caribbean. Where informal urbanization is concerned, the inadequacies of housing provision systems are the factor that accounts for the cycle of land invasion and subsequent regularization by means of site and service programmes. Although action of this type has proved very effective in remedying the lack of basic services that results from informal settlement, in the long term it has contributed to the horizontal expansion of cities. As regards land markets, the region has been lacking in policies to regulate the externalities generated by the working of these, and in land policies that can accommodate a growing urban population sustainably. Transport policies have also contributed to a form of modal development that has reinforced the tendency towards urban sprawl; the need for this sector to be integrated into urban policies is increasingly accepted, however, and there are impressive examples of successful management (expansion of underground railway systems and innovative models, as in the case of Curitiba, Brazil).

Since 1992, many of the region's metropolises have created or strengthened public agencies to deal with the main environmental problems on the basis of a conurbation approach. In some cases urban environmental authorities have been appointed, but the challenges are still daunting. The main one, without a doubt, is to provide housing and services to the poorest groups by creating new patterns of urbanization that prevent illegal settlement, with all the negative consequences this entails. In the final analysis, the solution to this problem must lie with reforms to urban land tenancy which, like the exclusion of the poorest from productive land in the rural sector, is one of the sources of inequity in the region. Some steps are being taken towards solving this problem, such as land banks and urban capital gains taxes.

Some measures now being taken to reduce air pollution and to solve public transport and road congestion problems could, if followed up, provide a realistic solution to these issues in developing countries. Examples are the trolleybus system in Quito and the Transmilenio initiative in Bogotá, which draw on the experience of Curitiba. In Bogotá, citizens agreed in a referendum that the use of private cars should be banned during the eight hours of greatest congestion with effect from 2015, when the new transport system should have city-wide coverage.

The fact is, though, that populations are concentrated to such a degree and in such an unbalanced way that national States cannot keep up with the growing volume of infrastructure and public services that are needed in the form of roads, housing, drinking water, sewage facilities, education and healthcare infrastructure, energy, pleasant public spaces and security. The situation described shows what an urgent need there is for proper urban environmental management, the first priority being to internalize environmental costs and remove perverse subsidies. The subject is beginning to be taken more seriously by central and local governments, which are starting to give consideration to land-use criteria, seek alternative ways of collecting and handling solid wastes (privatization of services, recycling projects, etc.) and explore options for achieving smoother, better ordered vehicle flows, among other things.

Lastly, one pressing challenge being faced by large urban centres arises from the occurrence of disasters, be they natural, technological or complex. Thus, the causes of pollution already referred to are compounded by the effects of extreme climate phenomena, cyclical events whose recurrence is frequent but not well enough predicted, and the risks from dangerous activities that are planned and carried out without sufficient regulatory control. The size, scale and infrastructure gaps and shortcomings of the region's cities make them acutely vulnerable to disasters whose negative consequences are felt locally, regionally and nationally at both the microeconomic and macroeconomic levels.

Infrastructure deficiencies take the form not just of problems with the provision of essential services to outlying areas —often over great distances, and at a very high cost (water, power, drainage, waste disposal, etc.— but also of physical and organizational unpreparedness to cope with emergencies or even recurrent seasonal phenomena. These problems are accentuated by inappropriate land use, unplanned distribution of businesses and services and inadequate rules for essential services provision and construction. Regulatory gaps are compounded by the inadequacy of local authority funding, but even appropriate standards or regulations cannot be applied in the economic and social circumstances of these urban conglomerations. On the one hand, private commercial and industrial businesses do not make provision for risk internalization and management or offsetting investment, so that these responsibilities are transferred to the State at either the local or national level, while on the other, irregular or informal settlements and activities account for a large percentage of urban development and growth.

D.   Pollution

In Latin America and the Caribbean, the problem of pollution seems to be taking a worrying turn for the worse as a result of economic and population growth and the accentuation of certain production and consumption patterns.

Generally speaking, the causes of the increasing air, land and water pollution being experienced by the region, and the health consequences of this, are to be sought in agriculture and unplanned urbanization. The scale of urban growth has led to a large proportion of the region's population suffering the consequences of worsening air quality, contamination by solid and hazardous wastes, coastal deterioration and water pollution (UNEP, 2000b). Overcrowding and infrastructure deficiencies are factors that increase exposure to pollutants, so it is the poorest strata that generally experience the worst effects of pollution.

Ironically, the health problems now being caused by deteriorating air quality and the presence of toxic substances as a result of development are as worrying as the traditional health problems deriving from underdevelopment, such as gastrointestinal diseases. If we compare this region with others, we find that it is less densely populated, water resources are abundant and relatively unpolluting activities account for a large share of the economy. Despite this, levels of pollution are high, suggesting serious planning failures and other deficiencies in environmental management.

1.   Air

The main causes of atmospheric pollution in the region are:

- the quantity and quality of fuels consumed, the inadequacy of controls on vehicle emissions and the growth in vehicle numbers, accelerated by the growing practice of importing used vehicles;

- industrial activities;
- inefficient energy use;
- human settlements and the high density of urban areas;
- the use of pesticides in rural communities;
- particle emissions produced by soil erosion and the burning of agro-industrial mass; and
- in some cities, unfavourable climate conditions, and particularly the burning of fuel in homes located in poor outlying areas.

Of all these causes, vehicle use is the most serious, while household pollution goes virtually unmonitored.

Pollution monitoring and control policies are largely confined to certain gases and particles whose health effects are of special concern. Monitoring of polluting emissions and concentration is complemented by studies on exposure and activity types to establish the links between health and the environment. The situation is made more complex by the fact that a range of pollutants are at work, with possibly synergistic or mutually reinforcing effects.

Predictably, records of the main pollutants in the region show a rising tendency over the decade. Between 1990 and 1999, emissions of suspended particles rose by 6.2%, of sulphur dioxide by 22%, of nitrogen oxides by 41%, of hydrocarbons by 45%, of carbon monoxide by 28% and of carbon dioxide by 37% (UNEP, 2001b).

Table IV.9
AIR POLLUTION
(Gas and particle emissions, in gigagrams)

Emissions of	1970	1980	1990	1999	Percentage 1990-1999
Particles	110.98	144.82	188.48	200.15	6.2
Sulphur dioxide	1,873.13	3,035.27	3,452.38	4,194.98	22.0
Nitrogen oxides	2,668.27	4,747.87	5,761.81	8,123.50	41.0
Hydrocarbons	665.17	1,121.36	719.99	1,043.28	45.0
Carbon monoxide	10,334.12	17,460.23	21,555.02	27,693.19	28.0
Carbon dioxide	420,282.79	750,205.14	922,273.89	1,165,237.71	37.0

Source: Global Environment Outlook (GEO), "Estadísticas ambientales de América Latina y el Caribe", San José, Costa Rica, 2001, forthcoming, pp. 34 and 174.

Lead emissions are still a major problem. While paint, batteries and certain foods are important sources of exposure, emissions from vehicles that run on leaded petrol, still widespread in most of the region's countries, are the main cause. The result is high concentrations of lead in the blood (see table IV.10).

Table IV.10
LEVELS OF LEAD IN THE BLOOD OF DIFFERENT URBAN POPULATION
GROUPS IN SELECTED COUNTRIES OF LATIN AMERICA AND THE CARIBBEAN

Country	Population	Age	Sample size	Range (•g/dl)[a]	Average (•g/dl)[a]	>10 •g/dl[a] (percentage)
Brazil	Adults	15-49	149	2.8-27.2	11.8 ± 5.2	75
	Children	4-5	199	0.6-35.7	9.6 ± 4.6	30
Chile	New-born babies	1	200	0.5-18.0	4.3 ± 1.8	5
Ecuador	Children	7	64	17.0-54.0	28.8	100
	Babies	0.1	27	6.0-20.0	14.4	60
	Women	Pregnant	83	...	18.4	60
Mexico	Children	< 5	200	1.0-31.0	9.0 ± 5.8	28
	Adults	15-55	200	1.0-39.0	9.7 ± 6.2	37
	Adults	15-45	3,309	5.0-62.2	10.6	42
Trinidad and Tobago	Women	...	94	1.2-14.4	4.8 ± 2.0	2
	Babies	0.1	94	0.0-8.7	3.4 ± 1.6	0
	Children	2-14	48	1.0-31	9.5	30

Source: M. Lacasaña and others, *El problema de exposición al plomo en América Latina y el Caribe*, Metepec, Pan American Centre for Human Ecology and Health, World Health Organization (WHO), 1996.

[a] Micrograms per decilitre.

In recent years, substantial progress has been made in controlling air pollution in large cities such as São Paulo, Rio de Janeiro, Buenos Aires, Santiago and Mexico City by means of complex strategies that include emission controls, changes in fuels and contingency controls. There would appear to be a turning point that depends on size and the measures taken to improve air quality. These programmes have not yet been extended to medium-sized cities, as in most of these the information needed for such measures to be taken is not available.

The progress made with efficiency and management may be jeopardized by a problem of scale. On current trends, the growth of vehicle numbers in the cities of the region could nullify the progress made in improving air quality. Rising real incomes, and the relationship between these and car purchases, which have been facilitated by the liberalization of used vehicle imports, could result in explosive growth in the number of cars in the fastest developing cities. One example is São Paulo, where population growth of 3.4% between 1990 and 1996 was accompanied by an expansion of 36.5% in the number of vehicles.[9] Mexico City has well over four million vehicles, while in Santiago, Chile, the number of cars is growing fast enough to double every five years.

Besides producing emissions pollution, which is compounded by functional segregation in cities, increased vehicle use has led to growing congestion in urban areas and longer journey times, with a strongly negative impact on urban productivity and quality of life.[10]

The effects of pollution have an economic aspect, because of the cost of alleviating them and the loss of working days that results from harm to workers' health. According to ECLAC, air pollution permanently affects the health of more than 80 million of the region's inhabitants and results in the loss of some 65 million working days. It is the main cause of over 2.3 million cases a year of chronic breathing difficulties among children and of over 10,000 cases of chronic bronchitis among adults. Its health effects are even more marked in the vulnerable population, consisting mainly of elderly people and infants (ECLAC, 2001d, p. 79).

2. Drinking water and sanitation

Drinking water supply and basic sanitation services have a very direct link with people's quality of life. Throughout the second half of the twentieth century, needs grew much faster than did the resources required to meet them, so that serious deficiencies built up in most of the countries.

The "lost decade" of the 1980s, designated as the International Drinking Water Supply and Sanitation Decade, and the weak and uneven recovery of the following decade, did not provide the conditions needed to rectify these shortcomings, which form part of the region's social deficit as the twenty-first century begins.

Efforts to measure secure access to drinking water and the adequacy of sanitation systems come up against methodological difficulties and discrepancies or changes in national criteria that complicate comparisons over time and among countries. Different United Nations agencies and development assistance organizations have made

---

[9] In a Chilean sample, the elasticity of the relationship between car ownership and family incomes was found to be 10.23 for the commune of Vitacura (ECLAC, 2001d, p. 150).

[10] ECLAC reports that urban transport consumes 3.5% of Latin American GDP, and the time spent making journeys the equivalent of a further 3%. By way of example, it is noted that in 1992 an average of 28 km in São Paulo were affected by severe congestion in the morning and 39 km in the evening. By 1996, the figures had risen to 80 km and 122 km, respectively (ECLAC, 2001d, p. 84).

valuable efforts to deal with this situation. These efforts are reflected in the updated information to which reference is made below. The general situation in the region can be appreciated from table IV.11.

Table IV.11
DRINKING WATER AND BASIC SANITATION: SITUATION OF
LATIN AMERICA AND THE CARIBBEAN
(Millions of inhabitants)

	1990				2000			
	Popula-tion	With service	Coverage (percentage)	Without service	Popula-tion	With service	Coverage (percentage)	Without service
Urban drinking water	313	283	90.4	30	391	353	90.3	38
Rural drinking water	128	72	56.4	56	128	74	57.6	54
Total drinking water	440	355	80.6	86	519	427	82.2	92
Urban sanitation	313	247	78.9	66	391	335	85.7	56
Rural sanitation	128	39	30.7	89	128	56	43.5	72
Total sanitation	440	286	64.9	155	519	391	75.3	128

Source: United Nations, *Progress Made in Providing Safe Water Supply and Sanitation for All During the 1990's* (E/CN.17/2000/13), New York. Information taken from sampling surveys among users.

As can be appreciated, progress in the region over the 1990s was disappointing where drinking water was concerned. In the last decade of the twentieth century, the percentage of the region's urban population with access to drinking water barely held steady, and the number of city dwellers without this service increased by 8 million. Nonetheless, the effort made was substantial; over the decade, the countries of the region brought drinking water services to 70 million new urban users, a figure which exceeds the current populations of Argentina, Bolivia, Chile, Paraguay and Uruguay combined. In the countryside —where the population has stagnated, chiefly owing to migration to the cities— greater progress was made, although some 60% of those without drinking water coverage in the region still live in rural areas.

The number of people in the region without drinking water coverage is 92 million, accounting currently for 8.2% of the world total. If current trends continue, the region will not achieve full coverage until 2040.

In the declaration that came out of the Millennium Assembly, the countries undertook to halve the number of people without access to drinking water in the countries by 2015. Assuming that the cost of a conventional connection remained at the current level,[11] this reduction in the accumulated deficit would cost the region some US$ 7.45 billion, not including the expansion of supply needed to cover the increase in population during the period concerned.

The coverage of sanitation services is less than that of drinking water. Nonetheless, far more progress was made with sanitation services in the 1990s than with drinking water. Over the decade, the region extended the coverage of sanitation infrastructure to an extra 105 million inhabitants, a number in excess of Mexico's entire population today. The number of people in the region without sanitation, at 128 million, now accounts for 5.2% of the world total in this situation.

3.   Waste

According to UNEP, the amount of solid waste generated in the region has doubled in 30 years. Furthermore, the composition of this waste has changed, with organic —and thus biodegradable— waste giving way to substances that remain in the environment for longer and are more likely to be toxic (UNEP, 2000a, p. 33 and UNEP, 2000b, p. 51) (see figure IV.3 and table IV.12).

---

[11]   In calculating the amount of financing required to eliminate the region's drinking water deficit, a unit cost of US$ 162 was taken, this being the average of the costs found to apply in Brazil (US$ 152) and Mexico (US$ 171.64) (PAHO-WHO, 2000).

Figure IV.3
ANNUAL PRODUCTION OF INDUSTRIAL WASTE PER INHABITANT, 1993
(Metric tons)

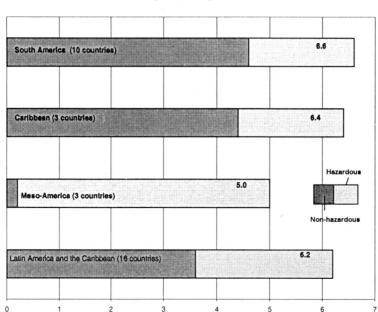

Source: G. Acurio and others, "Diagnóstico de la situación del manejo de residuos sólidos municipales en
América Latina y el Caribe", Ambiental series, No. 18, Washington, D.C., World Health Organization
(WHO)/Inter-American Development Bank (IDB), July 1997.

Table IV.12
LATIN AMERICA (SELECTED CITIES): SOLID WASTE PRODUCTION,
WASTEWATER TREATMENT AND WASTE COLLECTION

	Solid waste per capita (kg/year)	Wastewater treated (percentage)	Households with waste collection service (percentage)
Brasilia	182	54	95
Havana	584	100	100
La Paz	182	0	92
San Salvador	328	2	46
Santiago	182	5	57
For purposes of comparison:			
Toronto	511	100	100

Source: PAHO (Pan American Health Organization) (http://www.cepis.ops-oms.org/servicios/listados/
in_aseo.html), 2001. Adapted from the table "Coverage of urban sanitation", *Health in the Americas. 1998
Edition*, Scientific Publication, No. 569, Washington, D.C.

The situation within countries varies greatly as regards both the collection and the disposal of waste, as can be seen in table IV.13.

Table IV.13
LATIN AMERICA (23 COUNTRIES): COVERAGE OF URBAN SANITATION

Country	Percentage collected	Percentage disposed of in sanitary, secure or other landfills
Argentina	...	...
Bahamas	...	...
Bolivia	68	50
Brazil	71	28
Chile	99	83
Colombia	...	...
Costa Rica	66	68
Cuba	95	90
Ecuador	...	...
El Salvador	...	...
Guatemala	...	...
Haiti	30	20
Honduras	20	...
Mexico	70	17
Nicaragua	...	...
Panama	...	...
Paraguay	35	5
Peru	84	5
Dominican Republic	...	...
Suriname	...	...
Trinidad and Tobago	95	70
Uruguay	71	...
Venezuela	75	85

Source: PAHO (Pan American Health Organization) (http://www.cepis.ops-oms.org/servicios/listados/in_aseo.html), 2001. Adapted from the table "Coverage of urban sanitation", *Health in the Americas. 1998 Edition*, Scientific Publication, No. 569, Washington, D.C.

It will be noted that there is no information for many of the countries, and where there is information it may vary widely in the way it is collected. In any event, though, the data available reveal serious shortcomings in both infrastructure and management.

From the point of view of the "polluter pays" principle, most local governments are in the anomalous situation of being responsible for collecting waste at their own expense, and not at the expense of those who produce it. If the principle operated, waste collection would have to be costed and charged for by waste type and volume generated. This is not the situation, however. Charges and costs appear to be unrelated, and it is this that lies behind the inadequacies of coverage and disposal.

In European countries, for example, those generating certain types of urban waste have to make their own arrangements, while home collection services require waste to be sorted, and have volume limits. Differentiated charging has become an incentive to keep waste to a minimum. The countries of the Organisation for Economic Co-operation and Development (OECD) have developed the concept of extended liability for the waste producer and product security, whereby the producer also takes responsibility for the product when it is disposed of, under a variety of schemes such as direct collection, public collection or the use of centralized collection centres. This scheme extends responsibility to the entire cycle and encourages recycling, since producers of waste, knowing that they will have to take responsibility for the product, make provision for the materials to be recycled.

As regards hazardous waste, information about the way this is generated, stored and disposed of is generally scanty. The problem is made more complex by the prevalence of inappropriate and even clandestine handling of these substances.

UNEP reports that treatment, recycling or disposal infrastructure is in all cases inadequate in the region, even though some countries have legal provisions in place. The same is true of the human resources responsible for enforcing the law, so that a great deal of waste ends up in high-risk sites such as factory yards, wasteland, open tips or secure landfills where it is mixed in with municipal waste, with the consequent risks to the environment and health. The generation of hazardous waste is associated with the expansion of economic activity, which suggests that the quantity must have increased over the period.

4.   Changes in industrial pollution

During the 1990s industrial output increased substantially in absolute terms, led by the export sector. The composition of GDP changed in the same way as exports, although to a much lesser degree.

The information available on the relationship between the region's industrial and export dynamic and the scale of the resulting pollution is inadequate. The data available do allow an idea to be formed of these processes, however. One element is the change in the composition of exports over the decade (Schatán, 1999).

There were differences in the ways the countries of the region participated in international markets. Most of them increased their natural resource-intensive exports because of the difficulty of maintaining competitiveness in more technology-intensive sectors, owing to the combined effects of greater competition in open international markets and the withdrawal of many domestic incentive measures.

In many smaller countries, output of primary products or primary product-intensive goods was increased.

Meanwhile, a small group of countries managed to reorient their exports on the basis of sectors using more advanced technology, such as electronics, motor vehicles and other types of machinery, which are less polluting than traditional exports such as hydrocarbons and chemicals.

The effect of technological change on industrial pollution needs to be researched in greater depth, however.

5.   Rural and diffused pollution

Agricultural run-off is the largest source of ground and water pollution in the countryside. The use of agrochemicals has risen disproportionately and it is estimated that the quantity of heavy metals, chemicals and hazardous residues doubles every 15 years. Agrochemical use gives a rough idea of the pollution problem in the countryside, where fertilizer consumption alone rose by some 42% between 1990 and 1998 (GEO, 2001, p. 15). Nitrogen fertilization in bodies of water is increasingly widely used, and affects flora and fauna by boosting the growth of species such as algae.

Other causes of pollution require further study in the region, examples being the presence, risk and environmental impact of persistent organic pollutants,[12] characterized by their ability to spread over large distances, and the consequences of this for human health and wildlife. Concern about proper handling of chemicals has received renewed

---

[12]   The Stockholm Convention on Persistent Organic Pollutants, whose objective is to limit and gradually phase out their use, was approved in May 2001 and needs to be ratified by the countries to come into force. Negotiations on the Rotterdam Convention on the Prior Informed Consent Procedure for Certain Hazardous Chemicals and Pesticides in International Trade were concluded in 1998.

attention recently around the world. A new source of contamination that requires more careful analysis is the release of modified living organisms into the natural environment.

E.   Energy trends in the region and global climate change

1.   Energy trends in Latin America and the Caribbean over recent decades[13]

Around 2000, Latin America and the Caribbean, with 519 million inhabitants, accounted for 8.46% of the world's population and 4.5% of world GDP. According to ECLAC figures, per capita GDP in 1999 was US$ 2,690 per inhabitant, or about 35% below the world average estimated by the International Energy Agency (US$ 4,443 dollars per inhabitant). In 1999, per capita energy consumption in the region was 9.4 barrels of oil equivalent (BOE) per inhabitant, while the world average was 11.46 BOE. Although per capita energy consumption is thus 20% below the world average, it has been rising steadily over the last 20 years. The rate of energy demand growth in Latin America and the Caribbean is expected to follow the same trend as in other developing regions over the coming decades, as the following figure shows.

Total energy consumption worldwide has been growing at an average of 1.6% a year, owing mainly to the strong rise seen in developing countries in general, and in China and the other Asian countries in particular. The position of Latin America and the Caribbean in the regional composition of consumption did not change greatly between the 1970s and the 1990s; consumption in the region, in other words, grew in line with the world average, accounting in 1999 for no more than 5.2% of total energy consumption.

---

[13]   This study has been taken from an ECLAC work presented by José Antonio Ocampo at the Regional Seminar on Climate Change: National Strategic Studies, organized jointly by the World Bank and ECLAC.

Figure IV.4
PROJECTED ENERGY DEMAND

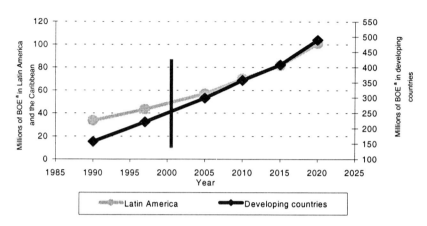

Source: United States Department of Energy.

^a Barrels of oil equivalent.

(a)   The region's energy reserves[14]

Over the last two decades, the oil reserves of Latin America and the Caribbean have increased substantially, from 24 billion to 121 billion barrels, so that the region's share of total world reserves has risen over this period from 5% to 11%. From 1990 to 1999, these reserves grew moderately to stand at some 120 billion barrels in the latter year, the region's share in the world total remaining unchanged.[15] These oil reserves are mainly situated in Mexico and Venezuela, which account for 40% and 50%, respectively, of the region's total.

The region's reserves of natural gas have grown considerably. Between the 1970s and the 1980s they rose from 1.926 trillion to 6.75 trillion cubic metres, and in 1994 they stood at 7.087 trillion cubic metres. Between the same two decades, however, the region's share of world natural gas reserves rose only slightly, from 5% to 6%, and by 1994 they had fallen back to 5%, owing to the strong growth in the reserves of Middle Eastern countries and the former Soviet Union. As in the case of oil, most of these reserves are in Mexico and Venezuela, which control 51% and 28%, respectively, of the region's natural gas reserves.

[14]   See Altomonte and Albavera (1997).
[15]   Estimate by *Oil & Gas Journal*, cited by the United States Department of Energy (DOE, 2000).

Figure IV.5
COMPOSITION OF FINAL ENERGY CONSUMPTION WORLDWIDE, 1973 AND 1999

By region, 1973

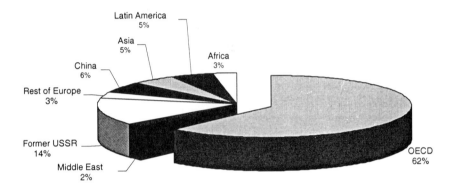

By region, 1999

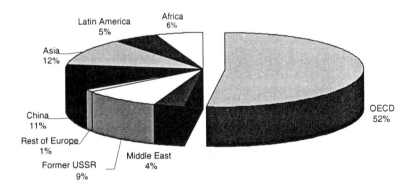

Source: H. Altomonte and S. Albavera, "Las reformas energéticas en América Latina", Medio ambiente y
desarrollo series, No. 1 (LC/L.1020), Santiago, Chile, 1997.

The region has modest coal reserves by world standards. Between 1980 and 1999 its share of world reserves rose slightly, from 1.2% to just 1.6%. Most of these reserves are in Brazil and Colombia, which account for 80% of the regional total. At current production levels, these reserves are good for 435 years, while the figure for oil is just 40 years.

The hydroelectric potential of the region is put at 728,591 megawatts (MW), or about 22% of world potential. The use made of these resources in Latin America and the Caribbean is still very limited, representing only 15% of their potential at the end of the century. Non-traditional renewable energy sources are used on a limited scale or are little developed. For example, the region's installed capacity for exploiting geothermal energy is 900 MW, equivalent to 14% of the capacity of the geothermal power systems installed worldwide.[16]

(b) Trend of energy intensity between 1980 and 1999

It is commonly said in the literature on the subject that energy policy has tended towards a sustainable approach to the exploitation and use of energy sources. Despite this general orientation, though, and notwithstanding the growth seen in per capita energy consumption, the region is a long way from having achieved adequate levels of efficiency in energy transformation and use. This is demonstrated by the stagnation of energy intensity (measured by energy consumption per unit of output), which is accounted for, among other factors, by the limited use made of energy-efficient technologies, the obsolescence of the industrial base and the high and inefficient consumption of the region's vehicles. It should be noted that the shift in the industrial composition of certain countries in the region (particularly Brazil) towards energy-intensive industries and, again in Brazil, the shift in the composition of tradable exports towards energy-intensive products, one example being cellulose, have led to a large rise in the energy content of the industrial sector, and thence in overall energy intensity.

As figure IV.6 shows, the evidence indicates that the effect of reform on energy efficiency/intensity has not lived up to expectations. As a result, this issue has come to form a crucial element in initiatives aimed at achieving more rational use of energy resources towards the end of the decade.

---

[16] Geothermal electricity generation is not carried out on a significant scale. At the end of the last decade, electricity of geothermal origin accounted for just 1.2% of the region's electricity output. The main developments are found in Mexico, Nicaragua and El Salvador, while there is interesting potential in Guatemala, Chile and Peru.

Figure IV.6
ENERGY INTENSITY, 1980-1999

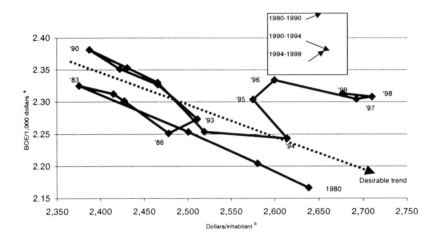

Source: Produced by the author on the basis of OLADE/ECLAC.

[a] Barrels of oil equivalent per 1,000 dollars.
[b] Dollars per inhabitant.

The erratic behaviour of this indicator in Latin America and the Caribbean shows that the fluctuations resulting from structural changes in economic behaviour in general were not matched by equivalent movements in energy-use behaviour. Thus, there was a strongly regressive movement in the period 1980-1985 (contraction in per capita income and rise in energy intensity), and this was repeated between 1987 and 1990. In the first three years of the 1990s this tendency was reversed as incomes recovered, but the energy intensity trend remained stable. What this means is that the economic recession of the 1980s was not accompanied by better energy utilization.

Progress in the Latin American and Caribbean countries has been modest, and in some periods the direction of change has been undesirable. After falling by a substantial 9% in the period 1970-1980, energy intensity rose in the 1980s, and in 1999 some 7% more energy was required to produce a given unit of output than in 1980. Over the last 20 years, the OECD countries have brought energy intensity down by some 20% on average by pursuing energy policies designed to diversify supply and achieve more effective use by eliminating waste and improving efficiency. Latin America and the Caribbean have significant scope for efforts in the same direction.

The following table shows a range of indicators proposed by the International Energy Agency to summarize the relative positions of the different regions in energy terms.

Table IV.14
REGIONS OF THE WORLD: SELECTED ENERGY AND CARBON DIOXIDE (CO_2)
EMISSION INDICATORS [a]

Region	Supply per capita (TOE/inhab)[b]	Supply/GDP (KTOE/1990 dollar)[c]	Electricity consumption/inhab (kWh/inhab)[d]	CO_2/TOE[e] consumed	CO_2/population[f] (CO_2/inhab)[g]	CO_2/GDP[h] (Kg CO_2/dollar)[i]
World total	1.64	0.37	2,252.3	2.36	3.86	0.87
OECD	4.63	0.25	7,751.2	2.36	10.92	0.58
Middle East	2.22	0.67	2,336.9	2.60	5.78	1.73
Former Soviet Union	3.06	1.69	3,617.2	2.47	7.56	4.17
Rest of Europe	1.91	0.74	2,925.1	2.53	4.83	1.88
China	0.84	1.16	895.2	2.76	2.32	3.19
Asia	0.55	0.7	508.5	1.88	1.03	1.31
Latin America	1.1	0.38	1,494.6	1.95	2.15	0.74
Africa	0.64	0.87	490.47	1.51	0.96	1.31

Source: International Energy Agency (IEA), "Key World Energy Statistics" (http://www.iea.org), 2001.

[a] The data for Latin America do not include Mexico, which is categorized as part of OECD.
[b] Tons of oil equivalent per inhabitant.
[c] Kilotons of oil equivalent per 1990 dollar.
[d] Kilowatt hours per inhabitant.
[e] Carbon dioxide per tons of oil equivalent consumed.
[f] Carbon dioxide produced in relation to population.
[g] Carbon dioxide per inhabitant.
[h] Carbon dioxide produced in relation to gross domestic product.
[i] Kilograms of carbon dioxide per dollar.

- In Latin America and the Caribbean, the total supply of primary energy per inhabitant is a quarter of the average for the OECD group of countries and close to the world average. In relation to GDP, the total primary energy supply is 40% higher than in the industrialized countries, which is indicative to some degree of energy underutilization.

- Per capita electricity consumption in Latin America and the Caribbean is a fifth of the level seen in industrialized countries and 30% below the world average. It exceeds only the levels of other developing regions such as Asia and Africa, being lower than in the transition economies.

- As regards carbon dioxide (CO_2) emissions, the figures are much lower in the developing regions, in relation to population, than in the other regions, including even the former Soviet Union and the countries of Central and Eastern Europe.

- Where CO_2 emissions per unit of output are concerned, the region's performance is bettered only by that of the OECD countries.

2.   Latin America and the Caribbean and global climate change

(a)   Trend in carbon dioxide (CO_2) emissions between 1980 and 1999

For the great majority of countries, a reasonable approximation can be arrived at for the level of CO_2 emissions from the burning of fossil fuels. This is not the case with CO_2 emissions from land use or changes in land use (deforestation), or with emissions of other greenhouse gases. This analysis will therefore focus on CO_2 emissions related to the energy sector, which are the ones that have the greatest influence on climate change. In what follows, unless otherwise stated, "emissions" will mean "CO_2 emissions from the burning of fossil fuels".

In Latin America and the Caribbean, CO_2 emissions were 34% higher in 1999 than in 1980, with most of the increase coming since 1994. In fact, in 1994 total CO_2 emissions were just 18% higher than in 1980, but between 1994 and 1999 they rose steadily by about 2.5% a year. The trend of emissions per unit of output in relation to per capita GDP does not show a clear or defined direction, as can be seen from the following chart. The behaviour of this indicator is associated with energy consumption structures (sectors and sources) and with changes in the region's production structures during the 1990s.

Figure IV.7
LATIN AMERICA: CARBON DIOXIDE EMISSIONS, 1980-1999

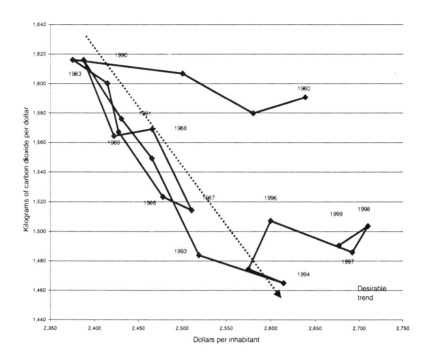

Source: Prepared by the author on the basis of OLADE/ECLAC.

3.   The contribution of Latin America and the Caribbean to total emissions

With 8.5% of the world's population, Latin America now accounts for 5.4% of world greenhouse gas emissions.[17] The largest share of emissions in the region is produced by Mexico, with 356 million tons a year. The emissions of Brazil and Mexico account for 53% of the regional total. Although the two countries between them have roughly the same population as the United States, their combined emissions add up to barely 12% of that industrialized country's total.

---

[17]   The data are only for emissions produced by the burning of fossil fuels. This publication does not count Mexico as part of "Latin America", as the country is included in the "OECD" category. For the purposes of the present document, Mexico's contribution has been counted in with that of Latin America and the Caribbean.

Two thirds of the region's emissions come from the burning of liquid fuels (oil and derivatives), while coal accounts for less than 8%. Emissions per unit of output are fairly small: 0.41 kg of CO_2/US$/GDP at purchasing power parity, as against a world average of 0.67 and an OECD average of 0.61. As regards the relationship between emissions and the total primary energy supply, the region produces 2.1 tons of CO_2 per ton of oil equivalent. This indicator is below the world average because of the substantial role of renewable sources, particularly water, in the regional energy structure. The following charts show the trend of this indicator, comparing the region with the rest of the world, and Brazil and Mexico with the rest of the region.

Figure IV.8
RELATIONSHIP BETWEEN CO_2 EMISSIONS AND GDP, AND CO_2 EMISSIONS AND POPULATION, 1977-1998

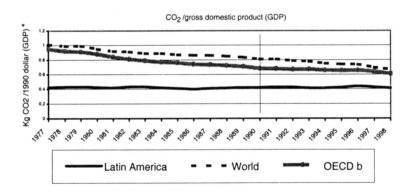

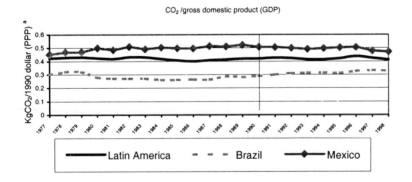

Where per capita emissions are concerned, the Latin America and Caribbean figure, at 2.45 tons per inhabitant, is strikingly low. The following charts show the changing relationship between the region and the rest of the world, and between Brazil and Mexico and the rest of the region, in respect of this indicator.

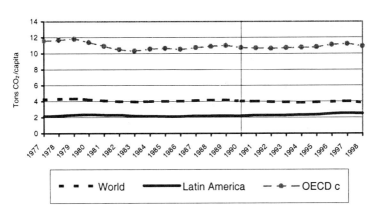

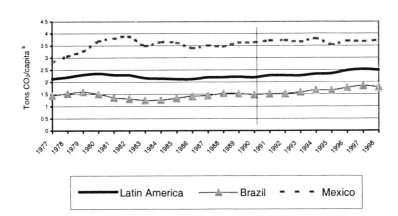

Source: Prepared by F. Tudela on the basis of International Energy Agency data, 2000.

[a] Kilograms of carbon dioxide per 1990 dollar (purchasing power parity).
[b] Tons of carbon dioxide per capita.
[c] Countries of the Organisation for Economic Co-operation and Development.

In the political sphere, lastly, the countries of the region have shown considerable commitment to world efforts to co-ordinate climate change mitigation measures. As of May 2001, 12 Latin American and Caribbean countries had submitted their first national reports to the authorities of the United Nations Framework Convention on Climate Change. In mid-2001, 15[18] of just 37 countries to have ratified the Kyoto Protocol were Latin American or Caribbean.

Latin America and the Caribbean are particularly vulnerable to climate change, a global upheaval that could compromise the sustainability of development in many parts of the region. If climate change were to take its course, the results in the region could include a rise in the frequency of extreme hydrometeorological phenomena, the intensification of climate-related disasters, progressive desertification, the loss of agricultural land, coastal effects caused by rising sea levels and widespread disruption to ecosystems that would compromise one of the planet's greatest reserves of biodiversity. Caribbean small island developing States are among the nations most threatened by climate change.

---

[18]   Antigua and Barbuda, Bahamas, Barbados, Bolivia, Ecuador, El Salvador, Guatemala, Honduras, Jamaica, Mexico, Nicaragua, Panama, Paraguay, Trinidad and Tobago and Uruguay.

Chapter V

Socio-environmental vulnerability

A.   The world context

The 1990s were designated by the United Nations as the International Decade for Natural Disaster Reduction (IDNDR). The community of nations intensified its efforts to increase and improve information, education and public awareness about natural disasters, and the systems for prevention, early warning, emergency aid, and rehabilitation and reconstruction or repair of damage were strengthened. Paradoxically, however, the incidence and intensity of natural disasters and the resulting damage have been increasing in recent years. Droughts, forest fires, floods, landslides, tropical storms, hurricanes, tornadoes, earthquakes, and volcanic eruptions have been claiming a growing number of victims and have given rise to losses which seriously affect the development of many communities, especially the poorest ones.

In the world as a whole, some 700,000 persons lost their lives between 1991 and 2000 as a result of natural disasters. This figure, while undoubtedly an underestimate, was lower than in the previous decade. However, the number of incidents, their intensity, the number of persons affected and the economic losses greatly exceeded the levels of the 1980s. Thus, while the average number of persons affected per year between 1981 and 1990 was 147 million, this figure rose to 211 million per year for the period from 1991 to 2000 (IFRC, 2001).

The insurance companies are viewing this situation with increasing concern and alarm. Up to 1988, there had never been a natural disaster which would have required the payment of more than US$ 1 billion per event in insurance claims, but between 1988 and 1996 there were 15 events in various parts of the world whose cost to insurers exceeded that amount. Compared with the average for the 1970s, the total number of disasters due to natural phenomena has trebled in the last decade, while the total amount of the economic losses caused has increased ninefold.[1] Half the insured losses due to natural disasters in the last 40 years have occurred in the last decade.[2]

The more serious nature of the disasters is particularly marked in the case of those connected with the climate or caused by extreme hydrometeorological phenomena, which represent rather more than half the total number of disasters but account for over 90% of the victims and at least 85% of the total calculated economic losses. Furthermore, over 90% of the victims of climate-related disasters are in developing countries. It is interesting to note that the International Red Cross reports that it dealt with 392 disasters of this type in the year 2000, whereas the average prior to 1996 was around 200 climatic disasters per year. Even so, the year 2000 was quite mild compared with the terrible year of 1998, when 50,000 lives were lost in disasters, there were 300 million displaced persons, and there were losses totalling over US$ 93 billion, of which only US$ 15 billion was covered by some sort of insurance. By way of comparison, it may be recalled that in the whole of the 1980s the economic losses due to climate-related disasters did not exceed US$ 55 billion.

The greater severity of climate-related disasters may be partly due to the heightening of meteorological extremes as a result of global climate change. The Munich Re reinsurance company estimates that if the international community allows this process of change to continue unchecked, losses from this cause may amount to over US$ 300 billion per year in the coming decades.

B.   Natural disasters in the region

The nature of the region's physical environment means that there is a particularly serious risk of the occurrence of phenomena capable of causing a disaster. The Sierra Madre, the chain of new volcanoes, the Central American isthmus and almost the whole length of the Andean

---

[1]   Data provided by the world's largest reinsurance company, Munich Re (http://www.munichre.com).
[2]   Reinsurance Association of America (RAA) (http://www.raanet.org).

range are very active tectonic elements responsible for the occurrence of large-scale earthquakes and volcanic eruptions. In tropical latitudes, the region is prone to tropical storms and hurricanes which occur seasonally in both the Atlantic and the Pacific. Droughts have occurred increasingly often even in humid and sub-humid ecosystems. Extensive areas of the Southern Cone region of South America suffer from severe flooding. Almost the whole of the region is affected by the periodical occurrence of the El Niño-Southern Oscillation phenomenon, which, depending on the location of the areas affected, intensifies rainfall or increases the severity of droughts which heighten the risk of forest fires.

The region's vulnerability to these phenomena became obvious from the devastating effects of recent disasters affecting the Andean region (the El Niño-Southern Oscillation phenomenon in 1997/1998), the Caribbean (hurricane Georges), Central America (hurricane Mitch) and Venezuela. There have also been smaller local disasters which, taken together, have likewise caused heavy damage. Among the factors which increase the region's vulnerability to disasters are:

- the increase and concentration of the population, rapid urbanization in unplanned human settlements, the location of many communities in high-risk zones such as deforested areas, the beds and primary terraces of rivers and streams, and hillsides and gullies, the existence of poverty conditions, the deterioration of public health conditions, the intensification of industrial and transport activities, the use of increasing amounts of energy, the adoption of unsuitable technologies, the lack of infrastructure or territorial planning, the deterioration of some public services, and the inadequacy of regulatory frameworks; and
- the degradation of ecosystems, deforestation, loss of plant cover and of biodiversity, soil erosion, the alteration of hydrological cycles, reduction of the recharging of aquifers and a corresponding increase in runoff, the accumulation of inflammable material and wastes, and various forms of pollution.

The occurrence of these and other disasters has to do both with the vulnerability of the socio-environmental systems involved and the incidence of the natural phenomenon responsible. All natural disasters are to some extent man-made and induced. Even though the phenomena capable of setting off a disaster are subject to patterns of natural variability and are generally beyond human control, measures can and must be taken to prevent such phenomena from bringing on a major disaster. The prevention and mitigation of natural disasters is one of the main challenges for the region, in view of its high level of vulnerability. It is estimated that one dollar spent on the prevention of disasters can save at least seven dollars in potential damage.

Within the region, the Caribbean is the subregion which has been most affected by natural disasters. Table V.1 below shows the biggest natural disasters it has suffered. Apart from volcanic eruptions, a notable feature is the frequent recurrence of climatic disasters, to which the Caribbean —like most of the world's small island States— is extremely vulnerable. Thus, for example, Antigua and Barbuda has been affected by nine hurricanes in the last 10 years. In 1999 —not a particularly bad year— the Caribbean was hit by 12 cyclones, 8 of which qualified as hurricanes, and 5 of which reached 4 on the Saffir-Simpson scale.

Table V.1
THE 10 WORST NATURAL DISASTERS OF THE TWENTIETH CENTURY
IN THE CARIBBEAN

Disaster	Date	Country	Number of dead	Number of persons affected
Volcanic eruption	8 May 1902	Martinique	40,000	-
Tropical storm (cyclone, hurricane, typhoon)	2 Oct. 1963	Grenada, Trinidad and Tobago, Bahamas, Dominican Republic, Haiti, Jamaica, Cuba	7,258	-
Tropical storm	3 Sep. 1930	Dominica, Dominican Republic	6,500	20,000
Tropical storm	9 Nov. 1932	Cuba	2,500	-
Tropical storm	12 Sep. 1928	Guadeloupe, Montserrat, Saint Kitts and Nevis, Puerto Rico	2,300	-
Tropical storm	22 Sep. 1998	Antigua and Barbuda, Cuba, Haiti, Dominican Republic	491	4,686,292
Torrential rain	15 Nov. 1994	Cuba, Haiti, Jamaica	1,124	1,697,558
Tropical storm	11 Sep. 1988	Haiti, Jamaica, Saint Lucia	148	1,680,000
Tropical storm	August 1979	Dominican Republic, Dominica, Puerto Rico, Haiti, Cuba	1,451	1,651,713
Floods	24 Aug. 1988	Dominican Republic	-	1,191,150

Source: Catholic University of Louvain, "EM-DAT, The OFDA/CRED International Disaster Database", Brussels, Belgium (http://www.cred.be/emdat/intro.html), 2001.

Like the Caribbean, the Central American subregion also suffers from the devastating effects of hurricanes and tropical storms. The vulnerability of the subregion is further increased by the location of settlements in the flood plains of the main rivers, in areas of high seismic risk, with highly active tectonic faults, and in areas of volcanic activity (proximity of some 30 active volcanoes). Most of the damage caused by natural disasters in this subregion is due to landslides and floods.

South America is affected above all by:

- The El Niño-Southern Oscillation phenomenon, which affects Peru and Ecuador in particular;
- Tectonic movements resulting in volcanic eruptions and earthquakes, such as that suffered by the department of Quindío, Colombia, in January 1999, which caused over 1,000 deaths;
- Floods, like those which affected Venezuela in 1999 and the recurrent flooding suffered by Argentina.

In both Central and South America, large-scale forest fires represent a growing threat to ecosystems, including those of the tropical rain forests. One disaster leads to another: the destruction caused by a hurricane produces dead material which serves months later as fuel for forest fires. Likewise, the unsuitable agricultural practices used include the use of fire, which in the present conditions is one of the most frequent causes of forest fires.

C.   The socio-economic impact of disasters in the region

Natural disasters have many serious consequences for national economies which, apart from the emergency attention required at the time, also have implications for economic policy management, the sustainability of development in the medium and long term, and the behaviour of production. In addition to the loss of human lives and assets, the reduction of countries' production capacity and their effects on macroeconomic variables, disasters also shift development priorities from the long term to the satisfaction of short-term needs, making it difficult to adopt sustainable development strategies.

Calculating the costs of damage, even in purely economic terms, makes it possible to gain a better idea of the threat that natural disasters represent for the development of the region as a whole. The Economic Commission for Latin America and the Caribbean (ECLAC) has developed a methodology for calculating direct and indirect costs in the short, medium and long terms. Thus, economic damage from disasters caused by natural phenomena over the last 30 years is calculated by ECLAC at US$ 50.365 billion (in 1998 dollars) (see table V.2). Since the table only contains information on some of the natural disasters which have occurred in the region, however, the real socio-economic impact has been much greater. In Central America, for example, the economic damage done by natural disasters since 1972 comes to an annual average of nearly US$ 800 million, which is equivalent to 2% of subregional GDP (Jovel, 2000).

Table V.2
LATIN AMERICA AND THE CARIBBEAN: NATURAL DISASTERS BETWEEN
1972 AND 2001 *

Country and year	Type of disaster	Number of persons affected		Millions of 1998 dollars
		Deaths	Directly affected	Total damage
Nicaragua, 1972	Earthquake	6,000	300,000	2,968
Honduras, 1974	Hurricane Fifí	7,000	115,000	1,331
Grenada, 1975	Tropical storm			29
Antigua and Barbuda, 1975	Earthquake		4,200	61
Guatemala, 1976	Earthquake	23,000	2,550,000	2,147
Dominica, 1979	Hurricane David	42	60,060	118
Dominican Republic, 1979	Hurricanes David and Federico	2,000	1,200,000	1,869
Nicaragua, 1982	Floods	80	70,000	599
El Salvador, 1982	Earthquake, droughts and flooding	600	20,000	216
Guatemala, 1982	Heavy rains and drought	610	10,000	136
Nicaragua, 1982	Floods and drought			588
Bolivia, Ecuador and Peru, 1982-1983	El Niño		3,840,000	5,651
Mexico, 1985	Earthquake	8,000	150,000	6,216
Colombia, 1985	Eruption of Nevado del Ruiz volcano	22,000	200,000	465
El Salvador, 1986	Earthquake	1,200	520,000	1,352
Ecuador, 1987	Earthquake	1,000	82,500	1,438
Nicaragua, 1988	Hurricane Joan	148	550,000	1,160
Nicaragua, 1992	Eruption of Cerro Negro volcano	2	12,000	22
Nicaragua, 1992	Pacific tsunami	116	40,500	30
Anguilla, 1995	Hurricane Luis			59
Netherlands Antilles, 1995	Hurricanes Luis and Marilyn			1,112
Costa Rica, 1996	Hurricane Cesar	39	40,260	157

(continued)

Table V.2 (concluded)

Country and year	Type of disaster	Number of persons affected		Millions of 1998 dollars
		Deaths	Directly affected	Total damage
Nicaragua, 1996	Hurricane Cesar	9	29,500	53
Costa Rica, 1997-1998	El Niño		119,279	93
Andean Community, 1997-1998	El Niño	600	125,000	7,694
Dominican Republic, 1998	Hurricane Georges	235	296,637	2,193
Central America, 1998	Hurricane Mitch	9,214	1,191,908	6,008
Colombia, 1999	Earthquake	1,185	559,401	1,580
Venezuela, 1999	Torrential rain	...	68,503	3,237
Belize, 2000	Hurricane Keith	10	57,400	265
El Salvador, 2001	Earthquakes	1,159	1,412,938	1,518
Total		**84,249**	**13,625,086**	**50,365**

Source: Economic Commission for Latin America and the Caribbean/Inter-American Development Bank (ECLAC/IDB).

* Natural disasters whose effects have been evaluated by ECLAC.

In Meso-America, over 20,000 persons lost their lives through hydrometeorological disasters between 1990 and 1999, and the total number of persons affected came to nearly 4.5 million, compared with 1,640 victims in the subregion in the period from 1980 to 1989. The tragic effects of hurricane Mitch on Central America in 1998 were mainly responsible for the difference between the two decades.

Hurricane Mitch

The most serious natural disaster in the recent history of Central America began on 21 October 1998, when a tropical depression formed in the Caribbean and on the next day was given the name Mitch. It gained force, especially between the 23rd and 26th of that month, until it finally became a category 5 hurricane on the Saffir-Simpson scale. The centre of the hurricane moved slowly and erratically, with some gusts exceeding 280 km/hr. Mitch was probably the most violent hurricane suffered by the subregion since that of 1780, which caused over 22,000 victims. The tragedy took place when the hurricane had already begun to lose strength, and was due to the intensity and persistence of the rains which affected the whole of the Central American isthmus, but especially Honduras. In a very few days Mitch caused over 1,500 mm of rainfall and wiped out almost a decade of development in that country. After causing impressive devastation by flooding in Central America, on 4 November the erratic vestiges of Mitch were affecting even the west coast of Florida.

Estimates of the economic and environmental damage caused by Mitch amount to over US$ 6 billion. Most of the damage was in Honduras, where the losses were equivalent to nearly 80% of GDP (49% of GDP in Nicaragua) (ECLAC, 1999b). A preliminary summary of the damage is given in table V.3 below, although some of the data are very unreliable.

Table V.3
THE DAMAGE CAUSED BY HURRICANE MITCH

Country	Dead	Missing	Number of persons affected	Number of dwellings destroyed or damaged
Honduras	7,000	8,052	1,393,669	70,000
Nicaragua	1,849	1,287	800,000	24,975
Guatemala	258	120	105,000	19,093
El Salvador	239	235	67,300	10,000
Total	**9,346**	**9,694**	**2,365,969**	**124,068**

Source: Office for the Coordination of Humanitarian Affairs (OCHA), *Situation Report*, No. 13, 12 November 1998.

In the effects of hurricane Mitch, an important role was played by the prior environmental degradation which existed. On the one hand, in 1997 the El Niño phenomenon had already caused droughts and forest fires, with the loss of 1.5 million hectares of forest in Central America. On the other hand, the deforestation of protection areas exposed the soil to erosion and sharply reduced its infiltration capacity, thus heightening the devastation. River beds were obstructed by buildings and dumped rubbish, and with the subsequent heavy rains this blocked the natural drainage channels of rivers and lakes. Mitch, in turn, has further weakened the environment's capacity to mitigate the effects of extreme natural events, thus increasing the risks in the event of future hydrometeorological events. Like other disasters of this type, Mitch caused the displacement of population groups both within and between countries, thus increasing the vulnerability of both urban (makeshift settlements) and rural areas (occupation of more fragile areas and/or expansion of the agricultural frontier).

The experience derived from hurricane Mitch was a turning point for the subregion and indeed for the region as a whole. It was clearly perceived that this time it was not enough simply to provide support during the emergency and replace or repair the damaged infrastructure; rather, it was necessary to carry out an in-depth review of the reasons for the increased vulnerability, put a stop to the accumulated deterioration of ecosystems, which undoubtedly made the tragedy worse, make changes in regulatory frameworks and planning systems, beginning with territorial planning, and prepare for future phenomena of the same type. As well as being a national-scale tragedy, Mitch was also an opportunity to revise the sustainable development strategies of various countries in the region.

Chapter VI

Public policies

A.   The institutional framework for the environment

The Declaration of the United Nations Conference on the Human Environment (Stockholm, 1972) recognized the need to adopt large-scale measures on the environment and made an appeal in this respect. In response to this, the governments of all the countries of the region, to a greater or lesser extent, began to incorporate the issue of the environment into their administrative and legislative activities, the result being environmental policies involving various legal, technical, institutional and economic initiatives.

Within the public administration of the State, in the 1970s environmental management was entrusted to sectoral organs and then to environmental bodies at the under-secretary or vice-ministerial level associated initially with the health sector and subsequently, in the 1980s, with the urban development sector. During the same period, environmental bodies in the most highly industrialized and urbanized countries were increasingly associated with the urban development and housing sector. In some cases environmental management was tackled from the planning standpoint, with an intersectoral approach in the form of high-level advisory bodies close to the executive (councils, commissions or secretariats associated with ministries of planning or offices of the president). The 1980s were difficult years for environmental management, however, because of the adjustment processes deriving from the economic crisis that affected the region, and this affected the ability of the public sector to slow the environmental deterioration of critical ecosystems and keep pollution in check (Bárcena, 2001).

The drive towards modern institutions for the environment in the region started with the Earth Summit in 1992, when most of the countries set up ministries to act as the highest environmental authorities, as part of a process designed to give environmental management the integral nature it needs in order to be efficient.

Natural resources have always been the main basis for the economic development of the countries of Latin America and the Caribbean, so it is not surprising that for over a century they have been establishing sectoral bodies for the promotion and development of those resources, but it must be acknowledged that these bodies have not all grown up in the same way in the region. In some countries, environmental functions were assigned to traditional bodies (in the fields of public health, agriculture, town planning, mining, etc.) and then passed on to intermediate authorities (advisory commissions at the highest levels of the executive). In the most recent stage, new bodies have been set up which have often been the result of the grouping together of existing areas of government, now defined with broader objectives.

This latter type of model now predominates in the region, although there are still cases of environmental matters being integrated in a single body, subordinate to other sectors. The highest authority for environmental matters therefore usually takes one of two forms. In most cases, it is a ministerial body, but in others the authorities concerned are collegiate (see table VI.1). In the latter case, the multisectoral nature of environmental management has led the countries to place it at a high level of government and, instead of establishing a ministry of the environment, they have preferred to set up a collegiate body with the participation of all the areas of the public administration whose decisions affect natural resources in some way. In some cases representatives of NGOs, academic circles, production sectors, etc., also participate in these bodies (UNDP, 1999).

The majority of the national-level environmental agencies have also taken responsibility for following up the sustainable development agenda. Bolivia is the only country which has set up a Ministry of Sustainable Development and given that body the functions of national planning, environmental protection, indigenous affairs and territorial planning, so that it will be responsible for integrating the country's economic, social and environmental policies and coordinating their implementation.

Table VI.1
HIGHEST ENVIRONMENTAL AUTHORITIES IN LATIN AMERICA AND THE CARIBBEAN

Countries where the highest environmental authority is a minister or official of similar rank	
Antigua and Barbuda	Ministry of Culture, Tourism and the Environment
Argentina	Ministry of Social Development and the Environment
Bahamas	Ministry of Agriculture and Fisheries
Barbados	Ministry of the Environment, Energy and Natural Resources
Belize	Ministry of Natural Resources, the Environment and Industry
Bolivia	Ministry of Sustainable Development and Planning
Brazil	Ministry of the Environment
Colombia	Ministry of the Environment
Costa Rica	Ministry of the Environment and Energy
Cuba	Ministry of Science, Technology and the Environment
Dominica	Ministry of Agriculture and the Environment
Ecuador	Ministry of the Environment
El Salvador	Ministry of the Environment and Natural Resources
Grenada	Ministry of Health, the Environment, Community Development and Cooperatives
Guatemala	Ministry of the Environment and Natural Resources
Guyana	Ministry of Health and Labour
Haiti	Ministry of the Environment
Honduras	Ministry of Natural Resources and the Environment
Jamaica	Ministry of Land and the Environment
Mexico	Ministry of the Environment and Natural Resources
Nicaragua	Ministry of the Environment and Natural Resources
Panama	National Environmental Authority
Paraguay	Ministry of the Environment
Dominican Republic	Ministry of the Environment and Natural Resources
Saint Kitts and Nevis	Ministry of Health and the Environment
Saint Lucia	Ministry of Development, Planning, the Environment and Housing
Saint Vincent and the Grenadines	Ministry of Health and the Environment
Suriname	Ministry of Labour, Technology and the Environment
Trinidad and Tobago	Ministry of the Environment
Uruguay	Ministry of Housing, Territorial Planning and the Environment
Venezuela	Ministry of the Environment and Renewable Natural Resources
Countries where the highest environmental authority is a coordinating or collegiate body	
Chile	National Commission for the Environment (Conama)
Peru	National Council for the Environment

Source: ECLAC, on the basis of the United Nations Development Programme (UNDP), "Estudio comparativo de los diseños institucionales para la gestión ambiental en los países de América Latina", document presented at the Fourth Meeting of the Inter-Sessional Committee of the Forum of Ministers of the Environment of Latin America and the Caribbean, Lima, 2 October 1999; Guillermo Acuña, Marcos regulatorios e institucionales ambientales de América Latina y el Caribe en el contexto del proceso de reformas macroeconómicas: 1980-1990 (LC/R.2023), Santiago, Chile, Economic Commission for Latin America and the Caribbean (ECLAC), April 2000; and data provided by the United Nations Environment Programme (UNEP), "Puntos focales técnicos de medio ambiente de los países de América Latina y el Caribe" (http://www.rolac.unep.mx/ForoALC/esp/), 2001.

A common feature of both models —ministries and commissions—
is the excessive number of responsibilities and functions assigned to them
in comparison with their limited capacities, which limits their
effectiveness (UNDP, 1999).

The new global international agreements resulting from the 1992
Rio Conference have also given rise to a number of important changes in
institutions and new cooperation mechanisms. For example, the majority
of the countries have set up or are in the process of setting up specific
bodies such as commissions, institutes or national programmes for
biodiversity, in response to the Convention on Biological Diversity. New
appraisals have also been undertaken, such as the national reports on the
amount of greenhouse gases prepared by each country in pursuance of
the United Nations Framework Convention on Climate Change. In the
case of the United Nations Convention against Desertification, the system
of regional units has been used in order to implement it in a decentralized
manner.

Meanwhile, national commissions for sustainable development,
which are at executive level and are of an intersectoral nature, are new
kinds of institutions designed to tackle sustainable development at the
national level, although they are only beginning to operate in the region.

Progress in the institutional field has also extended to
supranational subregional integration and cooperation, through the
generation of specific spaces for discussion and work.[1]

In the Central American subregion, the Central American
Commission on the Environment and Development (CCAD) was set up in
1989 as part of the Central American Integration System (SICA), a
Commission which is taking on great importance as a subregional forum
for ministers of the environment or similar authorities. On the basis of
common positions, these have proposed a number of subregional
agreements on biodiversity, hazardous wastes, forests, etc., accompanied
by a portfolio of environmental projects and a successful financial
strategy.[2] This boost for sustainable development issues was ratified by
the signing of the Central American Alliance for Sustainable Development
(ALIDES) in 1994, which considerably strengthens the integration of
the subregion on the basis of a common approach to sustainable
development.

---

[1]   For more details on this subject, see the analysis in chapter VII.
[2]   Mexico has recently applied to join this Commission, which currently consists of the
      environmental authorities of the seven Central American countries.

In the case of the Caribbean, in 1994 the United Nations Conference on the Sustainable Development of Small Island Developing States adopted a full programme of action which the Caribbean ministers undertook to apply in the subregion.

In South America, the same type of evolution has taken place within the MERCOSUR trade agreement, with the creation in 1996, subsequent to the 1991 Treaty of Asunción, of the Working Sub-group on the Environment. The member countries of the Andean Community, for their part, followed the same lines by approving in 1999 the establishment of the Andean Committee of Environmental Authorities, as a forum for discussion and consensus on this matter.

Mexico, which is a contracting party to the North American Free Trade Agreement (NAFTA), is also a party to the parallel agreement on the environment among the NAFTA countries and their trinational Environmental Cooperation Commission (ECC), which is designed to further cooperation on environmental matters among Canada, Mexico and the United States.

At the regional level, one of the most effective forms of cooperation among environmental authorities is the Forum of Ministers of the Environment of Latin America and the Caribbean, for which UNEP acts as the secretariat. The Forum, which was set up in 1982, groups together the 33 ministers or equivalent who are heads of environmental agencies or commissions in the region and who meet periodically to agree on joint positions vis-à-vis global agencies and to sign regional cooperation agreements. To this end, the Forum has identified priority issues which have been expressed in a regional plan of action, providing an important means of cooperation. The performance of the Forum of Ministers is also strengthened by the support it receives from the Inter-Agency Technical Committee (ITC) set up in 1999 by ECLAC, UNDP, UNEP, the World Bank and IDB, whose main task is to support the recommendations and goals adopted by the member countries of the Forum. For this purpose, the agencies in question have strengthened their programmes in the field of the environment, taking an approach based on sustainable development.

Another important effort which has been made is the follow-up to the Bolivian Summit on Sustainable Development held in 1996, which is coordinated by OAS. Among its achievements are the creation of the Inter-American Network on Environmental Law and the Inter-American Biodiversity Network, as well as the strengthening of the Inter-American Dialogue on Water Resources. The main aim of these mechanisms is to share information and management experience among the countries of the hemisphere.

B.   Evolution of regulatory frameworks

As in the case of institutions, regulatory frameworks for the environment also went through a process of evolution after the 1992 Rio Conference. That Conference gave a boost to the development and application of environmental legislation, one of the most pressing reasons for this being the need to bring that legislation into line with the new international instruments adopted in other areas (first climate change and biodiversity, and subsequently the struggle against desertification), Agenda 21, the Rio Declaration on Environment and Development, the Principles for a Global Consensus on Management, Conservation and Sustainable Development of All Types of Forests, and the inherent concept of sustainable development underlying all of them. This new stage has led to some qualitative advances as regards the definition of the public authorities responsible for environmental management and various material aspects of the national legislation of the countries of the region (Brañes, 1996 and 2001).[3] These countries have updated most laws relating to the direct regulation model, whereby regulations to establish controls on environmental quality and the emission, dumping and concentration of solid wastes are adopted, with penalties for non-compliance. The direct regulation approach[4] has been complemented with other regulations which open the way for the establishment of economic instruments for environmental management and greater participation by society as a whole.

Among the areas where there has been the greatest legislative progress in Latin America and the Caribbean in the last decade are: evaluation of environmental impact; territorial planning; new offences and penalties; responsibility for damage to the environment; scales of charges for pollution and other economic instruments; full endorsement of legal action to protect the environment; citizen participation mechanisms; and limitations of property rights for environmental reasons. Also important are reforms of sectoral laws regulating the exploitation, use and conservation of renewable and non-renewable natural resources. These processes have given rise to wide-ranging

---

[3]   In his studies on this subject for UNEP (2001c), Raúl Brañes carries out a full comparative analysis of the environmental rules adopted by the countries of the region in recent decades, with emphasis on a description of the extent to which the principles and commitments arising from the Rio Conference have been incorporated into national legislation and their effects on the institutional structure for environmental management in those countries.

[4]   Also known in the region as "command and control".

discussion in the countries concerned, and some of them have been resisted both by public actors and by civil society (Acuña, 2000).[5]

Most of the Constitutions of the countries of the region contain a number of provisions on the environment and sustainable development, especially those which formally recognize the idea of sustainable development and stipulate that the State and society have a duty to protect the environment and that all persons have the right to live in a suitable environment.[6] Constitutional status has also been given to one of the most widespread environmental management instruments, the evaluation of environmental impact.[7] Some central principles of the Rio Declaration, such as the precautionary and "polluter pays" principles, have also been incorporated into some Constitutions, although they have mainly been incorporated into framework environmental regulations.

These constitutional principles have created the right conditions for the courts of law and other bodies participating in the jurisdictional functions of the State to begin to play a more prominent role in protecting the environment. Civil, administrative and criminal responsibility for damage to the environment has been incorporated into the legislation of a number of countries. In addition to imposing penalties, the laws generally also require those responsible to make good or compensate for the damage caused. Constitutions and framework laws have also made provision for various types of legal action to safeguard environmental rights, such as class actions, actions seeking legal protection, etc., thus opening up new spaces for citizen participation in defence of the environment (Ocampo, 1999).

There has also been a trend in the region towards environmental laws which complement direct regulation and preventive measures with the use of diagnostic studies and environmental evaluations. This new approach is helping to give a broader dimension to the important role of municipalities and local action in preserving the environment.

In spite of the positive aspects of environmental legislation in the region, however, the experience gained over the last decade indicates that the challenge is not so much to reform or expand the environmental regulations in force as to strengthen the capacity to enforce them. This approach became even clearer in the light of the international agreements resulting from the Rio Declaration and its subsequent protocols. This situation warrants careful evaluation that takes account of the actual

---

[5] See also Trellez Solís, 1997.
[6] The first Constitution to incorporate these concepts was that of Peru, in 1979.
[7] This was done by Brazil in its 1988 reform of the Constitution, which is currently in force.

capacity of the countries to fulfil the commitments entered into and to clarify their implications in the environmental, economic, trade and social fields.

C.   Integration of public policies

The process of integrating environmental policies into other sectoral policies has also had its ups and downs. In all the countries of the region, generally speaking, the concept of sustainable resource use and environmental conservation is only just beginning to be incorporated into the different production and services sectors. Traditionally, macroeconomic policy and sectoral policies in the fields of health, education, agriculture, mining, etc. have taken very little account of the environmental dimension. Numerous "market failures", which are identified as one of the main underlying causes of environmental deterioration, are a reflection of this situation. This is also the case in those sectors which make direct use of biodiversity or act upon the elements on which it is based, such as the agricultural, forestry, fishery and water resources sectors. Likewise, alongside the main environmental authority, many public agencies often have mandates for the administration of renewable natural resources (i.e., ministries responsible for fisheries, forestry or agriculture and the various agencies responsible for water resources, energy, etc.) which frequently overlap and give rise to inter-agency conflicts.

With regard to economic and social policies, the balance-sheet of what was achieved in the 1990s is mixed. In the economic field, there has been considerable progress in the correction of fiscal imbalances, the reduction of inflation, speeding up the growth of exports, reviving regional integration processes or starting new ones, attracting new flows of foreign direct investment, and restoring economic growth. Significant progress has also been made in the development of strong macroeconomic institutions and, albeit with some delay, new institutional challenges have been tackled in other fields, such as the regulation of financial services, the promotion of competition, and the regulation of public services. With regard to social matters, public social expenditure has increased, and the proportion of the population in a state of poverty has been reduced, although not sufficiently.

On the negative side, the achievements in terms of economic growth and increasing productivity over the same period have been frustrating. The ups and downs of the economy and the frequency of financial crises indicate that not all the causes of instability have yet been eliminated, and some of them may even have got worse.

The structural heterogeneity of production sectors has further increased; the region now has more "world class" enterprises, many of them subsidiaries of transnational corporations, but it also has many enterprises, especially medium-sized and small ones, which have not been able to adapt to the new context. As a result, the labour market has deteriorated in many countries, the result being a rise in open unemployment or informal-sector employment in a number of them, while on the whole income distribution displays long-term deterioration in many countries of the region, in line with a universal trend. This is undoubtedly an important factor in the problems of social cohesion which are increasingly affecting many countries, and also in problems of governance.

In this context, the scope for orienting public policies towards sustainable development becomes more uncertain, since priority tends to be given to sectoral-type policies rather than integrative policies such as those for sustainable development (ECLAC, 2000a, pp. 10-11).

Nevertheless, it is becoming increasingly necessary for explicit environmental policies to be integrated with implicit ones. Some progress has come from new laws and management models, such as measures to integrate the environmental dimension into national planning processes along with the social and economic dimensions, or decisions to give the environmental authorities the right to define some sectoral policies, in conjunction with other agencies. The growing tendency to deal with environmental matters on the trade agenda and vice versa and the need to organize training campaigns on environmental issues, among others, are examples of the need for different public policies to be integrated (Gligo, 2001).

Some countries of the region are also noteworthy for their tendency to increasingly consider river valley areas as the units for planning and environmental management, so that territorial planning, deforestation, cleaner production methods and the promotion of suitable soil use become elements to be taken into account, thus integrating the efforts made by different policies from different perspectives to promote sustainable development and eliminate pollution.

D.   Experiments with the use of economic instruments in environmental management

The institutions regulating environmental matters in Latin America and the Caribbean face the growing challenge of designing environmental management instruments that can be both effective and economically efficient in the pursuit of environmental objectives, especially in view of the perception that traditional regulatory schemes have not been successful in dealing adequately with the processes of environmental deterioration that affect the region. Furthermore, because of the fiscal restrictions faced by most of the countries of the region, environmental authorities have less scope for strengthening their capabilities through higher budget allocations and must therefore explore other means for self-financing progress in environmental management.

Direct regulation has been the most popular way of approaching environmental problems in the world, with quality and emission or discharge standards being the most frequently used instruments. The main reasons why it is used are the importance of having objective values to guide environmental management and the capacity for direct control by the authorities over the conduct of economic actors.

During the last decade, an option which has found favour in the developed countries is that of using economic instruments[8] in environmental management to complement traditional direct regulation schemes. These instruments provide greater flexibility, through price/cost incentives, as well as the possibility of obtaining income to finance environmental management and investment through specifically dedicated funds. One new development in this respect is the use of environmental taxes as an integral part of the fiscal reform plans of the most highly developed countries.

The OECD countries, for example, are making more and more use of taxes linked with environmental parameters in their pollution control strategies. The environmental taxes collected in the OECD countries in 1995 were equivalent to 2.5% of those countries' GDP in that year, or almost 7% of all taxes collected (OECD, 1999, p. 5). The bulk of those taxes comes from a specific tax base relating to the transport and energy sectors, but they also include taxes on waste and effluent management, which are becoming increasingly common.

In view of the amount of work that still needs to be done to consolidate the institutions responsible for regulating the environment

---

[8]   Economic instruments are all those which affect the costs and benefits associated with the alternative courses of action open to agents, by affecting for example the profitability of alternative processes or technologies or the relative price of a product and thereby influencing the decisions of producers and consumers (ECLAC/UNEP, 1997). Other arrangements which can also be regarded as "economic instruments" for environmental management are informal regulation programmes based on the public dissemination of official information on environmental performance, certification, labelling, and other forms of external pressure based on the transparency of information. All these act through incentives associated with public image and market reputation, with economic consequences for the agents.

in Latin America and the Caribbean, and the budget constraints that affect them, the objective of enabling them to collect their own funds will necessarily play a key role in the design of instruments. The fiscal restrictions introduced by most of the countries in the region mean that increasing the capacity to collect resources of their own will be of vital importance if environmental institutions are to become stronger and develop the technical capabilities they need to operate effectively. The evidence indicates that great political credibility and technical capabilities are needed for the successful application of economic instruments that can bring about changes in the environmental performance of the agents subject to regulation which are effectively reflected in substantial improvements in the quality of the environment. Obviously, these conditions are not present in the initial stages of development of environmental regulatory agencies. As long as those agencies suffer from limitations in terms of budgetary and human resources, the possibility of self-financing even part of the resources needed for environmental management will continue to be an important objective when the relevant instruments are designed. Table VI.2 gives a number of examples of the way such instruments are being used in some countries of the region.

The foregoing examples reflect isolated experiments, and so far there has not been any evidence of vigorous and systematic application of economic instruments for environmental management in Latin America and the Caribbean.

There is a need for more in-depth analysis of the factors behind the successful application of economic instruments in the region and for the identification of the barriers standing in the way of implementation, given the legal, institutional and economic context of the countries of Latin America and the Caribbean. Most of the cases shown in table VI.2 reveal a number of conditioning factors and shortcomings in the institutional structure which limit the possibilities of success in the application of economic instruments for environmental management. These conditioning factors (Acquatella, 2001) may be classified in the following subject-groups: (i) the nature of the relationship between the environmental authorities and the fiscal authorities; (ii) the generation and availability of information for environmental management; (iii) adaptation of the legal and institutional framework to make possible effective environmental management; (iv) special territorial/regional features of environmental management instruments; and (v) the level of political priority and institutional strength attained by the environmental authorities.

Table VI.2
EXAMPLES OF THE USE OF ECONOMIC INSTRUMENTS IN LATIN AMERICA AND THE
CARIBBEAN

Country	Instruments used
Caribbean subregion Barbados and Jamaica	• System of returnable deposits on mass-consumption bottles (Barbados) • Environment tax on imported durable goods (Barbados) • Differential tariffs for solid waste collection (Barbados) • Fiscal exemptions for solar water heaters (Barbados) • Charges to users for the volume of water extracted (Jamaica) • Fiscal incentives for the construction of rainwater collection tanks and imported equipment for saving water in hotels (Barbados)
Brazil	• Financial compensation for the exploitation of petroleum deposits • Payment for water use rights • Tariffs for industrial effluent emission • Goods and Services Circulation Tax and use of environmental criteria in respect of its transfer to municipalities • Official recognition and rewards for improvements in the environmental performance of industries (non-governmental initiative)
Colombia	• Compensatory tax for water pollution, applied at the river basin level by the autonomous regional corporations
Chile	• System of compensatory payments for emissions of particulate material in the metropolitan region • Differential charges for collection of solid household waste • Transferable individual fishery quotas • Eco-labelling for ozone-friendly products and organic agricultural products
Guatemala	• Tradable water use permits • Certification schemes (organic agriculture and ecotourism) • Incentives (subsidies) for reforestation • Finance for clean production projects at preferential rates • National fund for environmental projects • Unified charges for municipal water, power, gardening and solid waste collection services
Mexico	• Zero tariffs and accelerated depreciation for pollution control and prevention equipment • Petrol surcharge • Charges for the use or exploitation of public goods such as wildlife • Charges for the emission of industrial waste waters • Systems of repayable deposits for car batteries, tyres and lubricants • Finance on preferential terms and subsidies for the planting and management of forests in severely deforested areas
Venezuela	• System of returnable deposits on mass-consumption bottles • Exemption from company taxes on investments in pollution control and prevention • Taxes on deforestation • System of charges, according to volume, for industrial waste generated in the Caracas metropolitan area

Source: Jean Acquatella, *Aplicación de instrumentos económicos en la gestión ambiental en América Latina y el Caribe: desafíos y factores condicionantes*, Medio ambiente y desarrollo series, No. 31 (LC/L.1488-P), Santiago, Chile, Economic Commission for Latin America and the Caribbean (ECLAC), January 2001. United Nations publication, Sales No. S.01.II.G.28.

Lastly, some subsidies are used in Latin America and the Caribbean which are potentially harmful to the environment or could lead to non-sustainable practices. These are generally subsidies or fiscal incentives for factors of production (physical inputs or natural resources) which reduce the marginal costs determined by production and consumption decisions. Thus, for example, subsidies for fertilizers and pesticides lead to greater use of these factors, and this can be counter-productive for agricultural production and also destructive for the environment.

E. Participation for sustainable development: sustainable development at the national and local levels; participation of leading actors from civil society and the productive sectors

A novel component of the concept of sustainable development is promotion of the participation of civil society and the productive sectors in the decision-making process, as a way of sharing responsibilities between the public and private sectors. The possibility of developing sustainable societies requires the provision of the necessary information to civil society, so that its members can take part in the adoption of decisions affecting them and play a constructive, leading role. In the same way, the valuable experiments being carried out at the national and local levels, together with training for responsible participation, are vital elements for taking full advantage of the potential of civil society (Zavala, 1999).

Thus, the ways in which participation for sustainable development has taken place in Latin America and the Caribbean since the Earth Summit may be analysed from three standpoints: (i) action at the national and local level and the mechanisms for it; (ii) the ways in which civil society and the main groups have taken part; and (iii) the behaviour of the business sectors.

1. Sustainable development at the national and local levels

One of the lines of action generated by the United Nations Conference on Environment and Development (UNCED) was the creation of mechanisms for collaboration between society, economic agents and the government in order to achieve a development model that takes account of environmental, social and economic factors in order to link together the different dimensions of sustainable development.

This approach resulted in the institutionalization of citizen advisory bodies of varied and representative composition, and this process speeded up in Latin America and the Caribbean from 1997 onward, when many national sustainable development councils or commissions were set up. Their function is to ensure that national plans comply with the objectives of Agenda 21. The establishment and implementation of the national agendas will be governed by the consensuses established between the population, the different levels of government, and the main groups. One of the objectives of national sustainable development councils is to promote participation in the process of generating public policies and open up spaces for the discussion of medium- and long-term strategies. The following table shows how the region has acted to fulfil the need for such national spaces.

Table VI.3
LATIN AMERICAN AND CARIBBEAN COUNTRIES WHICH HAVE NATIONAL
SUSTAINABLE DEVELOPMENT COUNCILS

Argentina: National Sustainable Development Council	Grenada: National Sustainable Development Council of Grenada
Barbados: National Sustainable Development Commission	Honduras: National Sustainable Development Council (CONADES)
Bolivia: National Sustainable Development Council	Jamaica: National Sustainable Development Council of Jamaica
Brazil: Political Commission for Sustainable Development and the National Agenda 21	Mexico: National Advisory Council for Sustainable Development
Chile: National Sustainable Development Council	Nicaragua: National Sustainable Development Council
Costa Rica: National Sustainable Development Council	Panama: National Sustainable Development Council of Panama
Dominica: Sustainable Development Council	Dominican Republic: National Follow-up Commission for the UNCED
El Salvador: National Sustainable Development Council	

Source: Earth Council "National experiences of integrative, multistakeholder processes for sustainable development", *NCSD Report, 1999-2000*, San José, Costa Rica, 2000, with updated information from the Earth Council.

Various factors militate against the consolidation of these spaces at the national level, however. The fact that their functions are not clearly defined, the conflicts that hinder them from ensuring multisectoral composition and the difficulty of exerting real influence on other sectors which regard them as merely "reactive" to the prevailing types of economic and social development, are all obstacles that limit the influence of this type of organ at the national level in Latin America and the Caribbean.

These difficulties in forming fully participatory national spaces that will make it possible to attain sustainable development are somewhat lessened when it is local actors who undertake these actions. The decentralization processes which have taken place in the region have made a contribution in this respect, furthering the democratization of the countries and bringing government closer to the citizens. Decentralization is seen to be a way of increasing efficiency in the provision of services, because it makes possible more flexible management and facilitates access to information on the real preferences and needs of the population.

Generally speaking, the decentralization of environmental authority has been more hesitant in the countries of the region with a strong centralist tradition than in others, with the role of municipalities being limited to managing some urban services. The areas of authority decentralized usually cover such matters as the handling of solid and liquid wastes, green areas in towns, and soil conservation (ECLAC, 2000a). With regard to promotion of the economic instruments which require more highly developed local capabilities, these instruments have been transferred to the sub-national levels only to a lesser degree.

The process of valuing the municipalities more highly as organs for promoting development at the local level is supported by the provisions of Agenda 21, chapter 28 of which specifically identifies the sustainable development activities that are to be carried out at the local level. Thus, there are initiatives at the municipal level such as those promoted by the International Centre for Local Environmental Initiatives (www.iclei.org), which links together groups of municipalities to promote local versions of Agenda 21. Although concrete results are not yet sufficiently widespread, there is a very proactive tendency among the local authorities of the region to use long-term local development strategies adopted on the basis of participatory planning processes which many of these authorities actually refers to as Local Agenda 21.

The ways in which Agenda 21 is applied at the local level in the region are very heterogeneous. Among the actions taken are sustainable land use, the fight against unemployment and social disintegration, the application of appropriate population and spatial population distribution policies, rational use of energy, the establishment of sustainable systems of transport and communications, conservation and rehabilitation of the historical and cultural legacy, and the development of rural settlements.

In order for local-level sustainable development strategies to have a greater impact, there must be coordination both among the different levels of government and among municipalities themselves. An integrated and coherent management strategy must be formulated, establishing intraregional administrative arrangements and giving associations of municipalities the possibility of playing a role in encouraging cooperation among municipalities located in the same area for the purpose of exchanging experiences and forming broader territorial management units in order to further competitiveness and make up for the differences between "winning" and "losing" areas (ECLAC, 2001d).

2.   Civil society and citizen participation

There is a growing movement in the region towards changes in terms of the organization of civil society and the main groups in the countries, which are increasingly demanding greater spaces for participation: indigenous groups, different types of NGOs (in such areas as gender, the environment, economic and social development, the role of municipalities, etc.), business and trade associations, and employers' groups. From their own standpoints and interests, these groups converge to create a sort of sensitivity to sustainable development, which is reflected in more active forms of behaviour (ECLAC, 2000a).

This tendency has been strengthened in recent years by the explosive growth of information and communications technologies, which has meant that organizations in civil society that, 10 years ago, were slow to make contact and adopt common positions, now do so digitally through the establishment of networks which enable them to obtain information very rapidly and to work quickly, in close coordination. Nowadays, these organizations are stronger, more specialized, and have more resources to support their operations.

Another area of participation is that of the legislature. The countries have provided in their legislation for various forms of specialized participation in environmental matters, including mechanisms to give citizens access to information at different levels, representation of citizens' organizations on various collective bodies (national, regional or local councils on sustainable development or the environment, councils on protected areas or river valley areas, national commissions on climatic change or biodiversity, etc.), and public hearings to reach agreement or consult on the granting of environmental licences or other matters. In order to strengthen the role of these forms of representation, it is recommended that institutions reporting to the legislature, with express or implicit authority in environmental matters, should be set up to keep checks on the executive, as in the case of ombudsmen (ECLAC, 2000a; Rodríguez, 2001).

Table VI.4 summarizes the participation mechanisms which have been set up by law in Latin America and the Caribbean. Such mechanisms provided for in general legislation can be used in the environmental field, as for example in the case of referendums on matters of general interest. So far, however, they have only been used in exceptional cases.

The region has to its credit many fruitful examples of the formation of new leaders and support for initiatives designed to link together all the social actors for sustainable development at the national level. It is this line of progress which has led to the objectives and results of the activities envisaged in Capacity 21, a UNDP initiative.[9] It should be noted that the aim has been to complement existing processes and strengthen their orientation towards sustainability; to help them, in other words, to develop a long-term approach which takes account of the environmental, economic, social and political dimensions (UNDP/Capacity 21, 2001).

The lessons learned in the region over the last ten years make it possible to distinguish between internal or operational factors, which have to do with the way projects are executed and therefore correspond to elements which are under the countries' control, and external or conditioning factors, which refer rather to elements which are outside the project but nevertheless have a very strong influence on it. Detecting internal factors makes it possible to determine which of them can be incorporated into the project or to correct their operation, while the identification of external factors leads to the awareness that they must be taken into account either to make use of them, if they are favourable, or to guard against their effects, if they are unfavourable.

This differentiation of the factors affecting projects is very important because the results obtained and even the way projects are executed are not determined solely by their own dynamics —that is to say, by internal or operational factors— but also by the dynamics of the environment in which they are executed. It should be borne in mind that certain factors, while external and strongly influential, are not immutable, as they may be modified even by the working of the project itself. It is of crucial importance, however, to take them into account during project design and execution, because they can strongly influence the range and scope of the activities and initiatives in question (UNDP/Capacity 21, 2001).

---

[9]　Capacity 21 is a special UNDP programme designed to strengthen the ability of individual countries to achieve sustainable development. It has been operating in Latin America and the Caribbean since 1993.

Table VI.4
SUMMARY OF PARTICIPATION MECHANISMS PROVIDED FOR IN THE LEGISLATION
OF LATIN AMERICAN AND CARIBBEAN COUNTRIES

Type of mechanism	Main instruments
Participation for reaching an informed prior consensus	• Right to request environmental information • Obligation of the government to periodically publish information or put it in readily visible places so that citizens may be informed of decisions on environmental matters
Participation in processes designed to give rise to policies and regulations on the environment	• Participation in national councils to decide on, recommend or coordinate national policies or propose negotiating positions in international forums in connection with global, regional, subregional or other conventions or agreements (for example, national councils on sustainable development, biodiversity, climate change, Convention on the Law of the Sea, etc.) • Participation in national, regional or local collegiate bodies with authority to issue or recommend policies and rules (for example, national councils on the environment or on forests or protected areas, technical committees responsible for formulating standards, etc.) • Popular initiatives for rules or standards • Special procedures for participation by any individual citizen
Political participation	• Popular consultations • Monitoring by citizens • Town meetings • Presentation in parliament of amendments to proposed laws • Referendums to approve or cancel a rule or regulation • Popular legislative initiatives at the national, subnational or local levels
Participation in the taking of administrative decisions	• Right to request environmental information • Intervention in administrative matters regarding the environment • Public hearings on the environment • Public consultations in connection with particular decision-making processes (for example, territorial planning, environmental licences, evaluation of environmental impact, setting of rules and standards, permission to exploit a resource) • Consultations among indigenous communities • Participation in collegiate bodies with authority to take administrative decisions
Direct administration of areas of special ecological value	• Rights and obligations of indigenous peoples with regard to the conservation and sustainable use of the biodiversity of their traditional territories, granted in the form of collective ownership, collective use, and other forms (for example, reservations, *ejidos*, indigenous territories) • Delegation to NGOs of responsibility for the total or partial administration of public protected areas

(continued)

		Table VI.4 (concluded)
Participation in the administration of justice	•	Legal actions to defend fundamental rights
	•	Class actions to defend collective rights
	•	Legal actions to force the authorities to take action
	•	Legal actions to force the repair or compensation of environmental damage
	•	Legal actions to declare measures unconstitutional
	•	Legal actions to declare measures null and void
	•	Legal actions under criminal legislation
	•	Legal actions to enforce administrative civil responsibility

Source: M. Rodríguez Becerra, "Anotaciones para promover una reflexión subregional andina sobre el desarrollo sostenible", consultant document, Mexico City, June, unpublished, 2001.

3. Participation of the business sector in sustainable development

The growing integration of sustainability issues into business management has been an important feature of the process of internationalization of economies in the quest to increase companies' competitiveness. This process began in the 1990s and continues today. Nowadays, gaining a reputation as an environmentally responsible company has become an asset which is just as important as many other competitive advantages, especially for Latin American enterprises exporting to the United States and the European Union, which are the markets with the most demanding consumers in environmental matters. Latin America and the Caribbean, therefore, have not been an exception to this trend, and have witnessed the creation by business corporations of many local and regional organizations for the purpose of debating environmental issues and incorporating them into their strategies.

In this respect, two significant efforts made in the region should be noted: the establishment of business councils for sustainable development, and the creation of national clean production centres. The range of issues covered, such as climate change, eco-efficiency, certification of environmental management systems (ISO 14000), health, social development, training and business education, has enabled the region to play its part in the international debate on environmental matters, the development of clean technologies, clean production, and production development in general.

Another initiative which has been carried out quite effectively in the region during the past 10 years is the establishment of national centres for clean production and technology, which arose as a result of proposals sponsored by international organizations[10] and joint projects between technical cooperation agencies from developed countries. These centres seek to promote the use of and access to clean technologies by the various industrial sectors, as part of the concept of sustainable development. The goal is for the national institutions selected (where the centres are established) to subsequently take over the project. There are at present six centres in Latin America (Brazil, Costa Rica, El Salvador, Guatemala, Mexico and Nicaragua).

Table VI.5
COUNTRIES WHICH HAVE BUSINESS COUNCILS OR ORGANIZATIONS FOR
SUSTAINABLE DEVELOPMENT

Country	Organization
Argentina	Consejo Empresario Argentino para el Desarrollo Sostenido (CEADS)
Brazil	Conselho Empresarial Brasileiro para o Desemvolvimento Sustentável (CEBDS)
Chile	• Compañía de Acero del Pacífico (CAP)
	• Centro de Estudios Públicos (CEP)
Colombia	Promoción de la Pequeña Empresa Ecoeficiente Latinoamericana (PROPEL)
Costa Rica	Consejo Empresarial Costarricense para el Desarrollo Sostenible (CEMCODES)
Ecuador	Banco del Pacífico
El Salvador	Consejo Empresarial para el Desarrollo Sostenible de El Salvador (CEDES)
Guatemala	Fundación para el Desarrollo Sostenible (FUNDES)
Honduras	Consejo Empresarial Hondureño para el Desarrollo (CEHDESO)
Mexico	• Centro de Estudios del Sector Privado para el Desarrollo Sustentable (CEPEDES)
	• Consejo Empresarial para el Desarrollo Sostenible del Golfo de México (CEDES-GdeM)
	• Iniciativa de Gestión del Medio Ambiente Mundial (Iniciativa GEMI)
Paraguay	Fundación Moises Bertoni
Peru	Perú 2021
Uruguay	Administración Nacional de Usinas y Transmisiones Eléctricas (UTE)
Venezuela	Consejo Empresarial Venezolano para el Desarrollo Sostenible

Source: Business Council for Sustainable Development for Latin America (BCSD-LA), *Global Climate Change: A Basis for Business Strategy and Practice in Latin America*, Monterrey, Nueva León, 1999.

Lastly, another of the mechanisms which make it possible to measure the degree of commitment of enterprises to the environment is the certification of environmental management through the ISO 14000 standards. The number of enterprises certified in this way has grown steadily since this standard was established in 1997. In December 1998, 7,887 enterprises in 72 countries had ISO 14000 certification, but by December 2000 this figure had trebled to 22,897 companies in 98 countries, and in March 2001 there were

[10] United Nations Environment Programme (UNEP) and United Nations Industrial Development Organization (UNIDO).

27,509 companies with this certification.[11] Although the number of enterprises certified in Latin America and the Caribbean is not very large, it has grown considerably since the establishment of ISO 14000. The first place is held by Brazil, with 270 companies, followed by Mexico with 188 and Argentina with 114, representing increases of 81%, 27% and 14%, respectively. As of March 2001, Colombia and Costa Rica had 20 certified firms, Chile 11, Peru and Uruguay 10, Venezuela 7, Barbados 3 and Honduras 2, while the Dominican Republic, Ecuador, Guatemala, Paraguay, Saint Lucia and Trinidad and Tobago had one certified firm apiece.

---

[11]   According to figures provided by the International Standardization Organization (ISO) (www.isoworld.org).

Chapter VII

International framework

An unparalleled planetwide phenomenon which stems from the expanding scale of human activity has been scientifically documented over the past three decades. This phenomenon has had worldwide environmental impacts, such as global warming, the thinning of the ozone layer (the "ozone hole"), the loss of biodiversity, the transboundary movement of hazardous wastes, and the gradual encroachment of desertification processes and drought. The acceleration of economic globalization and worldwide environmental deterioration has given rise to greater ecological and economic interdependence, making this a unique moment in history (MacNeill and others, 1991).

An unprecedented international environmental regime, as represented by a new generation of multilateral environmental accords, began to take shape after the Earth Summit. As was reaffirmed in the Rio Declaration, environmental issues are a dimension of development that goes to the very heart of production and consumption and that consequently influences every aspect of economic and social growth.

As noted by Brañes (2001), "the environmental changes promoted by the Earth Summit were designed to be implemented as part of a process of unprecedented international cooperation".[1] In this regard, the

---

[1]   This process of cooperation was conceived as having three dimensions: first, cooperation to promote a favourable international economic system, as provided for in principle 12 of the Rio Declaration; second, cooperation in the form of a substantial increase in official development assistance; and third, the proposal of new institutional

Rio Declaration constitutes a political platform that combines a series of comprehensive ethical principles and concepts with a view to laying a more equitable foundation for international cooperation and thus helping to establish sustainable development as the new development paradigm on the global, regional and local levels.[2] Agenda 21 then established lines of action for putting these policies into effect.

This new environmental and institutional era gives rise to new and different imperatives for global management of the environment and, hence, for international cooperation. On the one hand, Governments are being induced to play a more proactive international role in safeguarding global public goods through innovative multilateral arrangements. On the other, the private sector is being called upon to play an increasingly prominent role, particularly in relation to various multilateral environmental accords and their protocols, such as the Framework Convention on Climate Change and the Kyoto Protocol, and the Convention on Biological Diversity and the Cartagena Protocol.

A.   Pre- and post-Rio multilateral environmental accords

The Stockholm Conference in 1972 marked the starting point for a series of international environmental agreements. In the 1980s, these agreements were converted into full-fledged multilateral conventions with a view to protecting each country's globally-beneficial environmental goods and services.[3] One of the major institutional outcomes of this conference was the creation of the United Nations Environment Programme (UNEP), whose purpose is to develop and strengthen environmental management capabilities within the United Nations system and to facilitate the negotiation of multilateral environmental accords. The number of multilateral environmental accords, together with the scope and number of organizations responsible for their follow-up, began to increase sharply in the 1980s.

---

arrangements and closer cooperation among both global and regional programmes, agencies and organizations of the United Nations system.

[2]   Through its 27 principles the Rio Declaration lays the groundwork for the integration of the environmental dimension with the economic and social aspects of development based on a recognition of: common but differentiated responsibilities among nations, particularly the most vulnerable ones; the urgent need for an economic and trade system that is conducive to sustainable development; the importance of internalizing environmental costs; and the need to strengthen endogenous capacity-building and to promote the transfer of technologies, including new and innovative ones.

[3]   Several international environmental agreements were signed before the 1970s, but their main thrust was to conserve natural ecosystems and certain species of flora and fauna.

Until the 1980s, environmental accords were designed mainly to protect endangered species (CITES 1973, CMS 1979), to protect specific ecosystems (RAMSAR 1971) or to control transboundary movements of pollutants (Basel Convention 1989). During this period two major treaties marked the beginning of a process leading towards a system of global environmental regulation: the 1982 United Nations Convention on the Law of the Sea (most notably part X), which attempts to link development with the environment; and the Antarctic Treaty of 1959, which has safeguarded an ecologically important, multinational region by proposing the introduction of a system that makes it possible to avert conflicts of sovereignty. Interestingly, three of these accords have relied on commercial measures to make their implementation more effective.[4]

The 1992 United Nations Conference on Environment and Development was a landmark event because it produced agreements that afforded more comprehensive treatment of global environmental issues by focusing on the goal of sustainable development. The five Rio agreements represented the most universal and coordinated political step taken in the early 1990s towards establishing an international system of cooperation for mainstreaming the environmental dimension into development.[5] These instruments explicitly incorporate the concept of "common but differentiated responsibilities", which was developed in Stockholm and fully acknowledged in principle 7 of the Rio Declaration.

Thanks to the worldwide awareness of countries' interdependence in the face of global environmental problems, the legally binding instruments formulated in Rio de Janeiro were adopted and ratified more quickly than in previous decades and by practically all members.

---

[4] The Convention on International Trade in Endangered Species of Wild Fauna and Flora, the Basel Convention, and treaties to protect the ozone layer (the 1985 Vienna Convention for the Protection of the Ozone Layer and the 1987 Montreal Protocol on Substances that Deplete the Ozone Layer).

[5] The five Rio agreements are: the Rio Declaration on Environment and Development; Agenda 21; the Non-legally Binding Authoritative Statement of Principles for a Global Consensus on the Management, Conservation and Sustainable Development of All Types of Forests; the United Nations Framework Convention on Climate Change; and the Convention on Convention on Biological Diversity. After the summit, agreement was reached on other major multilateral instruments, such as the United Nations Convention to Combat Desertification, the Kyoto Protocol, the Cartagena Protocol on Biosafety, the Global Programme of Action for the Protection of the Marine Environment from Land-based Activities, the Rotterdam Convention on the Prior Informed Consent Procedure for Certain Hazardous Chemicals and Pesticides in International Trade and the Stockholm Agreement on Persistent Organic Pollutants.

Other post-Rio gains have taken the form of additional multilateral accords that focus on environmental concerns which, due to advances in scientific knowledge, have reappeared as emerging issues.[6] The key difference in the post-Rio multilateral accords is that they explicitly acknowledge the correlation between environment, health, and production and consumption patterns, on the one hand, and, on the other, economic, commercial and social policies.

As one of the outcomes of the Earth Summit, the Commission on Sustainable Development was incorporated into the international institutional structure in order to provide more comprehensive, cross-sectoral follow-up for the Rio agreements. As provided for in Agenda 21, the Commission is to hold annual sessions for the purpose of assessing the progress made and anticipating new challenges based on an integral development perspective. This has fostered the gradual involvement of other sectors (energy, agriculture and health care, among others) and of national authorities responsible for environmental protection. Over the nine years that have elapsed since then, however, the Commission on Sustainable Development has faced two major difficulties: incorporating the environmental dimension into the concept of sustainable development, and the lack of integration with socio-economic policies. These difficulties have hindered policy coordination efforts to further integral development. One of the positive aspects of the situation, however, has been the growing involvement of both global and regional agencies and bodies of the United Nations system which have been using innovative approaches in the follow-up to specific chapters of Agenda 21 (UNDP, UNEP, FAO, WHO, UNCTAD, UNESCO, WHO, ILO and the World Bank, and at the regional level, the regional development banks, the regional commissions and PAHO, among others).

The post-Rio multilateral environmental accords established their own institutional structure in the form of separate secretariats having specific mandates arising from the corresponding intergovernmental processes. Also created was the Global Environment Facility (GEF), which provides financing for the activities and policies agreed upon at multilateral conferences dealing with such global issues as climate change, biodiversity, international waters, preservation of the ozone layer and, more recently, actions taken to combat soil degradation, desertification and persistent organic pollutants.

---

[6]   This is particularly evident in the Kyoto and Cartagena protocols and in the Rotterdam and Stockholm Agreements.

B.   The region and global environmental problems

The treaties mentioned above are a response to global problems that stem primarily from production and consumption patterns and processes used in the developed countries, to which the developing countries are contributing to a growing extent (with the exception of the current loss of plant cover throughout the world).

According to an assessment prepared by UNEP, the main source of environmental pressure in the region of global proportions is the destruction of forests and the resulting habitat loss, which threatens a considerable number of species. The next most serious problem is soil degradation (UNEP 2000), as discussed in section A of chapter IV.

As noted in section D of chapter IV, the region's contribution to the mounting level of total emissions of greenhouse gases is a modest 5.4% of worldwide emissions (Earth Trends 2001). Nevertheless, emissions stemming from changes in land use and deforestation are quite high even in global terms. Total carbon emissions from the burning of fossil fuels and cement production amounted to 6,518 megatons in 1996, while carbon emissions from the combustion of biomass totaled 3,940 megatons (slightly more than half of industrial emissions). Latin America and the Caribbean accounted for 4.3% of worldwide industrial emissions but 48.3% of the emissions caused by changes in land use, which attests to how important the loss of plant cover is in terms of its effect on the global atmosphere.

Another group of pollutants that affect the entire planet —ozone-depleting substances— has declined considerably as a result of the implementation of the Montreal Protocol. The region's output of these substances increased during the first half of the decade, but their production and use then began to decline, although quite gradually (see figure VII.1). In 1996, the region's production of such substances accounted for 14.9% of the total. The expectation is that this decline will continue in the years to come; there are, however, some worrisome developments, such as the smuggling of chlorofluorocarbons (CFCs), although efforts to control such activities are being increased.

The countries of the region have been taking the lead in the negotiations on two particularly important environmental issues on the global agenda: climate change and biodiversity. One clear example of this is the Clean Development Mechanism within the framework of the Kyoto Protocol. The governments of the region have played a pioneering role in the international negotiations concerning the design of this mechanism, which could generate some income for the region to support the sustainable development agenda.

Figure VII.1
LATIN AMERICA AND THE CARIBBEAN: PRODUCTION OF
CHLOROFLUOROCARBONS (CFCS), 1986-1996
*(Thousands of metric tons, multiplied by ozone-depleting potential,
in the four main producing countries)*

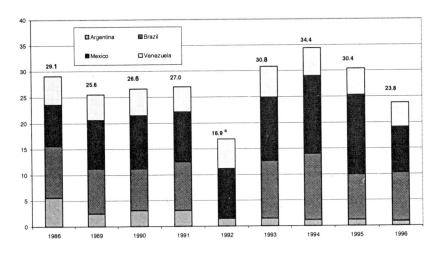

Source : UNEP Ozone Secretariat, 1999.

[a] No data are available for Brazil in 1992.

Special mention should be made of the future potential of an economic valuation of the environmental services rendered by that the region's natural ecosystems. Numerous initiatives have been developed in this regard. In Brazil, for example, there is a system under which revenues from the ICMS (Merchandise and Services Tax) are rebated to municipalities that are protecting natural ecosystems that render environmental services. Another interesting case is Costa Rica, where some of the environmental services rendered by forests have been acknowledged and a mechanism has been established for paying their owners for those services. Colombia and Guatemala have also set fees for the use of water resources from river basins to be paid by downstream beneficiaries. The funds thus raised are used to finance conservation activities in the upper basins. This is a very interesting tool, but its use requires proper (and complex) institutional support, as is discussed in chapter VI.

The region offers considerable potential for providing environmental services to strategic sectors of the economy, such as tourism and the sale of organic products and other commodities bearing environmental sustainability certificates. Some of the particularly promising products in this regard are coffee, bananas and cotton (ECLAC, 2000d).

Other global environmental services in the region, such as the preservation of global biodiversity and bioprospecting to enhance knowledge of the region's biodiversity, open up the possibility of greater scientific and technological capacity-building and are potential sources of income for the region if they are used prudently.

Whether these economic opportunities are taken advantage of not will depend on the ability of the countries in the region to take integrated, joint action. On the strength of common stands on these matters, the countries of the region can become leading players in a new global alliance for planetwide sustainability. In some instances, the nature of environmental problems and the need to protect the renewable resource base of the region's economies call for joint responses, such as watershed management and other land management planning modalities based on a bioregional or ecoregional approach. In others, intraregional cooperation affords an economic advantage by permitting the harmonization of environmental regulations in order to promote the unhindered circulation of goods and services, expand the market and ward off the danger of "ecodumping".

C.   The Latin American and Caribbean response

A worldwide comparison shows that the vast majority of Latin America countries have ratified at least 10 legally binding multilateral environmental accords (see table VII.1). Their speed in ratifying these instruments stands in contrast, however, to their limited implementation for a variety of reasons. One of those reasons has to do with the failure of the developed countries to fulfil the basic commitments undertaken at the Earth Summit.

Table VII.1
CURRENT STATUS OF MULTILATERAL ENVIRONMENTAL AGREEMENTS IN THE REGION

Countries	Pre-Rio RAMSAR Signed 02/02/1971 In effect 1975	CITES Signed 03/03/1973 In effect 01/07/1975	CMS Signed 23/06/1979 In effect 01/11/1983	CONVEMAR Signed 10/12/1982 In effect 16/11/1994	OZONE (Vienna Convention) Signed 1985 In effect 22/09/1988	OZONE (Montreal Protocol) Signed 1987 In effect 01/01/1989	BASEL Signed 1989 In effect 1992	Post-Rio FCCC Signed 09/05/1992 In effect 21/03/1994	CBD Signed 5/06/1992 In effect 29/12/1993	CBDD Signed June/1994 In effect 26/12/1996
Caribbean										
Antigua and Barbuda	X	A 08/07/97	X	S 02/02/89	A 03/12/92	A 03/12/92	a 05/04/93	R 02/02/93	R 09/03/93	R 06/06/97
Bahamas	E 07/06/1997	A 20/06/79	X	S 30/05/85	A 01/04/93	A 04/05/93	a 12/08/92	R 29/03/94	R 02/09/93	A 10/11/00
Barbados	X	A 09/12/92	X	S 12/10/93	A 16/10/92	A 16/10/92	a 24/08/95	R 23/03/94	R 10/12/93	A 14/05/97
Cuba	E 12/08/2001	A 20/04/90	X	D 15/08/84	A 14/07/92	A 14/07/92	a 03/10/94	R 05/01/94	R 02/03/94	R 13/03/97
Dominica	X	A 20/08/95	X	S 24/10/91	A 31/03/93	A 03/03/93	a 05/05/98	R 21/06/93	R 06/04/94	A 08/12/97
Dominican Republic	X	A 17/12/86	X	S (no date)	A 18/05/93	A 18/05/93	a 10/07/00	R 07/10/98	R 25/11/96	A 26/06/97
Grenada	X	A 30/08/99	X	S 25/04/91	A 31/03/93	A 31/03/93	X	R 11/08/94	R 11/08/94	A 28/05/97
Guyana	X	A 27/05/77	X	S 16/11/93	A 12/08/93	A 12/08/93	a 04/04/01	R 29/08/94	R 28/08/94	A 26/06/97
Haiti	X	X	X	S 31/07/96	A 29/03/00	A 29/03/00	X	R 25/09/96	R 25/09/96	R 25/09/96
Jamaica	E 07/02/98	A 23/04/97	X	S 21/03/83	A 31/03/93	A 31/03/93	X	R 06/01/95	R 06/01/95	A 12/11/97
Saint Kitts and Nevis	X	A 14/02/94	X	S 07/01/93	A 10/08/92	A 10/08/92	a 07/09/94	R 07/01/93	R 07/01/97	A 30/06/97
Saint Vincent and the Grenadines	X	A 30/11/98	X	S 01/10/93	A 02/12/92	A 02/12/96	a 02/12/96	R 02/12/96	A 03/06/96	R 16/03/98
Saint Lucia	X	A 15/12/82	X	S 27/03/85	A 28/07/93	A 28/07/93	a 09/12/93	R 14/01/93	A 28/07/93	A 02/07/97
Trinidad and Tobago	E 21/04/93	A 19/01/84	X	S 25/04/86	A 28/08/89	A 28/08/88	a 18/02/94	R 24/01/94	R 01/08/96	A 08/06/00

(continued)

Table VII.1 (continued)

Countries	Pre-Rio							Post-Rio		
	RAMSAR Signed 02/02/1971 In effect 1975	CITES Signed 03/03/1973 In effect 01/07/1975	CMS Signed 23/06/1979 In effect 01/11/1983	CONVEMAR Signed 10/12/1982 In effect 16/11/1994	OZONE (Vienna Convention) Signed 1985 In effect 22/09/1988	OZONE (Montreal Protocol) Signed 1987 In effect 01/01/1989	BASEL Signed 1989 In effect 1992	FCCC Signed 09/05/1992 In effect 21/03/1994	CBD Signed 5/06/1992 In effect 29/12/1993	CBDD Signed June/1994 In effect 26/12/1996
Meso-America										
Belize	E 22/08/98	DS 19/08/86	X	S 13/08/83	A 06/06/97	A 09/01/98	a 23/05/97	R 31/10/94	R 30/12/93	A 23/07/98
Costa Rica	E 27/04/92	R 30/06/75	X	D 21/09/92	A 30/07/91	A 30/07/91	a 07/03/95	R 26/08/94	R 26/08/94	R 08/01/98
El Salvador	E 22/05/99	A 30/04/87	X	S (no date)	A 02/10/92	A 02/10/92	R 13/12/91	R 04/12/95	R 28/09/94	A 27/06/97
Guatemala	E 26/10/90	R 07/11/79	X	S & D 11/02/97	A 11/09/87	A 07/11/89	R 15/05/95	R 15/12/95	R 10/07/95	A 10/09/98
Honduras	E 23/10/93	A 15/03/85	X	S 05/10/93	A 14/10/93	A 14/10/93	a 27/12/95	R 19/10/95	R 31/07/95	R 25/06/97
Mexico	E 04/11/86	A 02/07/91	X	S 18/03/83	R 14/09/87	a 31/03/88	R 22/02/91	R 11/03/93	R 11/03/93	R 03/04/95
Nicaragua	E 03/11/97	A 06/08/77	X	D 03/05/00	A 05/03/93	A 05/03/93	a 03/06/97	R 31/10/95	R 20/11/95	R 03/04/95
Panama	E 26/11/90	R 17/08/78	E 01/05/89	S & D 01/07/96	A 13/02/89	R 03/03/89	R 07/10/98	R 23/05/95	R 17/01/95	R 04/04/96
South America										
Argentina	E 04/09/92	R 08/01/81	E 01/01/92	D 01/12/95	R 18/01/90	R 18/09/90	R 27/06/91	R 11/03/94	R 22/11/94	R 06/01/97
Bolivia	E 27/10/70	R 06/07/77	X	D 28/04/95	A 03/10/94	A 03/10/94	R 15/11/96	R 03/10/94	R 03/10/94	R 01/08/96
Brazil	E 24/09/93	R 06/08/75	X	D 22/12/88	A 19/03/90	A 19/03/90	a 01/10/92	R 28/02/94	R 28/02/94	R 25/06/97
Chile	E 27/11/81	R 14/02/75	E 01/11/83	D 25/08/97	R 06/03/90	R 26/03/90	R 11/08/92	R 22/12/94	R 09/09/94	R 11/11/97
Colombia	E 18/10/98	R 31/08/81	X	S 21/06/94	A 16/07/90	A 06/12/93	R 31/12/96	R 22/03/95	R 28/11/94	R 08/06/99

(continued)

Table VII. 1 (conclusion)

Countries	Pre-Rio							Post-Rio		
	RAMSAR	CITES	CMS	CONVEMAR	OZONE (Vienna Convention)	OZONE (Montreal Protocol)	BASEL	FCCC	CBD	CBDD
	Signed 02/02/1971 In effect 1975	Signed 03/03/1973 In effect 01/07/1975	Signed 23/06/1979 In effect 01/11/1983	Signed 10/12/1982 In effect 16/11/1994	Signed 1985 In effect 22/09/1988	Signed 1987 In effect 01/01/1989	Signed 1989 In effect 1992	Signed 09/05/1992 In effect 21/03/1994	Signed 5/06/1992 In effect 29/12/1993	Signed June/1994 In effect 26/12/1996
Ecuador	E 07/01/91	R 11/02/75	X	X	A 10/04/90	A 30/04/90	R 23/02/93	R 23/02/93	R 23/02/93	R 06/09/85
Paraguay	E 07/10/95	R 15/11/76	E 01/01/99	S 26/09/86	A 03/12/92	A 03/12/92	X	R 24/02/94	R 24/02/94	R 09/11/95
Peru	E 30/03/92	R 27/06/75	E 01/06/97	X	A 07/04/89	A 03/03/93	a 23/11/93	R 07/06/93	R 07/06/93	R 09/11/95
Suriname	E 22/11/85	A 17/11/80	X	S 09/07/98	A 14/10/97	A 14/10/97	X	R 14/10/97	R 12/01/96	A 01/06/00
Uruguay	E 22/09/84	R 02/04/75	E 01/05/90	D 10/12/92	A 27/02/82	A 08/01/91	R 20/02/90	R 18/08/94	R 05/11/93	A 17/02/99
Venezuela	E 23/11/88	R 24/10/77	X	X	A 01/09/88	R 06/02/89	R 03/03/98	R 28/12/94	R 13/09/94	A 29/06/98

R = Ratification
A = Accession
S = Signed
E = Effective date
a = Acceptance
D = Declaration
DS = Declaration of succession
X = Not applicable, no account of agreement, or not ratified or signed

Source: Data provided by the Environmental Law Unit of the Regional Office for Latin America and the Caribbean (ROLAC) of the United Nations Environment Programme (UNEP), August 2001.

BASEL: Basel Convention on the Control of Transboundary Movements of Hazardous Wastes and their Disposal
CBD: Convention on Biological Diversity
CITES: Convention on International Trade in Endangered Species of Wild Fauna and Flora
CCDD: United Nations Convention to Combat Desertification in those Countries Experiencing Serious Drought and/or Desertification, particularly in Africa
UNFCCC: United Nations Framework Convention on Climate Change
CMS: Convention on the Conservation of Migratory Species of Wild Animals
Vienna Convention: Vienna Convention for the Protection of the Ozone Layer
CONVEMAR: United Nations Convention on the Law of the Sea
Montreal Protocol: Montreal Protocol on Substances that Deplete the Ozone Layer
RAMSAR: Convention on Wetlands of International Importance Especially as Waterfowl Habitat

It bears recalling here how ineffective international cooperation with developing countries has proven to be when the time comes to furnish additional resources and to transfer technologies on concessional or preferential terms, pursuant to the principles set forth in the Rio Declaration. This is an obstacle that developing countries have mentioned time and again in international negotiations and forums, and it was the subject of a wide-ranging debate at the special session held by the United Nations General Assembly to review and appraise the implementation of Agenda 21 (the "Rio+5" Summit), but the prospects for resolving this question do not appear to be very bright. Almost 10 years after the Earth Summit, it has become obvious that the principles agreed upon in Rio de Janeiro need to be bolstered at the international level.

For example, in accordance with principle 16, production processes must internalize environmental costs to fully reflect the loss of resources and environmental degradation they entail. This is closely tied to the incorporation of the environmental dimension into national accounts and into measurements of the progress being made towards sustainability.

Given the problems facing the region, the Convention on Biological Diversity is the instrument that may have the most potential for addressing the problems involved in the loss of ecosystems, species and genetic material. Nonetheless, the follow-up to the agreement has not led to the expression of its objectives in quantifiable, geographic terms, nor has it been tied in, as was initially intended, with other conventions relating to nature conservation.

A great deal of attention and effort were devoted to the negotiation of the Cartagena Protocol on Biosafety;[7] this is an important issue because it poses an emerging threat particularly to countries in which organisms used to produce transgenic products originate and diversify. Implementation of the agreement has not attached enough importance to conservation *in situ*. Therefore, it has been these countries that have been working to bolster this aspect of the Biodiversity Convention under their own national programmes and regional agreements.

Multilateral environmental agreements, along with the Rio Declaration and Agenda 21, have, however, had a major impact on the enhancement of regulatory frameworks, policies and programmes and on institutions for environmental management on the national and regional level, as is discussed in chapter VI.

---

[7] Cartagena Protocol on Biosafety (29 January 2000, Montreal, Canada).

Some efforts have also been made to develop general instruments for promoting the inclusion of environmental concerns in national, regional and local planning processes, particularly under the auspices of international agencies.

Many projects aimed at conserving biodiversity or reducing greenhouse gases are being developed or implemented in the region with financing from the Global Environment Facility (GEF), which is the funding agency of the conventions, or from bilateral cooperation agencies to which various international agencies (e.g., UNDP, UNEP, the World Bank and IDB) contribute large amounts of national (and sometimes subregional) technical resources and counterpart funding.

In addition, the countries of the region have undertaken multilateral cooperation efforts that have given rise to national sustainable development programmes and strategies (biodiversity, climate change) pursuant to their commitments as parties to the corresponding multilateral accords.

The region has also made further efforts to fulfil its multilateral commitments in the hemisphere. Initiatives in this connection have included the revitalization of the Forum of Ministers of the Environment of Latin America and the Caribbean based on its Regional Action Plan and the establishment of the Inter-Agency Technical Committee,[8] the Summit Conference on Sustainable Development held in Bolivia in 1996 within the framework of the three Summits of the Americas (Miami, 1994; Santiago, Chile, 1998; and Quebec, 2001), and the gradual incorporation of environmental issues into other ministerial forums dealing with such matters as energy and mines, housing and urban development, and economic affairs.

Efforts have also been made to establish cross-sectoral dialogues between ministers for the environment and ministers of health under the auspices of PAHO and UNEP, and between ministers for the environment and ministers responsible for energy and mines under the auspices of ECLAC and OLADE. In addition, the involvement of regional development banks and ECLAC has increasingly allowed environmental considerations to be linked to economic and social development issues.

Nonetheless, macroeconomic stabilization in a climate of volatility and the need to boost social spending have been the main focus of national agendas, and less priority has consequently been attached to environmental issues.

---

[8]   The Regional Action Plan was agreed upon in 1998 in Lima, Peru, along with the establishment of the Inter-Agency Technical Committee by UNEP, ECLAC, UNDP, the World Bank and IDB.

D. Subregional integration and sustainable development agendas

Three processes are involved in the relationship between subregional integration and sustainable development. First, the concept of sustainable development is being explicitly incorporated into economic integration agreements, as may be seen in resolutions of the Andean Community, MERCOSUR, the Central American Integration System and CARICOM.

Second, numerous subregional treaties seek to conserve shared natural resources and to incorporate sustainable development considerations (e.g., the Regional Seas Programme,[9] the Treaty for Amazonian Cooperation and the accords concluded by the Central American Commission on Environment and Development (CACED).

Third, the agreements reached at the Earth Summit have given rise to subregional instruments such as the Programme of Action for the Sustainable Development of Small Island Developing States, the Alliance for the Sustainable Development of Central America (ALIDES) and the proposal of a strategy for protecting Central America's biodiversity.

The Central American subregion enjoys a particularly sound institutional base in the form of the Central American Integration System (SICA), which is in charge, *inter alia*, of executing and coordinating the mandates issued at the Summit Meetings of Central American Presidents and the decisions of the Council of Ministers. In this case, the System's priority is to develop a new perspective on Central American development through ALIDES; one example of this effort is the Meso-American Biological Corridor initiative.[10]

In the Andean Community, the Andean Committee of Environmental Authorities has been created to build consensus and promote joint programmes concerning sustainable development issues of interest to member countries. Two outstanding examples, among many others, are the Regional Biodiversity Strategy and the innovative proposal

---

[9] In the case of Latin America and the Caribbean, this programme takes the form of the Convention for the Protection and Development of the Marine Environment of the Wider Caribbean Region and the Convention for the Protection of the Marine Environment and Coastal Area of the South-East Pacific.

[10] Each country in Meso-America has developed a national biodiversity strategy. These plans are being used as the basis for the development of a biodiversity strategy for the entire area which will set priorities for the conservation and sustainable use of biodiversity; it is estimated that 80% of the area's biodiversity is shared.

contained in the Common Regime on Access to Genetic Resources.[11] In addition, in the Act of Carabobo of June 2001, the heads of State of the subregion emphasized the importance of setting guidelines for environmental management and sustainable development.

Under the provisions of the 23-year-old Treaty for Amazonian Cooperation, the Special Commission on the Environment of the Amazon Region was created in 1989. The Commission has developed a programme consisting of eight lines of action: assessment of renewable natural resources, agro-ecological zoning and monitoring of changes in land use; ecology, biodiversity and population dynamics; wildlife; hydrobiological resources; the protection and utilization of forest resources; planning and management of protected areas; harmonization of environmental legislation and an exchange of experiences with national environmental protection programmes; and environmental research.

In the Southern Cone, the MERCOSUR Framework Agreement on the Environment was approved in June 2001 in an effort to foster sustainable development and environmental protection through the coordination of economic, social, and environmental policies, thus helping to improve the quality of the environment and the population's quality of life. The agreement calls for cooperation in fulfilling the international environmental accords signed by member countries and for the further development of principles set forth in the Rio Declaration that have not been the object of international treaties.

Special mention should be made of the Programme of Action for the Sustainable Development of Small Island Developing States. The specific traits of the planet's small island States, as discussed during the preparations for the United Nations Conference on Environment and Development and at the Conference itself, prompted the United Nations to convene a special conference aimed at seeking out means of making sustainable development a viable option for these countries. Accordingly, the Global Conference on the Sustainable Development of Small Island Developing States was held in Barbados in 1994. This Conference issued the Declaration of Barbados and the Programme of Action for the

---

[11]   M. Rodríguez Becerra (1999), says that the chief binding legal provisions having environmental implications that have been promulgated in the Andean Community are: Decision 344 of 1993 concerning the Common Regime on Industrial Property; Decision 345 of 1993 concerning the Common Provisions on the Protection of the Rights of Breeders of New Plant Varieties; Decision 391 of 1996 concerning the Common Regime on Access to Genetic Resources; Decision 435 of 1998, which created the Andean Committee of Environmental Authorities; Decision 182 of 1983, which created the "Jose Celestino Mutis" Andean System on Agriculture, Food· Security and Environmental Conservation; and Decision 436 of 1998 concerning the registration and control of chemical pesticides for agricultural use.

Sustainable Development of Small Island Developing States, which was adopted by 111 participating Governments and sets forth development principles and strategies aimed at protecting the fragile environment of small island developing States.

The Caribbean countries have strongly supported this new instrument and have developed their own model for implementing the Programme of Action based on the agreements adopted at the Ministerial Meeting of the Caribbean Countries in 1997.[12] The subregion has thus taken steps to develop and implement mechanisms to help overcome the financial, technical and other barriers to sustainable development in the island countries of the Caribbean, with special emphasis on vulnerability.

E. Imperatives for a new institutional structure

The increase in multilateral environmental treaties, the proliferation of forums and secretariats for these environmental treaties, and the growing number of intergovernmental organizations created to follow up on them have underscored the need to streamline the international management structure for sustainable development. Thus, the existence of more than 500 legal instruments —which, in many cases, have no practical connection between one another— has given rise to a multilateral environmental treaty "traffic jam".

Accordingly, a matter of particular concern to the countries is the almost complete absence of synergies among these accords, even though, when they are viewed from a territorial perspective, some major areas of common ground can be found.

As noted earlier, a majority of these multilateral environmental accords, with the exception of the Montreal Protocol and the Convention on International Trade in Endangered Species of Wild Fauna and Flora, have had very limited success in altering trends. Their wide geographic dispersion, the broad range of issues addressed, and the frequency and duration of meetings have caused the implementation of these agreements to come to represent a major technical and financial burden for the government institutions concerned.

---

[12] This model, as established by the Ministers attending that meeting, includes a Secretariat formed by the ECLAC Subregional Headquarters for the Caribbean and the Secretariat of CARICOM, a Bureau formed by small island States of the Caribbean, an Inter-Agency Cooperation Group made up of numerous agencies and programmes working in the subregion, and a Joint Programme of Work.

Countries are therefore considering the possibility of evaluating means of harmonizing the various processes that focus on similar issues and objectives,[13] such as biodiversity, chemical substances, the ozone layer and others.

The work done in looking into the possibility of linking environmental agreements negotiated before the Earth Summit (e.g., Convention on International Trade in Endangered Species of Wild Fauna and Flora, the Ramsar Convention and the Convention on the Conservation of Migratory Species of Wild Animals) within broader frames of reference (the Convention on Biological Diversity) are one of the examples to be considered in promoting greater consistency and avoiding duplications among accords with having common objectives. Agreements on the protection of biodiversity (both species and ecosystems) represent a particularly clear-cut case, since they all exhibit a high degree of territorial overlap as well. Although the agreements for the protection of species or ecosystems that were negotiated before the early 1980s approached conservation from a wholly environmental perspective, today they require more comprehensive frameworks for their more effective, coordinated implementation.

The relationship between multilateral environmental treaties and economic (and especially trade) agreements concluded between 1970 and 2000 has not been clearly understood.[14] Indeed, the environment has often been seen as posing a threat to economic goals and targets, and, as a result, the task of protecting natural resources and the environment has in many instances been left up to the community of experts and environmentalists. Thus far, attempts to reconcile commercial goals and environmental needs have failed, since a short-term approach is often taken to economic considerations and it is seen as necessary for a suitable value and price to be assigned to environmental and natural resources. The solution to environmental problems, however, is a long-term undertaking, and their nature and characteristics make a full economic appraisal of such resources difficult. Attempts to deal with these problems are hindered by uncertainties about the source, scope and magnitude of the harm done to health and the natural habitat by pollution, which makes it difficult to accurately calculate the costs of environmental damage (both past and present) and of the economic

---

[13] See the report of the Preparatory Meeting of the Southern Cone for the World Summit on Sustainable Development, Santiago, Chile, 14 and 15 June 2001.

[14] During the preparations leading up to the Stockholm Conference of 1971, the Secretariat of the General Agreement on Tariffs and Trade (GATT) was asked to conduct a study which brought to light officials' fears that environmental policies would become obstacles to trade. The recent Marrakesh Agreements (1994) did not succeed in laying these fears to rest either.

benefits of reducing pollution or protecting natural resources. In addition, in contrast to the multilateral trading system, the management of international environmental affairs is marked by a scattered, far from coherent structure. This interferes with the reconciliation of environmental and economic interests. Against this backdrop and once again using the issue of biodiversity as an example, the determination of correlations between environmental and trade agreements can be identified as a pending challenge.[15]

A final consideration is the importance of carefully reviewing the balance between international financial contributions and national funds for sustainable development. The concessional funding provided by GEF and the Multilateral Fund of the Montreal Protocol is clearly just a small fraction of the financing needed to solve global environmental problems. Furthermore, the official development assistance pledged at the Earth Summit to support the most vulnerable countries has not reached its targeted levels (0.7% of GDP) and has, in fact, declined significantly (0.2%) (ECLAC 2001e).

Hence, it must be emphasized that the transition towards sustainable development will require new and additional funding together with inventive, reliable financial mechanisms that will enable endogenous capabilities to be deployed and innovative technologies to be transferred to the developing countries.

---

[15] One of the most controversial issues in the negotiation of the Cartagena Protocol on Biosafety, which regulates transboundary movements of genetically modified organisms, is the relationship between the Protocol and world free trade agreements and the question as to which of the two would take precedence in the event of a conflict between them. Both in this instance and in the case of other international environmental agreements, there is no global mechanism for settling the disputes that are increasingly arising between environmental and trade accords.

Part two

Future prospects

Chapter VIII

The region's role in a global alliance

Although Latin America and the Caribbean enthusiastically adopted the agreements reached at the Earth Summit in 1992, the drive to implement them faded as the decade wore on. Domestic structural constraints, compounded by distortions in the interpretation and application of the accords, the biases introduced by various international negotiations and global asymmetries, among other factors, have steadily eroded the sustainable development agenda.

Although the region has made clear institutional and regulatory changes, it has failed to harness the reforming and mobilizing potential of the sustainability agenda. The foundations for this have been laid, but Latin America and the Caribbean are still in the preliminary stages of a transition to sustainable development.

A.   Recognizing the progress made

Environmental protection has become increasingly important in the countries of the region, and even though it is not yet an "integral" part of either the policies or processes of development, in the full sense of that word, the progress that has been made constitutes a better institutional and social platform than was available 10 years ago. The new generation of national institutions, laws and management tools, and international and regional agreements, renewed and extended processes of social intervention, public awareness and communication, and the tidal wave of technological change, information and capacity-building have all helped pave the way for a more decisive effort to achieve sustainable development.

The region's more consolidated democratic systems can also help to move the process in this direction, as can the increasing acceptance of development concepts that take a broader gender perspective, are more inclusive of minorities and more respectful of ethnic and cultural diversity, the existing cooperation and integration mechanisms between subregions, and today's more advanced international cooperation agreements. The social perception of problems has also changed. Nowadays there is a greater awareness of the seriousness of unsustainable trends and a stronger commitment to protect the environment.

B. A disturbing assessment

An assessment of the economic, social and environmental situation, together with a review of the efforts made, reveals a disturbing situation. Development has failed to attain the pace and direction needed to assure people a better and more productive life that is more in harmony with nature.

The post-Rio decade has witnessed intensive economic change in the region, which is now more integrated into global currents and subject to tensions that generate new and heightened uncertainty and instability. At the same time, the benefits of recent global processes have not yet reached the vast majority of Latin American and Caribbean people, and progress towards the goals of equity has stagnated.

Economic performance has been insufficient to overcome the deficits that were already affecting the region at the time of the Earth Summit, and more progress has been made in improving macroeconomic variables than in enhancing social well-being. Levels of inequality and inequity have failed to improve in most countries and have actually worsened in comparison to the developed world. Relative poverty has decreased very little, and the number of people unable to cover even a minimum of basic expenditures has grown. As a result, the region is no more socially or economically sustainable that it was 10 years ago.

The environmental situation is not showing any clear signs of progress towards sustainability either. Environmental degradation continues at alarming rates, although there are clear differences between individual processes in this regard. Ecosystems continue to feel the impact of unsustainable production, consumption and urbanization patterns. The natural resource base continues to be subject to increasing human pressure, and environmental services are now absorbing a greater burden of pollution. On the other hand, some advances are beginning to take root in the area of environmental protection and sustainable resource use, thanks to the efforts of those economic organizations that have risen to the challenge of producing in a sustainable manner.

Over the last decade the region has exhibited a marked degree of vulnerability to a series of more intense and frequent natural phenomena that are impacting on increasingly fragile ecological and social systems. This has resulted in greater human, environmental and economic insecurity, further undermining sustainability and generating heightened uncertainty, especially for island States.

Poverty and exclusion deprive over 200 million Latin American and Caribbean people of their right to share equitably in the fruits of development. Poverty continues to be associated with environmental deterioration in rural and urban sectors alike. The rapid pace of environmental degradation is preventing the generations of today from enjoying a healthy environment and from safeguarding the environmental rights of future generations. The most significant conclusion to be drawn from an assessment of the situation one decade one year after the 1992 Earth Summit is therefore that widespread progress towards sustainable development has not been made, although there are many concrete cases which demonstrate that sustainability is possible.

C. The main challenges

The steps taken along the road to sustainable development need to be appreciated and recognized, but the disturbing situation being faced today by Latin America and the Caribbean must be confronted as a major challenge for the region. Between the Rio and Johannesburg summits, 80 million people will have been added to the region's population, and when that population eventually stabilizes (sometime after the middle of the twenty-first century), Latin America and the Caribbean will have 300 million additional inhabitants. These new generations, like our own, are fully entitled to a decent, healthy and long life, to a healthy environment, to the creation and ownership of knowledge, culture and information, and to the ability to participate in public affairs.

Latin America and the Caribbean need to define a vision for the future and a vision of the viability of the development process that is both needed and desired for the region and the countries comprising it. Diversity in the biological, cultural, knowledge and information domains may be crucial to sustainable development in Latin America and the Caribbean during the twenty-first century.

Given the present situation and current trends, sustainability is coming to be seen not simply as a desirable future, but as an essential requirement for human survival and social coexistence at the national, regional and global levels. Recognizing and adopting this premise, and assuming it as a commitment, entails reviving regional and national commitments to sustainable development, mobilizing a common effort and sustaining it as a governing priority in public affairs. Thus, as the region moves towards the 2002 summit, a central task is to motivate governments, sectors of civil society, business organizations, parliaments, local governments and others to reconsider and renew their commitments towards this goal.

D.   Constraints in national and global agendas

The obstacles that will have to be resolved if the region is to move decisively towards sustainable development also need to be identified. These are the main constraints that are delaying the effort to achieve sustainable development or limiting its scope, both in the national domain and in the global framework. The assimilation, creation and dissemination of technical progress continues to act as a key constraint on wealth creation and market expansion, and the lags existing in these areas continue to act as structural limitations of the development process. Sustainability is also restrained by cultural inertia, compounded by vested interests in the unequal distributional structure, the absence or insufficiency of general and applied knowledge, the severity of cumulative processes of environmental deterioration and the high cost of reversing them, and a variety of institutional shortcomings. the experience gained over the last decade reaffirms the fact that, while national societies and the region as a whole need to take responsibility for their own affairs, global problems must be tackled in a spirit of worldwide solidarity based on the principle of common but differentiated responsibilities. Latin America and the Caribbean must take responsibility for their own tasks and must make a determined effort to promote common actions, and the 2002 Summit offers new opportunities in both areas.

The road to the upcoming summit offers an opportunity to renew and relaunch the region's own agenda —in its various dimensions and expressions— and to refine and consolidate the global agenda to promote the common interests of Latin America and the Caribbean more forcefully in international forums. The distinction between "own" and "global" agenda is not artificial, but the two are gradually converging as global environmental processes increasingly require local actions, since real possibilities for sustainable development are more and more conditioned —economically, socially and politically— by the globalization boom that has gathered momentum since 1992.

E.   The uniqueness of the region

The uniqueness of Latin America and the Caribbean stems not only from its natural resource wealth and the global importance of the environmental services it generates, but also from the global hazards inherent in the region's rapid environmental deterioration. Projecting this uniqueness, consolidating the regional effort to protect ecosystems and obtaining worldwide support for this, represent the starting point for a platform of action for the new summit. This has the objective of redoubling regional efforts to safeguard the stability of the most important ecosystems of importance for global diversity. This is a basis upon which a common regional agenda could be shaped, and it is what could persuade the developed world to stand shoulder to shoulder with the region on environmental protection. Other priorities need to be reinforced at the same time, for example those relating to the urban and industrial environment, or the oceans.

Given the divided opinions that exist on environmental processes and policies, strengthening and implementing approaches that involve conservation and sustainable use of biological and cultural resources is crucial for the region. At the start of the twenty-first century, this integrating view of human development and environmental protection is increasingly relevant, not only because it has proved impossible to slow down the alarming pace of environmental deterioration, but because of the higher goal of overcoming poverty in the region.

Thus arises a very broad agenda, and given the large number of existing deficits, priorities need to be defined to address common interests in protecting the stability of critical ecosystems and avoiding dispersion of effort. Such priorities will need to be monitored, and a small number of indicators chosen as the basis for a precise appraisal and comprehensive measurement of progress made towards sustainable development.

F.   Domesticating globalization for sustainable development

The region's involvement in globalization processes has failed to generate better conditions for sustainable development. Controlling the risks of globalization and exploiting its advantages for sustainability requires collective negotiation of better conditions for participating in the world economy, fairer and more stable rules of market access for exportable goods, greater security and stability in financial flows, more realistic conditions for external debt service and specific mechanisms for funding key sustainability projects.

All this does not obviate the need to reassert the commitment to raise official development assistance by industrialized nations to 0.7% of GDP, particularly targeting the poorest and most vulnerable countries, such as the island developing States of the Caribbean. Under the principle of shared but differentiated responsibility, one should also not forget developed-world recognition of previously accumulated environmental damage as an ecological cost in developing countries. This environmental debt needs to be assumed to the benefit of sustainability in the region.

The external debt problem has worsened and is obstructing developing countries' efforts to achieve sustainable development. The forthcoming summit should urge financial organizations and other relevant bodies to put mechanisms in place to ease the external debt burden and free resources to tackle the sustainable development agenda.

At the same time, environmental cooperation mechanisms associated with open regionalism need to be strengthened both within countries and regionally, and an appropriate environmental outlook needs to be incorporated into agreements currently being negotiated. A special priority for the next few years will be to address the issue of sustainability in negotiations for the Free Trade Agreement of the Americas (FTAA).

G.   Synergy between agreements and more efficient environmental institutions

Based on the understanding that protection of biological diversity and soils, sustainable resource use and disaster prevention are all inextricably linked, it is increasingly important for the region that global conventions come together with actions to protect high-priority ecosystems, while at the same time addressing other environmental problems and critical regions. What has prevailed until now is an uncoordinated set of actions with no common vision. The same is true of conventions on pollution and the urban environment.

Convergent action to protect the stability of priority ecosystems in Latin America and the Caribbean requires closer coordination between convention secretariats, additional earmarked financial resources per agreement, a strengthening of global environmental institutions to ensure such conventions are implemented more efficiently, and political strengthening in the leading environmental bodies of the United Nations system, so as to avoid dispersion. The international management of sustainable development also needs to be rationalized, given the proliferation and geographic dispersion of the forums and secretariats of multilateral environmental conventions and inter-governmental organizations, and the diversity of corresponding information requirements. At the Johannesburg summit, a recommendation could be made for a gradual evolution towards the harmonization of processes dealing with similar issues and objectives. Convergence of trade and environmental agreements and the reconciliation of their provisions are also needed.

H.   Convergence between global agreements and the regional position

Until now the main obstacles to sustainable development in Latin America and the Caribbean have included a lack of global co-responsibility, growing inequality in the world economic system, and inefficiency in adopting and applying global environmental agreements. It will be impossible to improve the global environment for sustainable development, or even for environmental protection, through environmental agreements and institutions alone; convergent action is required between reforms to the financial, trade and technology systems, and worldwide environment agreements, institutions and governance. This reality has crystallized particularly in the years following the Rio accords, giving rise to two prongs of the overall Latin American and Caribbean agenda: one aimed at the world economic system and the other at the global and regional environmental system.

I.   Knowledge and technology for sustainable development

The obstacles to the achievement of a more favourable integration into the international market, with production arrangements based on modern processes of scientific and technological innovation, have shown very eloquently that education, research, development, technology transfer and adaptation, and access to information are going to play an increasingly decisive role in sustainability.

In addition, in the face of increasing natural, technological and social hazards, evidence of growing human and ecological fragility stemming from cumulative environmental damage on a variety of scales continues to accumulate. The precautionary principle has gained renewed and more urgent significance for Latin America and the Caribbean. Protection efforts are no longer sufficient, as now there are increasing needs for adaptation and mitigation, along with the corresponding costs.

Today, more than ever, the region needs to make progress in science, technology, innovation and adaptability in order to deepen knowledge of its natural resources, undertake research that addresses its own priorities, restore appropriate technologies and promote the sustainable use of biotic resources based on appropriate risk assessment using a precautionary approach. Mechanisms for protecting intellectual property —in terms of both formal and informal knowledge— relating to biodiversity are becoming especially important. In this respect there is an ongoing demand for international financial agencies and the mechanisms of the United Nations system to support the development of scientific and technological capacities in the region, in compliance with principle 9 of the Rio Declaration.

J.   Towards a new stage of policy integration

Current achievements in institutional, legal, regulatory and instrumental development can be projected towards new forms of management that support policy integration. In addition to strengthening current management tools, a new generation of more effective preventive instruments now needs to be developed, aimed at economic-environmental integration. These should be associated with voluntary compliance and be more widespread and more accessible for small and medium-sized producers and firms, and be supported by other economic and financial measures to stimulate their development.

K.   Public participation

Given new capacities developed for public participation and intervention, it will be possible to move towards more advanced forms of collaboration between State and society. This will involve strengthening public intervention processes by institutionalizing participation mechanisms nationally and locally and consolidating national sustainable development councils, while also expanding other schemes of participation and direct intervention.

Chapter IX

Proposals for future action

It is now a commonplace to say that globalization brings both risks and opportunities. Although globalization has given most Latin American and Caribbean countries more dynamic access to capital markets and investment, the financial volatility it entails has also increased the economic vulnerability of the region. Owing to the fragility and instability of Latin American and Caribbean financial systems, the speculative capital flowing into and out of the region has precipitated a number of crises that have affected the real economy, the sustainability of development, and the environment. It is essential that the need for reform of the world financial system should be recognized and that the merits of introducing mechanisms and instruments to control speculative capital movements and thus reduce the impact of today's volatility should be discussed.

Meanwhile, it is not enough just to recognize that globalization brings risks and opportunities. The essential thing is to realize that the balance between the two is neither predetermined nor unchangeable. The risks can be lessened and the opportunities increased by working on two fronts. Internationally, new rules can be developed to "tame" globalization and direct it along channels that facilitate sustainable growth in all countries. At the same time, the region can minimize the risks and take advantage of the opportunities if it promotes a set of policies that link the environmental dimension with the economic and social one by applying the appropriate strategies and instruments at both the domestic and international levels, which are interrelated. International performance is conditioned by domestic policies, whose room for manoeuvre is determined in turn by international circumstances.

Domestically, it has been shown that the countries which can benefit most from globalization are the ones that have well-developed capabilities of their own, a solid production base and a stable, appropriate, effective and efficient institutional and regulatory environment. Subjecting the influences of globalization to a solid national regulatory framework is a positive strategy, but one that, now more than ever, requires national States to be fiscally sound, politically strong, socially cohesive and institutionally democratic if they are to be able to deploy their full regulatory capabilities in this way. One pending item on the agenda is the harmonization of fiscal policy with the needs of effective environmental management. International cooperation in this area can extend the reach of national strategies.

To make the transition to sustainable development, the region needs to introduce far-reaching economic and social changes, starting by restructuring production in a way that meets the threefold objective of increasing the region's competitiveness, reducing social disadvantage and checking the environmental deterioration associated with current patterns of production specialization. This will involve increasing domestic saving, which has hitherto been inadequate to sustain the level of domestic capital accumulation needed to make inroads into the poverty that afflicts a large percentage of the population. Also essential is higher social spending, particularly on education and health care, and the creation of high-quality employment, with particular attention to gender equity and better labour market opportunities for the region's young. Achieving substantial volumes of real saving within countries would also help to reverse the environmental deterioration and the loss of natural and human capital that are now taking place, and that are largely responsible for the loss of production capabilities.

If restructuring in the economy is to have a firm orientation, qualitative changes will have to be made to the patterns of public, private and social investment, which will need to be redirected to sustainable projects that offer a high social return.

As part of this effort, there is a vital need for effective national systems of technological development and knowledge creation that are capable of driving technical progress of a kind appropriate to the circumstances of the region, which has large reserves of natural resources and whose workforce is largely employed in low-productivity activities.[1]

In the legal and institutional sphere, the region is faced with the task of adapting current systems to make it easier for environmental management instruments to operate at the different levels of government, ensuring consistency among sectoral policies. The territorial specificity of environmental management means there is a need to establish solid operational links with local authorities by means of strategies that tie the whole range of administrative structures to a widening of management instruments, including those of an economic nature.

In view of the above considerations, it may be concluded that, from the point of view of sustainability, it is not feasible to expect the rapid economic growth required by the countries of the region to be achieved on the basis of current production and export patterns.

Forms of production that are based on abundant natural resources, cheap, low-skilled labour, a low level of scientific and technological development and slow diffusion of technical progress tend to lose ground to economies whose output is based on knowledge and on systematic technological and organizational innovation. Extending the coverage and quality of education systems is a key strategy for achieving greater social justice and global competitiveness. For this to happen, it is essential for the pattern of competitiveness in the region to be reshaped and 'for the limitations that currently compromise its social, economic and environmental viability to be overcome.

The viability of the domestic agenda is largely determined by the progress made with the international agenda. Globally, it is indispensable for consideration to be given to reforming the world financial system in the light of sustainable development imperatives, and the Johannesburg Summit could be a good opportunity to progress with this debate on the basis of the results that come out of the United Nations Conference on Financing for Development.

In this context, it seems advisable for participants at the Monterrey and Johannesburg summits to look again at the need to explore innovative, more effective international mechanisms for financing the protection of national and international public goods that are of global benefit. Given the realization that the external debt problem is still an obstacle to efforts by the region's countries to achieve sustainable development, the two summits may provide governments with a good

---

[1]   See, for example, the proposals made for an approach based on "export substitution" as the economic foundation for technical progress and as a means of changing over to environmentally and socially sustainable production patterns (Guimarães, 2001a).

opportunity to revive the spirit of resolution 44/228, which called the Rio Conference, and encourage international financial organizations and other relevant bodies to take efficient, urgent steps to implement mechanisms that reduce the burden of external debt and free up resources for the sustainable development agenda.

In pursuit of the same goal of identifying instruments to finance the transition from the development styles still being followed to sustainable development, there is a particular need to expand the operational areas currently eligible for disbursements from the funds created since the 1992 Rio Conference (such as the Global Environment Facility) so that these mechanisms can respond to the needs and concerns of developing countries. This will involve reviewing the criteria for allocating resources to the mechanisms used to implement the Rio agreements, administering funds, accounting and reporting.

It is also indispensable for the complex relationships among trade, investment and the environment to be reshaped by means of rules designed to operate in a way that is not detrimental to any of these, but rather makes them mutually reinforcing.

One of the main opportunities that a redirected form of globalization can open up is the prospect of returning to a comprehensive approach to development whereby measures can be taken at the appropriate level to solve global environmental problems that compromise the health of human beings and ecosystems. Climate change, the thinning of the stratospheric ozone layer, the loss of biodiversity, new types of pandemics and other processes are becoming problems of global proportions that reveal the growing interdependence among countries and can clearly be addressed only through concerted global action.

The urgent thing now is to put principles and declarations into practice. The Johannesburg negotiations represent an opportunity to design concerted approaches that strengthen the prospects for building on what has been achieved so far. This will involve consolidating operational approaches that mobilize international resources to address global problems on the basis of common but differentiated responsibility and extension to the international sphere of the "polluter pays" principle expressed in principle 16 of the Barbados Declaration.

National, regional and global sustainable development strategies need to be supported by systems of indicators based on criteria that combine qualitative and quantitative factors and focusing not just on what is happening to the world's air, water, soil and biodiversity, but also on quality of life, expressing new forms of well-being that harmonize with ecological and cultural processes.

There need to be a few, well-chosen indicators that cover the different aspects of sustainability, are able to reflect national peculiarities, facilitate dialogue among sectoral authorities, incorporate global implications and are closely tied in with decision-making.

A set of priorities will now be proposed on the basis of the key needs identified at the four subregional meetings held as part of the preparations for the Latin American and Caribbean Regional Preparatory Conference for the World Summit on Sustainable Development, to be held in Johannesburg in 2002. The choice of priorities needs to be made by identifying which processes require stronger joint action in the current period, both within the community of nations and the global environmental system and within the region.

This proposal, while it sets out from existing undertakings, seeks to focus the attention and efforts of Latin American and Caribbean society and governments, and of international institutions, on issues that are only now emerging, or that are of renewed interest because environmental damage has tended to accelerate or the pressure on natural resources to increase.

There are undoubtedly more important issues to consider now than before, and this is manifested in national and subregional agendas and in the various programmes of action adopted by international agencies and different institutions. The aim, however, is to put forward a set of priority issues to provide the basis for common positions at the 2002 Summit.

If priorities are more accurately identified, it will be possible to allocate such cooperation resources as may be channelled to the region more efficiently, and to provide a clearer direction for the work of international agencies. The following subject areas are proposed.

A.   Protection and sustainable use of natural ecosystems and biodiversity, and access to genetic resources

1.   Protection and sustainable use of natural ecosystems and biodiversity

Considering that Latin America and the Caribbean have the greatest diversity of species and ecosystems in the world, that this wealth represents great development potential, that it is the responsibility of the region to preserve it, that critical ecosystems have sustained extensive damage, which is placing biodiversity at risk, and that the best preserved ecosystems are inhabited by indigenous and campesino communities living in extreme poverty, regional initiatives need to be undertaken urgently to ensure that highly damaging processes in areas whose environmental wealth and services make them strategic are halted and even reversed, and that production in these areas is sustainable and thus compatible with conservation, and is carried out in a way that allows their inhabitants to achieve better living conditions.

In addition to the relevant national measures, the following regional measures are proposed:

(i)   *Strengthen the activities of governments and international organizations* that focus on the conservation and sustainable management of priority natural ecosystems by giving rural development policies an environmental orientation.

- Have priority natural land and marine ecosystems identified by a working group composed of government experts.
- Foster a policy providing for the integral, sustainable management of natural ecosystems based on economic incentives. This policy should reflect the social, economic and environmental importance of timber and non-timber resources and should offer solutions to small-scale rural producers that allow them to derive their livelihood from the forest. It should also create linkages with other measures for the promotion of production activities and avoid changes in land use.
- Draw up conservation, natural resource use and sustainable development plans for priority natural ecosystems. These plans, which need to be based on environmentally-friendly land use and river-basin strategies, should provide for the creation and strengthening of protected natural areas and biological corridors; support for production activities that are in land ecosystems certified as sustainable, such as ecotourism; sustainable logging and non-logging forest use. The promotion of environmentally sound commercial forestry plantations, sustainable agriculture and agro-ecological conversion; incentives for the environmental restoration and reforestation of priority areas included in clean development projects so that carbon capture can take place; and the application of programmes to guard against forest fires and the eradication of exotic species in biologically valuable areas. In the case of marine ecosystems, the

emphasis should be on sustainable fishing and the restoration of coastal areas.

- Integrate intersectoral, institutional coordination and social participation policies relating to the implementation of conservation plans, use of natural resources and sustainable development.
- Make particular efforts to ensure the suitability of these plans in areas belonging to indigenous communities.
- Monitor the process of environmental degradation and develop methodologically comparable indicators that can be used to measure actual progress towards environmental, economic and social stabilization and improvement of priority natural ecosystems.

(ii)   *To achieve these objectives, in the spirit of the Rio Summit principles,* it is proposed that a global alliance be formed in the interests of greater world commitment to the conservation of biodiversity and ecosystems *in situ,* expressed in quantitative targets and measures to attain these, and based on the central objectives of the Convention on Biological Diversity.

(iii)   *Increase the amount of funding available for in situ conservation* by making existing mechanisms more effective and efficient, fostering the development of synergies with other innovative economic instruments and analysing the possibility of setting up a compensatory fund based on a recognition of the globally *beneficial* environmental services provided by the countries' priority natural ecosystems; this fund could provide financing for conservation, sustainable production and restoration, thus serving as an explicit application of the principle of common but differentiated responsibilities.

(iv)   *Promote the establishment of a multinational compensation fund* that recognizes *the* environmental services of global benefit produced within individual countries by priority natural ecosystems and that can be used to finance conservation, sustainable production and restoration measures as a specific way of applying the principle of common but differentiated responsibility.

(v)   *Generate synergies* among multilateral, global, national and regional *environmental* conventions and instruments concerned with the protection and sustainable use of biodiversity and ecosystems.

2.   Access to genetic and transgenic resources

(i)   *Harmonize national biosecurity regulations across the region.*
Regional regulations, as well as dealing with cross-border movements of
modified living organisms, should help strengthen the national
institutions responsible for this issue, both by enhancing their authority
and by giving them greater risk analysis capabilities. This will contribute
to the development of different types of horizontal cooperation among the
countries of the region, stimulate technology transfer and protect our
countries from unauthorized experimentation, while safeguarding the
region's endemic species against transgenic contamination and helping
preserve the knowledge, innovations and traditional practices of
indigenous communities.

(ii)   *Open up national systems of access to genetic resources* for
participation by indigenous and campesino communities that have
experience in conserving and improving these resources, and strengthen
their ability to negotiate access to the intangible component of these
resources.

3.   Regional and global alliances

(i)   *Work for the creation of a programme of action for in situ*
conservation, a central objective of the Convention on Biological
Diversity, that specifies quantitative goals and the means to achieve them.

(ii)   *Pursue synergy in the implementation of the conventions and
Protocol* to make them more effective in conserving ecosystems and
species.

(iii)   *Contribute to implementation of the Cartagena Protocol* by
ratifying it and encouraging other signatories to do the same, and apply
the mechanisms approved by the Protocol so that the risk to biodiversity
from modified living organisms can be analysed.

(iv)   *Work for the creation of a protocol* to regulate access to genetic
resources.

(v)   *Encourage the international community to establish financial
mechanisms* that can be used to give recognition to the role played by
indigenous and campesino communities in understanding, improving
and conserving genetic resources.

B. Vulnerability

1. Natural disasters

In respect of natural disaster-related public policies, most of the region's countries recognize that existing systems could be inadequate to deal with a rising loss rate.

Possible approaches to reformulating these systems include in particular:

(i) *Priority for preparation and prevention measures*. This is the area where most remains to be done in the region. The success of any new policy to cope with natural disasters will depend more than anything on what action is taken before the phenomenon giving rise to any disaster occurs. Education, organization, the installation of early warning and information systems, systematic drills and the mobilization of communities and different civil society organizations will all contribute to the gradual construction of a *risk culture*.

(ii) *Introduction of decentralization schemes* that increase the responsibility and participation of local government agents in disaster prevention and response.

(iii) *Better* security *for human settlements* through clear planning and construction rules for urban infrastructure.

(iv) *Progressive reduction of vulnerability to natural disasters*. This is the most complex of the tasks, and the one that will take longest. Ecological land-use management is a key part of this medium-term strategy, as it allows the occupation and use of territory to be matched to the biophysical conditions of each area. An unavoidable part of this is the relocation of settlements located in high-risk areas.

(v) *Reconstruction of ecosystems whose deterioration has increased* vulnerability *to certain types of disaster*. Reforestation, for example, is a way of fixing the soil in areas affected by erosion or subject to landslides.

(vi) *Immediate disaster response*. A great deal still needs to be done to improve efficiency and coordination. Initial response systems need to be reviewed, as do the relevant regulatory frameworks. It is proposed that subregional and regional mechanisms be created to increase cooperation and improve efficiency in the specific field of disaster management.

(vii)   *More* rapid *progress with the development of a vulnerability index* that can be used to orient the allocation of prevention work and resources and to monitor progress.

(viii) *Creation* of *financial mechanisms* incorporating systems of international insurance based on pre-established vulnerability indices.

As was pointed out in relation to the problem of climate change, general efforts to reduce vulnerability to natural disasters of various kinds need to take account of the particular urgency of the problem in small island States and some other areas in the region that have been affected disproportionately in the past, and whose sustainability prospects have thereby been compromised.

2.   Vulnerability and sustainable development in small island States

Small island developing States (SIDS) in the Caribbean have recommended that the Programme of Action for the Sustainable Development of Small Island Developing States and all related issues be given higher priority on the international agenda, particularly where the creation of comprehensive development strategies that seek to reconcile economic, social and environmental parameters is concerned. The primary concern is to ensure that this Programme and related issues are actually integrated into the international, national and regional sustainable development framework. The following are some of the main focuses:

(i)   *Periodic review of implementation of the Programme of Action.* The idea is to carry out a "full and comprehensive analysis" of Programme implementation in 2004, 10 years on from the Barbados *conference.* For this purpose, it is proposed that a second world conference on the sustainable development of small island developing States be held.

(ii)   *Climate change and rising sea level.* Among the most critical aspects are the impact of a rising sea level on coastal areas, the need to *strengthen* vulnerability assessment capabilities, and the planning of control and adaptation measures. To this end, the SIDS recommended that the international community should provide support for projects and programmes to build institutions and create education and training centres in these countries.

(iii)   *Marine and coastal resources.* Emphasis is put on the need for support in developing and strengthening institutional, administrative, scientific and technological capabilities so that resources in exclusive economic zones can be managed and used effectively and sustainably. In addition, a comprehensive inventory of existing resources in these zones needs to be drawn up and protection extended to additional sea areas.

(iv)   *Freshwater resources.* Demand for freshwater is still growing in the Caribbean subregion, mainly owing to economic and demographic *changes* in the countries. One important measure required to deal with this situation is the establishment of a subregional institution that can design cost-effective, efficient freshwater resource management capability-building projects and programmes and interact with national governments and the relevant subregional, regional and international organizations.

(v)   *Trade.* It is recommended that at the World Summit on Sustainable Development, heads of State and government should adopt measures to ensure that SIDS are integrated effectively into the international economy, including measures to counteract inequity in the distribution of gains from faster globalization and trade liberalization. SIDS also recommend the adoption of measures to mitigate the fall-off in official development aid, the rolling back of preferential market access and the worsening of many countries' external debt situation.

(vi)   *Vulnerability indicator.* The need for quantitative and analytical work on a SIDS vulnerability indicator is re-emphasized.

(vii)   *Financing.* It is recommended that the Johannesburg Summit should reaffirm the commitment entered into at UNCED whereby the *international* community recognized the need to optimize the availability of appropriate, reliable new resources in addition to those already existing, and that this commitment should be acted on urgently. For the countries of the Caribbean, the commitment accepted by the United Nations for 0.7% of GDP to go to official development assistance, as agreed at UNCED, is a particularly important one.

C.   Water management

Approaches to reforming water management and public water policies that seem to have found favour with many Latin American and Caribbean countries include:

(i)   *Changes in culture and in the social perception of water.* For many decades, water has been regarded by part of society as a limitless, freely available good. The culture of waste will have to be ended and a culture of scarcity constructed on the basis of the interaction between the problems of *quantity* and *quality.*

(ii)   *A new economic approach to reflect conditions of growing scarcity.* For many generations, water has been perceived as a free good. Indeed, it is still free in many contexts and for a variety of uses, such as *agriculture.* No water user in the region pays the full *cost* of access or supply, or of the damage caused by the resultant contamination. This failure to value water needs to be rectified, and direct regulation, while it should continue, needs to be supplemented in a socially sensitive way by a range of economic management instruments.

(iii)   *Integrated water management with an ecological and bioregional approach.* For *many* decades, water has been subject to a variety of unrelated management practices, most of them hydraulic in nature rather than hydrological, much less ecological. There needs to be integrated, intersectoral management that sets out from the functionality of water in relation to the systems that support life.

(iv)   *Involvement of private enterprise in water management.* Traditionally, the State has been the only important economic actor in water management. Particularly over the last decade, however, a number of the region's countries have experimented with private-sector involvement in the provision of water services in the context of a general reshaping of the *role* of the State. Some of these innovations have been highly successful, while others have been abandoned after failing badly. It would be very useful for these experiments to be studied objectively and in detail, and for general conclusions to be drawn. It is clear, however, that very few national States in the region are in a position to bear the whole cost of water management on their own.

(v)   *Decentralized management.* Until recently, local governments had little say in water management, which was mainly conducted by central government. At a time when public powers in *general* are being decentralized and regulatory frameworks revised, convergence needs to be achieved and a balance struck among the capabilities, resources and powers of different levels of government.

(vi)   *Social participation.* In a context of decentralization and increased dissemination of transparent, timely information, society and, in particular, users' groups need to have mechanisms for effective participation in water management. Some countries in Latin America and the Caribbean have now returned to river basin-oriented approaches, with which the region has had some valuable experience in the past.

(vii)   *Measurement and* monitoring. It would be of the greatest use for agreement to be reached on standards for measuring and monitoring regional progress with water management sustainability.

(viii)   *International cooperation.* There is a need to review and enhance international cooperation at the global, regional and subregional levels. As regards the subregional level, the region has done valuable work with inland basins and shared seas. As is happening at the national level, greater coordination is needed at the multilateral international level among the many authorities involved in water management.

D.   Energy management

1.   Climate change

Because of the region's vulnerability to this global process, climate change represents a challenge of huge proportions for Latin America and the Caribbean. It would make sense for the region to work for remedial action on a global scale, in accordance with the principle of common but differentiated responsibility among countries, on the basis of the United Nations Framework Convention on Climate Change, and to promote adaptation activities, something that will be very important over the coming decades, when climate patterns will undoubtedly change as this very slow-acting phenomenon takes effect.

The region could jointly explore planning approaches that included the following.

(i)   *Support for the Kyoto Protocol.* The recent Bonn Accord provides grounds for cautious optimism about the immediate prospects for the Kyoto Protocol which, with one striking exception, has received the support of the international community. As things stand, the Protocol is the only multilateral instrument that has achieved a consensus for concerted international action to put into effect the commitments of the Convention.

The countries of the region can work jointly to increase the likelihood of the Kyoto Protocol coming into force at the Johannesburg Summit. Among other measures, those countries that have not so far ratified the instrument should do so promptly.

(ii)   *Strengthening of regional capabilities.* The region has still not made sufficient progress in building the institutions its countries require if appropriate measures are to be taken in response to climate change. There is a need to generate capabilities and establish or reinforce intersectoral coordination mechanisms and information, follow-up, education, social participation and research systems, and to promote programmes and projects that could benefit from the international funding agreed on and from the clean development mechanism. This can provide the basis for effective action to make good the commitments entered into and take advantage of the opportunities opened up by the Convention and Protocol.

(iii)   *Regional programme of adaptation to climate change.* There are many measures and strategies that can begin to be adopted now to prevent or mitigate future disasters resulting from climate change and enhance the sustainability of development in the climatic conditions expected in future. The prospects of successful adaptation to climate change would be improved if a regional programme were launched to enhance and supplement national efforts. Coordination of ecological management efforts would play an important role. Adaptation funding from the clean development mechanism and from other funds that are expected to be set up could contribute to the regional adaptation programme.

(iv)   *Focus on areas of greatest vulnerability.* Efforts to enhance capabilities and to adapt to climate change should take into consideration the priority that attaches to the most vulnerable areas, namely the Caribbean and certain parts of Meso-America. In particular, Caribbean SIDS have repeatedly called upon the international community to provide support for the implementation of projects and programmes to strengthen capabilities and improve adaptation prospects. The same is true of Central American countries threatened by climate disasters.

(v)   *Synergy between natural ecosystem conservation and climate action.* Conservation and restoration of ecosystems can converge with climate measures, to the benefit of both. Dealing with the two objectives jointly can enhance the benefits from the institutional arrangements put in place, particularly reforestation and forestation projects that might be implemented by way of clean development mechanisms.

Meanwhile, the region could enhance its already considerable contribution to international efforts to identify approaches and methodologies for dealing with problems associated with the climatic implications of land use and changes in land use, such as measurement of the scale and duration of capture benefits.

2.   Energy efficiency

In view of the region's energy situation, the following general recommendations may be made as regards the priorities of regional energy policy and its contribution to efforts to mitigate global climate change:

(i)   *Change the trend of energy intensiveness in the region* by means of policies to promote better energy efficiency. These would also have positive effects on local environmental quality.

(ii)   *Diversify the energy supply* by evaluating the potential of conventional energy sources and renewable ones such as geothermal energy, biomass, solar and wind energy and other sources that have not been much developed in the region.

(iii)   *Establish long-term synergies between energy and environmental policies in the region* so that efforts to achieve progress with energy efficiency are combined with the application of new clean technologies.

(iv)   *Promote integrated strategies* that can extract economic benefits from energy efficiency, pollution reduction measures, the conservation of fossil fuel reserves and action to meet social demands and improve the lot of the disadvantaged, and that can help to mitigate climate change.

E.   Urban management

One strategic objective in cities is to improve urban productivity. A necessary starting point for this is a system for monitoring progress. Human health is an important productive resource that is very closely linked to the state of the environment. As a result, there is a need to:

(i)   *Improve urban* productivity, *by*

- Measuring urban productivity and the effects of the worst bottlenecks, thus establishing a baseline for future comparisons.
- Recognizing the economic cost of working days lost because of health problems and monitoring this as an indicator of the interaction among pollution, health and the economy. Thence, reducing the number of days lost by improving environmental quality.
- Monitoring journey times within cities as a quality of life indicator, and improving them.
- Reducing the amount of waste and emissions produced per unit of urban output, and monitoring this relationship.
- Improving health indicators that have a clear environmental link, such as morbidity and mortality in populations that are particularly vulnerable to certain pollutants.

(ii)   *Monitor pressures created by the exploitation of natural resources and by emissions,* and thus:

- Estimate and monitor the ecological footprint of urban centres.
- Stabilize or reduce this footprint.

(iii)   *Increase the density of urban centres.*

(iv)   *Develop and apply follow-up and evaluation programmes,* and in particular:

- Monitor and take steps to increase wastewater treatment.
- Use planning instruments to measure and reduce urban vulnerability.
- Measure, monitor and reduce solid waste generation.
- Estimate the role played by emissions from small and medium-sized enterprises, measure them and take steps to reduce them.

F.   The institutional underpinnings of sustainable development

In its environmental aspect, the international system requires the consolidation of national regulatory mechanisms and institutions on the one hand and, on the other, the creation of a comprehensive, consistent and integrated framework that can provide the basis for an agenda and a consensus to achieve, among other things:

(i)   A stronger *environmental* dimension in the system of global development institutions;

(ii)   More *coordinated* action by international bodies, particularly those providing financing;

(iii)   Synergy among *the* different international agreements that have consequences for the sustainability of development;

(iv)   The involvement of all countries in the adoption and implementation of commitments; and

(v)   The *consolidation* of regional cooperation among international and regional bodies around priorities set by governments.

Existing institutional structures in the environmental field should be rationalized, the first step required being the consolidation of dialogue among ministerial forums in different sectors as a way of achieving regional debate and coordination, followed by measures to improve communication between environment ministers and those responsible for other areas of sustainable development.

The countries will need to decide on the future agenda for this institutional rationalization in the appropriate forums. In particular, cooperation among organizations, convention secretariats, the Global Environment Facility and the World Trade Organization is vital for the region, as is the effective working of sustainable development agreements that require greater integration of environmental, financial and trade policies and consistency among specific programmes, strategies and projects. All of this will require stability and substantial financing.

A first step could be to use single issue coordination systems to group those treaties and agreements that share objectives and agendas around strategic issues, such as biodiversity, chemicals and the atmosphere.

If global environmental institutions are to be strengthened, there will need to be better conditions for following up and evaluating the results of common agendas and conventions and for monitoring the state of the world and regional environment more systematically.

Bibliography

Acuña, Guillermo (2000), Marcos regulatorios e institucionales ambientales de América Latina y el Caribe en el contexto del proceso de reformas macroeconómicas: 1980-1990 (LC/R.2023), Santiago, Chile, Economic Commission for Latin America and the Caribbean (ECLAC), April.

Acquatella, Jean (2001), *Aplicación de instrumentos económicos en la gestión ambiental en América Latina y el Caribe: desafíos y factores condicionantes*, Medio ambiente y desarrollo series, No. 31 (LC/L.1488-P), Santiago, Chile, January. United Nations publication, Sales No. S.01.II.G.28.

Altomonte, Hugo and Fernando Sánchez Albavera (1997), "Las reformas energéticas en América Latina", Medio ambiente y desarrollo series, No. 1 (LC/L.1020), Santiago, Chile, Economic Commission for Latin America and the Caribbean (ECLAC).

Annan, Kofi (2000), *Globalization: The United Nations Development Dialogue: Finance, Trade, Poverty, Peace-Building*, Isabelle Grundberg and Sarbuland Khan (eds.), New York, United Nations University Press.

Bárcena, Alicia (2001), *La dimensión ambiental en el desarrollo de América Latina*, Libros de la CEPAL series, No. 58 (LC/G.2110-P), Santiago, Chile. United Nations publication, Sales No. S.01.II.G.67.

___ (1999), *Multilateral Diplomacy and the United Nations Today*, Boulder, Colorado, Westview Press.

BCSD-LA (Business Council for Sustainable Development for Latin America) (1999), *Global Climate Change: A Basis for Business Strategy and Practice in Latin America*, Monterrey, Nueva León.

Brañes, Raúl (2001), *Informe sobre el desarrollo del derecho ambiental latinoamericano y su aplicación después de diez años de la Conferencia de las Naciones Unidas sobre el Medio Ambiente y el Desarrollo*, Mexico City, Regional Office for Latin America and the Caribbean (ROLAC)/United Nations Environment Programme (UNEP).

___ (1996), *La recepción en los sistemas jurídicos de los países de América Latina y el Caribe de los compromisos asumidos en la Conferencia de las Naciones Unidas sobre Medio Ambiente y Desarrollo. Propuestas para la cooperación hemisférica*, Mexico City, Regional Office for Latin America and the Caribbean (ROLAC)/United Nations Environment Programme (UNEP).

Burkart, R. and others (1995), "Grandes ecosistemas de México y de América Central", *El futuro ecológico de un continente*, Gilberto Gallopín (ed.), Mexico City, United Nations University Press/Fondo de Cultura Económica (FCE).

Canuto, V.M. (1989), *Deforestation of Tropical Forests*, New York.

Castro, Gonzalo and Ilana Locker (2000), *Mapping Conservation Investments: An Assessment of Biodiversity Funding in Latin America and the Caribbean*, Washington, D.C.

Constanza, Robert and others (1997), "The value of the world's ecosystem services and natural capital", *Nature*, No. 387.

Elizalde, A. (2001), "Anotaciones para promover una reflexión subregional del Cono Sur sobre desarrollo sostenible", Santiago, Chile, August, unpublished.

Earth Council (2000), "National experiences of integrative, multistakeholder processes for sustainable development", *NCSD Report, 1999-2000*, San José, Costa Rica.

ECLAC (Economic Commission for Latin America and the Caribbean) (2001a), *Una década de luces y sombras. América Latina y el Caribe en los años noventa*, Bogotá, D.C., Economic Commission for Latin America and the Caribbean (ECLAC)/Alfaomega.

___ (2001b), *Crecer con estabilidad: el financiamiento del desarrollo en el nuevo contexto internacional*, Bogotá, D.C., Economic Commission for Latin America and the Caribbean (ECLAC)/Alfaomega.

___ (2001c), *Social Panorama of Latin America, 2000-2001* (LC/G.2128-P), Santiago, Chile. United Nations publication, Sales No. E.01.II.G.141.

___ (2001d), *El espacio regional: hacia la consolidación de los asentamientos humanos en América Latina y el Caribe*, Libros de la CEPAL series, No. 60 (LC/G.2116/Rev.1-P), Santiago, Chile. United Nations publication, Sales No. S.01.II.G.68.

___ (2001e), "Financiamiento para el desarrollo ambientalmente sostenible", document prepared for the Regional Preparatory Conference of Latin America and the Caribbean for the Worl Summit on Sustainable Development, September, forthcoming.

___ (2000a), *Equity, Development and Citizenship* (LC/G.2071/Rev.1-P), Santiago, Chile. United Nations publication, Sales No. S.00.II.G.81.

___ (2000b), Crecer con estabilidad: el financiamiento del desarrollo en el nuevo contexto internacional (LC/G.2117(CONF.89/3)), Santiago, Chile.

___ (2000c), *Economic survey of Latin America and the Caribbean 1999-2000* (LC/G.2102-P), Santiago, Chile. United Nations publication, Sales No. E.00.II.G.2.

___ (2000d), Informe de la Reunión preparatoria del Cono Sur para la Cumbre Mundial sobre el Desarrollo Sostenible (LC/L.1600), Santiago, Chile, 14-15 June.

___ (1999a), *Urban Consensus: Contributions from the Latin American and the Caribbean Regional Plan of Action on Human Settlements*, Medio ambiente y desarrollo series, No. 21 (LC/L.1330-P), Santiago, Chile. United Nations publication, Sales No. E.00.II.G.38.

___ (1999b), Centroamérica: evaluación de los daños ocasionados por el huracán Mitch, 1998 (LC/MEX/L.375), Mexico City, ECLAC Subregional Headquarters in Mexico, 18 May.

___ (1993), Remesas y economía familiar en El Salvador, Guatemala y Nicaragua (LC/MEX/L.154/Rev.1), Mexico City, ECLAC Subregional Headquarters in Mexico.

ECLAC-CELADE (Economic Commission for Latin America and the Caribbean, Population Division - Latin American and Caribbean Demographic Centre) (1999), "Latin America: urban and rural population projections, 1970-2025", *Demographic Bulletin*, year 32, No. 63 (LC/G.2052; LC/DEM/G.183), Santiago, Chile, March.

ECLAC/OLADE (Economic Commission for Latin America and the Caribbean/Latin American Energy Organization) (1999), *Energía y desarrollo sustentable en América Latina y el Caribe: guía para la formulación de políticas energéticas*, Santiago, Chile.

ECLAC/UNEP (Economic Commission for Latin America and the Caribbean/United Nations Environment Programme) (1997), "Instrumentos económicos para la gestión ambiental en América Latina y el Caribe", Mexico City, unpublished.

Erize, F. y otros (1993), *Parques nacionales de Argentina y otras de sus áreas naturales, segunda edición*, Madrid, El Ateneo.

FAO (Food and Agriculture Organization of the United Nations) (2001a), "Forest Resources Assessment, 2000" (http://www.fao.org/forestry/fo/fra/index.jsp).

___ (2001b), "FAOSTAT Agriculture Data" (http://apps.fao.org).

___ (2001c), *The Global Forest Resources Assessment, 2000. Summary Report* (COFO 201/INF.5), Rome.

___ (2001d), *Yearbook of Forest Products, 1999*, Rome.

___ (2001e), *Production Yearbook, 1999*, vol. 53, Rome.

___ (2000a), *Inventario de producción agropecuaria, 1999*, Rome.

___ (2000b), *Yearbook of Fishery Statistics, 1999*, Rome.

___ (2000c), *Inventario de producción forestal, 1999*, vol. 53, Rome.

___ (2000d), *El desarrollo forestal y la ejecución de las propuestas de acción del Grupo Intergubernamental de Bosques (GIB) países centroamericanos*, Santiago, Chile.

___ (1999), *State of the World's Forests, 1999*, Rome.

___ (1998), *FRA, 2000, Términos y definiciones*, Rome.

___ (1995a), "Evaluación de los recursos forestales 1990. Síntesis mundial", Estudio FAO Montes, No. 124, Rome.

___ (1995b), "Evaluación de los recursos forestales 1990. Países tropicales", Estudio FAO Montes, No. 112, Rome.

FSC (Forest Stewardship Council) (1999), *Opciones para las políticas sobre declaraciones basadas en porcentajes. Segunda Asamblea General del FSC*, Mexico City, June.

GEO (Perspectivas del Medio Ambiente Mundial) (2001), "Estadísticas ambientales de América Latina y el Caribe", San José, Costa Rica, forthcoming.

GESAMP (Group of Experts on the Scientific Aspects of Marine Pollution) (2001), *A Sea of Troubles*, United Nations Environment Programme (UNEP).

Gligo, Nicolo (2001), *La dimensión ambiental en el desarrollo de América Latina*, Libros de la CEPAL series, No. 58 (LC/G.2110-P), Santiago, Chile. United Nations publication, Sales No. S.01.II.G.67.

Goldewijk, Klein (2001), "Estimating global land use change over the past 300 years: the HYDE database", *Global Biogeochemical Cycles*, vol. 15, No. 2, June.

Guimarães, R. (2001a), "Tierra de sombras: Desafios de la sostenibilidad y del desarrollo territorial y local ante la globalización", Santiago, Chile, July, unpublished.

Guimarães, R. (2001b), *Fundamentos territoriales y biorregionales de la planificación*, serie Medio ambiente y desarrollo, N° 39 (LC/L.1563-P), Santiago, Chile, July. United Nations publication, Sales No. S.01.II.G.108.

IDB/ECLAC/CELADE (Inter-American Development Bank/Economic Commission for Latin America and the Caribbean/Latin American Demographic Centre) (1996), "Impacto de las tendencias demográficas sobre los sectores sociales en América Latina; contribución al diseño de políticas y programas", serie E, No. 45 (LC/DEM/G.161), Santiago, Chile.

IFRC (International Federation of Red Cross and Red Crescent Societies) (2001), *2001 IFRC World Disaster Report*, Geneva.

IOM/ United Nations (International Organization for Migration) (2000), *World Migration Report, 2000*, New York. United Nations publication, Sales No. E.00.III.S.3.

Jordán, Ricardo and Daniela Simioni (eds.) (1998), Ciudades intermedias en América Latina y el Caribe: propuestas para la gestión urbana (LC/L.1117), Santiago, Chile, Economic Commission for Latin America and the Caribbean (ECLAC).

Jouravlev, Andrei (2001), *Administración del agua en América Latina y el Caribe en el umbral del siglo XXI*, Recursos naturales e infraestructura series, No. 27 (LC/L.1564.P), Santiago, Chile, July. United Nations publication, Sales No. S.01.II.G.109.

Jovel, Roberto (2000), "El impacto económico y social de los desastres naturales en la región centroamericana", document presented at the Congress on medicine and disasters, San Salvador, Faculty of Medicine, University of El Salvador.

Katz, Jorge and Giovanni Stumpo (2001), *Regímenes competitivos sectoriales, productividad y competitividad internacional*, Desarrollo productivo series, No. 103 (LC/L.1578-P), Santiago, Chile, July. United Nations publication, Sales No. S.01.II.G.120.

Lacasaña, M. and others (1996), "El problema de exposición al plomo en América Latina y el Caribe", Serie ambiental, No. 16 Metepec, Pan American Centre for Human Ecology and Health (ECO), Pan American Health Organization (PAHO), World Health Organization (WHO).

LAFC (Latin American and Caribbean Forestry Commission) (1998), *Situación forestal en la región de América Latina y el Caribe. Período 1996/1997*, Havana.

León, R. (2001), "Anotaciones para promover una reflexión subregional del Caribe Insular sobre el Desarrollo Sostenible", consultant document, Havana, August, unpublished.

Mac Neil, Jim and others (1991), *Beyond Interdependence*, New York, Oxford Press.

Malingreau, J.P. and C.J. Tucker (1988), "Large-scale deforestation in the south-eastern Amazon basin of Brazil", *Ambio*, vol. 17, No. 1.

Mills, F. (1997), *1990-1991 Population and Housing Census of the Commonwealth Caribbean. Regional Monograph, Intraregional and Extraregional Mobility, the New Caribbean Migration*, Port of Spain, Caribbean Community (CARICOM).

Mittermeier, Russell and others (1999), *Biodiversidad amenazada: las ecorregiones terrestres prioritarias del mundo*, Mexico City, Cementos Mexicanos (CEMEX).

___ (1997), *Megadiversidad*, Mexico City, Cementos Mexicanos (CEMEX).

Monreal-Goméz, María Adela and others (1999), "Las surgencias costeras de América", *Geofísica*, No. 51, Mexico City, Pan American Institute of Geography and History (PAIGH).

Morelo, J. (1995), "Grandes ecosistemas de Sudamérica", *El futuro ecológico de un continente*, Gilberto Gallopín (ed.), Mexico City, Editorial de la Universidad de las Naciones Unidas/Fondo de Cultura Económica (FCE).

Morrone, Juan J. (2001), "Biogeografía de América Latina y el Caribe", Manuales y tesis SEA, vol. 3, Zaragoza.

Myers, F. (1988), "Threatened biotas: hotspots in tropical forest", *The Environmentalist*, vol. 8, No. 118.

Ocampo, José Antonio (2001), "Agricultura y desarrollo rural en América Latina", *Desarrollo rural en América Latina y el Caribe: la construcción de un nuevo modelo?*, M.B. de A. David (ed.), Bogotá, D.C., Economic Commission for Latin America and the Caribbean (ECLAC) / Alfaomega.

___ (1999), *Políticas e instituciones para el desarrollo sostenible en América Latina y el Caribe*, Medio ambiente y desarrollo series, No. 18 (LC/L.1260-P), Santiago, Chile, Economic Commission for Latin America and the Caribbean (ECLAC). United Nations publication, Sales No. S.99.II.G.37.

OECD (Organisation for Economic Co-operation and Development) (1999), *Economic Instruments for Pollution Control and Natural Resources Management in OECD Countries: A Survey* (ENV/EPOC/GEEI(98)35/REV.1/FINAL), Paris, OECD Environment Directorate, October.

PAHO-WHO (Pan American Health Organization- World Health Organization) (2000), *Evaluación, 2000*, Washington, D.C.

Pinto Santa Cruz, Aníbal (1976), "Styles of development in Latin America", *CEPAL Review*, No. 1, Santiago, Chile, First half. United Nations publication, Sales No. E.76.II.G.2.

PROCYMAF (Proyecto de Conservación y Manejo Sustentable de Recursos Forestales en México) (2000), *Balance de tres años de ejecución*, Mexico City, Secretariat of the Environment, Natural Resources and Fisheries (SEMARNAP).

Ramankutty, Navin and Jonathan A. Foley (1999), "Estimating historical changes in global land cover: croplands from 1700 to 1992", *Global Biogeochemical Cycles*, vol. 13, No. 4, December.

___ (1998), "Characterizing patterns of global land use: An analysis of global croplands data", *Global Biogeochemical Cycles*, vol. 12, No. 4, December.

Rodríguez Becerra, M. (2001), "Anotaciones para promover un reflexión subregional andina sobre el desarrollo sostenible", consultant document, Mexico City, June, unpublished.

___ (1999), "Las instituciones para la gestión ambiental: oportunidades y limitantes para la planificación biorregional", document prepared for the World Bank, unpublished.

Schaper, M. (1999), *Impactos ambientales de los cambios en la estructura exportadora de nueve países de América Latina y el Caribe: 1980-1995*, Medio ambiente y desarrollo series, No. 19 (LC/L.1241-P), Santiago, Chile, Economic Commission for Latin America and the Caribbean (ECLAC), October. United Nations publication, Sales No. S.99.II.G.44.

Schatan, Claudia (1999), "Contaminación industrial en los países latinoamericanos pre y post reformas económicas", Medio ambiente y desarrollo series, No. 22, Santiago, Chile, Economic Commission for Latin America and the Caribbean (ECLAC).

Shiklomanov, Igor (coord.) (1999), "World Water resources at the Beginning of the 21st Century", Paris, International Hydrological Programme, United Nations Educational, Scientific and Cultural Organization (UNESCO), unpublished.

Solanes, Miguel and David Getches (1998), "Prácticas recomendables para la elaboración de leyes y regulaciones relacionadas con el recurso hídrico", Washington, D.C., Inter-American Development Bank (IDB) (http://www.iadb.org/sds/doc/1085spa.pdf).

Tomlinson, P.B. (1986), *The Botany of Mangroves*, Cambridge, Massachusetts, Cambridge University Press.

Trellez Solis, E. (1997), *Legislación y gestión ambiental en los países andinos*, Buenos Aires, Konrad Adenauer Foundation/Interdisciplinary Centre for Latin American Development Studies (CIEDLA).

Tudela, F. and others (2001), "Disponibilidad de agua en América Latina y el Caribe", Mexico City, El Colegio de México, forthcoming.

UNDP (United Nations Development Programme) (1999), "Estudio comparativo de los diseños institucionales para la gestión ambiental en los países de América Latina", document presented at the Fourth Meeting of the Inter-Sessional Committee of the Forum of Ministers of the Environment of Latin America and the Caribbean, Lima, 2 October.

UNDP (United Nations Development Programme)/Capacity 21 (2001), "Actuar en proyectos, pensar en procesos – De Rio a Johannesburgo: Experiencias latinoamericanas hacia el desarrollo sostenible", Mexico City, Red Humana Agenda 21 de América Latina, unpublished.

UNEP (United Nations Environment Programme) (2002), "Caribbean Environmental Law Development and Application: Environmental Legislative and Judicial Developments in the English-speaking Caribbean Countries in the context of Compliance with Agenda 21 and the Rio Agreements", Mexico City, Regional Office for Latin America and the Caribbean, May.

___ (2001b), "Anotaciones para promover una reflexión subregional mesoamericana sobre el desarrollo sustentable", July, unpublished.

___ (2001c), *An Assessment of the Status of the World's Remaining Closed Forests*, (UNEP/DEWA/TR 01-2), A. Singh, H. Shi, Z. Zhu and T. Foresman (eds.), Division of Early Warning and Assessment (DEWA).

___ (2001d), *El desarrollo del derecho del ambiental latinoamericano y su aplicación. Informe sobre los cambios jurídicos después de la Conferencia de las* Naciones Unidas *sobre el Medio Ambiente y el Desarrollo (Río 1992)*, Mexico City, Regional Office for Latin America and the Caribbean, October.

___ (2000a), "Conservación y uso sustentable de las selvas tropicales de América Latina y el Caribe", document presented at the Meeting of the Forum of Ministers of the Environment of Latin America and the Caribbean, March.

___ (2000b), *GEO: América Latina y el Caribe. Perspectivas del medio ambiente*, San José, Costa Rica.

___ (2000c), "Final Report, Twelfth meeting of the Forum of Ministers of Environment of Latin America and the Caribbean" (UNEP/LAC-IG.XII/4), Barbados, March.

___ (2000d), "Regional preparation process for Rio + 10", Mexico City, Regional Office for Latin America and the Caribbean.

___ (1995), *Programa de Acción Mundial para la Protección del Medio Marino frente a las Actividades Realizadas en Tierra*, Washington, D.C.

___ (1993), "Situación Actual del Derecho Internacional Ambiental en América Latina y el Caribe", Documentos sobre derecho ambiental series No. 2, Mexico City, Regional Office for Latin America and the Caribbean.

Vargas, R. (2001), "Anotaciones para promover una reflexión subregional de Mesoamérica sobre el desarrollo sostenible", consultant document, San Salvador, August, unpublished.

Villa, Miguel (2001), "Globalización en América Latina y el Caribe", Santiago, Chile, Population Division - Latin American and Caribbean Demographic Centre (CELADE), forthcoming.

Villa, Miguel and Jorge Martínez (2000), "Tendencias y patrones de la migración internacional en América Latina y el Caribe", document presented at the Symposium on International Migration in the Americas (San José, 4-6 September).

WRI (World Resources Institute) (2001), *World Resources Report, 2000-2001*, Washington, D.C.

Wilson, E.O. (1988), *Biodiversity*, Washington, D.C., National Academy Press.

World Bank (1996), *Annual Report, 1996*, Washington, D.C. (http://www.esd.worldbank.org/envmat/vol2f96/latincard.htm).

World Conservation Monitoring Centre (2000), "Venezuela" (http://www.latinsynergy.org/ven_map_for.htm).

WWF (World Wildlife Fund) (2000), "Wild World Map" (http://www.wwf.org/wildworld).

Yáñez-Arancibia, Alejandro and Ana Laura Lara-Domínguez (1999), *Ecosistemas de manglar en América tropical*, Mexico City, National Ecology Institute.

Yánez-Arancibia, Alejandro (1994), "Los manglares de América Latina en la encrucijada", *Faro*, No. 1.

Zavala, Wilber (1999), "Integración centroamericana y participación de la sociedad civil: impacto sobre el medio ambiente y el desarrollo sostenible", *Hacia una integración desde abajo; participación sociedad civil e integración centroamericana*, San Salvador, Talleres Gráficos UCA.

Annex 1

Rio de Janeiro Platform of Action on the road to Johannesburg 2002

The ministers and representatives of the Governments of Latin America and the Caribbean gathered in Rio de Janeiro on 23 and 24 October 2001 to participate in the Regional Preparatory Conference of Latin America and the Caribbean for the World Summit on Sustainable Development hereby:

A.   Reaffirmation of principles and commitments

1. **Recall** the commitments made at the Latin American and Caribbean Regional Preparatory Meeting for the United Nations Conference on Environment and Development, held in Mexico City in March 1991, and at the United Nations Conference on Environment and Development itself, which was held in Rio de Janeiro in June 1992.

2. **Reaffirm** the principles and objectives set forth in the Rio Declaration on Environment and Development; Agenda 21; the non-legally binding Authoritative Statement of Principles for a Global Consensus on Management, Conservation and Sustainable Development of All Types of Forests; the United Nations Framework Convention on Climate Change and the Kyoto Protocol; the Convention on Biological Diversity; the Cartagena Protocol on Biosafety; the United Nations Convention to Combat Desertification in those Countries Experiencing Serious Drought and/or Desertification, particularly in Africa; the

Stockholm Convention on Persistent Organic Pollutants; and the Convention on the Prior Informed Consent Procedure for Certain Hazardous Chemicals and Pesticides in International Trade.

3. **Reaffirm also** the principles and objectives set forth in the Vienna Convention for the Protection of the Ozone Layer, the Montreal Protocol on Substances that Deplete the Ozone Layer and the Basel Convention on the Control of Transboundary Movements of Hazardous Wastes and their Disposal, which have laid the foundations for the various international instruments adopted at the United Nations Conference on Environment and Development and thereafter.

4. **Further reaffirm** the Declaration of the Global Conference on the Sustainable Development of Small Island Developing States approved in Barbados in 1994 and the subregional conventions and agreements which grew out of the United Nations Conference on Environment and Development (the "Earth Summit").

5. **Recall also** the commitments made during the World Summit on Social Development, the International Conference on Population and Development, the United Nations Conference on Human Settlements (Habitat II) held in Istanbul and the important contribution they have made to the enhanced implementation of Agenda 21, bearing in mind the need for more effective integration of economic and social development and environmental protection strategies within the sustainable development framework.

6. **Reaffirm** the sovereign right of all States to exploit their own resources pursuant to their national environmental and development policies, in accordance with principles 2 and 13 as set forth in the Rio Declaration.

7. **Reiterate** their commitment to the precautionary principle defined in the Rio Declaration as a key component of environmental policy.

8. **Reiterate also** their commitment to the principle of common but differentiated responsibilities, according to which the developed countries should assume a proportionally greater share of responsibility for ensuring sustainable development.

B. Obstacles and lessons learned

9. **Consider** the World Summit on Sustainable Development a unique opportunity to evaluate progress in meeting the commitments made at the United Nations Conference on Environment and

Development, and **acknowledge** that significant ground has been gained with regard to awareness raising and the codification of environmental law. Ten years later, however, the conditions for sustainable development are no better than those that prevailed in 1992. There has been a dramatic increase in the size of the world's population living in poverty, development needs are more pressing than ever, the deterioration of the environment has worsened and the rapid pace of globalization poses new challenges for sustainability and especially for equity.

10. **Believe** that the strengthening of democratic institutions throughout the region, the advances made in peace processes in some countries of the region and greater public awareness have helped to incorporate the environmental dimension into the development process and to make people-centered sustainable development the first priority of the political, economic and social programmes of the States of Latin America and the Caribbean.

11. **Recognize** the importance of the transparent and jointly responsible participation of civil society, including the main groups identified in Agenda 21, in the design, implementation and follow-up of sustainable development policies and of regional and international commitments on these matters, and that it is essential to strengthen the cultural, educational and environmental training base that makes it possible to engage civil society in the achievement of sustainable development.

12. **Recognize also** that, 10 years after the United Nations Conference on Environment and Development, and given the new global events and challenges that are affecting our peoples and environment, progress needs to be made in laying the foundations for a new ethic that will serve as the cornerstone of sustainable development.

13. **Emphasize** that the persistence of unsustainable production and consumption patterns and the negative impacts of some trade and financial mechanisms, especially in the developed countries, seriously jeopardize the achievement of sustainable development throughout the world, and **reiterate** the need to increase the efforts being made to comply with the provisions of the relevant international instruments.

14. **Regret** that, although the countries of the Latin American and Caribbean region have made progress in promoting a more favourable environment for technology transfer and for new clean, energy-efficient approaches to production, together with the corresponding technical knowledge, particularly through the establishment of suitable systems for the protection of intellectual property, the developed countries have not adopted effective measures for ensuring transfers of, in particular, the

most appropriate technologies in terms of environmental, social and economic sustainability.

15. **Recognize** that the viability of sustainable development in the region requires a stable, predictable, open and inclusive international economic system, in which the environmental dimension is acknowledged as an opportunity for investment and trade.

16. **Reject** any principle or policy that distorts international trade, investment or capital flows and **urge** that all export subsidies be eliminated, that market access be substantively improved and that national forms of support that distort trade or production be reduced with a view to their eventual elimination.

17. **Voice** their concern regarding the possible conditionality which developed countries could impose by linking environmental standards to the approval of official export credits.

18. **Express their concern** as to the importance of averting an abusive interpretation of the precautionary approach on the part of the industrialized countries which might lead them to use trade policy measures as a vehicle for arbitrary or unjustifiable discrimination or as a disguised restriction on international trade (principles 12 and 15).

19. **Recognize** the need to streamline the organizations, forums and initiatives devoted to promoting sustainable development, as well as the need to rationalize the calendar of meetings related to the sustainable development agenda, in order to ensure most efficient and effective use of resources in servicing these meetings, and **underscore** also the need to help strengthen developing countries' capacity to implement policies and fulfil commitments undertaken within those frameworks.

20. **Recognize** the importance of regional initiatives to promote sustainable development in Latin America and the Caribbean.

21. **Recognize also** the special needs of regional and subregional ecosystems, including arid and semi-arid, mountain, forest, marine, aquatic and island ecosystems, which are rich and diverse but generally fragile as well, together with the importance of ensuring their conservation, protection and sustainable use.

22. **Acknowledge and identify** with the concern of the United Nations, which, on the basis of the guidelines established in chapter 13 of Agenda 21, has declared 2002 the International Year of Mountains, bearing in mind that the importance of mountain ecosystems derives not only from their great vulnerability, but also from their role as the source of important resources for the future of humankind, such as water,

energy, biological diversity, mineral resources, cultural diversity and leisure, in addition to providing a physical space for many populations.

23. **Renew also** their commitment to the Global Environment Facility and other major multilateral finance agencies, which should broaden the criteria they use in selecting issues and activities that qualify for financing with a view to addressing areas prioritized by developing countries.

C.   Present considerations

24. **Believe** that extreme poverty, environmental degradation, underdevelopment, unsustainable production and consumption patterns, and the lack of equity in income distribution impact all the countries in the international community, particularly developing countries, and that it is in this light that international cooperation should be regarded as a unifying element for the efforts of the peoples and Governments of the entire world to build a common objective: to improve the living conditions of present and future generations.

25. **Reiterate** that multidimensional efforts to develop national and regional capacities should be promoted with a view to reinforcing regional and subregional cooperation schemes and meeting the needs of developing countries and the most vulnerable groups and regions.

26. **Recall** that during the special session of the United Nations General Assembly to review and appraise the implementation of Agenda 21, it was seen that globalization was manifesting itself as an uneven phenomenon that has both a positive and a negative influence on all societies, that some of its negative effects —such as economic and financial instability, social exclusion and depletion of national resources— have increased since then, especially in some developing countries, and therefore **urge** that policies and measures be adopted to facilitate equitable economic development by incorporating all social actors and protecting natural resources for the benefit of present and future generations.

27. **Emphasize** that in order to further sustainable development, social, economic and environmental policies need to be integrated so that trends that threaten human beings' quality of life can be reversed before they become irreversible and so that a sharp increase in the costs for society can be avoided, and that the ongoing degradation of the environment must be stopped by means of measures designed to mitigate the negative effects of economic and social development and to ensure the existence of a sustainable bond between humankind and nature.

28. **Recognize** the need to promote wider understanding, acceptance and application of the integrative sustainable development approach, particularly among policy-makers at the local, national and regional levels, which entails, as a matter of urgency, the participatory development of the foundations for a new ethic, and **recognize** also the need to promote a culture of sustainable development among communities, civil society and the private sector through education and public awareness strategies.

29. **Highlight** the importance of ensuring that the diffusion of scientific knowledge, the promotion of research, and the development of clean technologies serve the needs of the international community, especially of the developing countries, in regard to decision-making and policy formulation for sustainable development.

30. **Recognize** that scientific research, technological innovation, and new information and communications technologies can be instrumental in the formulation of economic, social and environmental policies, and should therefore be promoted and facilitated through regional and international cooperation.

31. **Recognize also** that indigenous and local communities embodying traditional lifestyles relevant to the conservation and sustainable use of natural resources constitute an important group for the sustainable production and consumption of goods and services, and that they should therefore participate in the design of policies and actions to achieve sustainable development; that the use and enjoyment of natural resources in the places in which they live should be approached with respect; and that their knowledge, innovations and practices should be legally protected and that continual feedback which benefits all concerned should thus be established.

32. **Recognize** that gender equality has been fundamental in advancing efforts to achieve sustainable development and that the full participation of women in policy formulation and implementation should be strengthened at the local, national, regional and global levels.

33. **Believe** that, in order to deal with the serious environmental damage and extreme poverty that persist in many countries, the actions of the international community in promoting sustainable development should be precise, efficient and effective.

D. Future commitments

The ministers and representatives of the Governments of Latin America and the Caribbean gathered in Rio de Janeiro on 23 and 24 October 2001 to participate in the Regional Preparatory Conference of Latin America and the Caribbean for the World Summit on Sustainable Development hereby decide:

1. Institutional structure for sustainable development

34. **To develop** local, national and regional capacities through a lasting strategic alliance among all development actors so that advantage can be taken at the local level of the potential of globalization through an exchange of experiences and best practices within and between countries, the promotion of formal and informal education for national and local leaders, and support for applied research and technological innovation at all levels.

35. **To promote** the reinforcement of open public and private institutions and clearly defined standards that will help all individual and collective actors to forge their own development process and strengthen institutional links among economic, social and environmental policies with the participation of the population, as set forth in Agenda 21, through national sustainable development councils.

36. **To strengthen** regional institutions in relation to the design and implementation of programmes and projects to promote the integration of economic, social and environmental policies through the organization of workshops, forums, high-level conferences and South-South cooperation programmes.

37. **To promote** more efficient ways of addressing the issue of sustainable development in multilateral forums through the use of flexible, suitable mechanisms for rationalizing efforts and the use of resources more fully and through the promotion of synergies among the relevant conventions, as set forth in Agenda 21, by national sustainable development councils, among others, in order to articulate economic, social and environmental policies with the participation of the population.

38. **To support**, in this regard, the efforts being made by the United Nations Environment Programme to examine and structure environmental policy and governance, while taking care not to impinge upon the jurisdictions or objectives of the different multilateral environmental agreements, in order to generate greater synergies among

them and to assess the possible standardization and harmonization of reporting requirements and procedures for their implementation.

39. **To reaffirm** the importance of achieving greater consistency and coordination among environmental, social and economic strategies and policies and, to that end, **to invite**, among other institutions, the United Nations Development Programme, the United Nations Environment Programme, the United Nations Commission on Sustainable Development and the Economic Commission for Latin America and the Caribbean to continue and to increase their support for the countries to help achieve that integration and to strengthen cooperation mechanisms at the global and regional levels.

2.   Financing and technology transfer

40. **To urge** the international community in general and the developed countries in particular to allocate a sufficient, predictable level of new and additional resources in order to ensure the effective implementation of Agenda 21, particularly chapters 33 and 34, and of other international agreements.

41. **To reiterate** the importance of the developed countries meeting the commitment to allocate 0.7% of their GDP to cooperation for development in the rest of the world.

42. **To define** economic and fiscal incentives that effectively encourage the participation of the private sector in public schemes to promote sustainable development and correct market failures that have a negative impact on the sustainability of development.

43. **To call upon** the major contributors to redouble their efforts to ensure that the Global Environment Facility will have additional concessional funds in the future and that those resources will be allocated and administered in a more transparent, efficient and timely manner.

44. **To recognize** that the burden of debt and debt servicing faced by many countries of the region, particularly in the face of declining official development assistance and their limited ability to attract new financing and investment, have continued to undermine strategies to mobilize resources for sustainable development; **to note** with concern that debt-to-output ratios in heavily indebted countries have not seen significant improvement; and **to underscore** the need for renewed consideration of the possibility of creating mechanisms to relieve the burden of highly-indebted countries, as well as the need to increase, through the creation of new, innovative financial instruments,

concessional multilateral funding for the implementation of sustainable development programmes.

45. **To recommend** that the participants in the International Conference on Financing for Development to be held in Monterrey, Mexico, in March 2002, address the need to explore innovative and more effective mechanisms for financing the protection of national public goods that afford global benefits and that they propose means of linking the environmental dimension with countries' fiscal policies in order to effectively incorporate financial sectors into the effort to achieve sustainable development goals.

46. **To reaffirm** that developing countries can succeed in fulfilling their international commitments regarding sustainable development only if they have access to adequate financing and technology transfers, bearing in mind that the promotion of development and the eradication of poverty are the overriding priorities for developing countries .

47. **To underline** the fact that. given the existing complementarities among trade, investment, environmental quality, social well-being, growth, the benefits of the sustainable use of natural resources and the formation of an open and inclusive world economic system, the environmental dimension constitutes an opportunity rather than a barrier to investment and trade.

48. **To ensure** market access for developing countries' products as an essential factor in sustainable development and **to promote** the competitiveness of developing-country goods and services that are handled and produced in a sustainable manner.

49. **To emphasize** the need to recommend at the Summit that multinational corporations adopt international principles and standards of social responsibility with regard to the environment and sustainable development, and that they set up regular mechanisms and procedures for reporting to the appropriate bodies.

50. **To call for** steps to be taken at the Summit to be held in Johannesburg to foster the establishment of effective means of facilitating technology transfer and new approaches to production under more favourable conditions, in keeping with principle 9 of the Rio Declaration, based, in particular, on the establishment by developed countries of financial mechanisms and preferential forms of tax treatment.

3.   Formulation of actions

51. **To call upon** all countries that have not yet done so to ratify the Convention on Biological Diversity as soon as possible so that it can serve as a key instrument for the conservation of biodiversity, the sustainable use of its components, and the achievement of a just and equitable share of the benefits afforded by the use of genetic resources.

52. **To ensure** equitable access to the benefits afforded by the use of genetic resources through the implementation of national and international regulatory schemes for this purpose, taking into account all rights pertaining to these resources and technologies, and through appropriate financing and the transfer of relevant technologies.

53. **To foster** cooperation aimed at achieving the conservation and sustainable management of the region's natural ecosystems for the purpose of deepening world commitments to conserve biodiversity *in situ* and to work to establish sustainable development plans in those ecosystems which incorporate, at the local level, the agreements that figure in all the relevant conventions and that provide for the creation and reinforcement of protected areas and biological corridors and for the promotion of sustainable production activities.

54. **To call for** the design of a strategy for the sustainable development of mountain ecosystems that promotes the comprehensive management of land, bodies of water and living resources through an ecosystemic approach to the prevention of natural disasters.

55. **To underline** the need to preserve, support and protect traditional knowledge as an important part of the efforts being made to ensure the harmonious development and use of natural resources in order to promote the achievement of sustainable development objectives.

56. **To call upon** the Economic Commission for Latin America and the Caribbean, the United Nations Development Programme and the United Nations Environment Programme to support a participatory discussion among the various actors of Latin American and Caribbean society regarding the ethical foundation for sustainable development.

57. **To urge** the international community to continue its efforts to implement and secure the early entry into force, as universally as possible, of the Cartagena Protocol on Biosafety, bearing in mind national constitutional procedures, with a view to ensuring that it enters into effect before the World Summit on Sustainable Development is convened.

58. **To strengthen** national and regional regulatory and institutional structures relating to biosafety.

59. **To underscore** the importance of assessing vulnerability and quantifying the progress made towards sustainable development; **to note** the lack of data and indicators that would permit such measurements; and **to stress** the need to develop a core set of data and indicators, including a vulnerability index, that will make it possible to measure progress towards sustainable development, taking into account the unique features of Caribbean countries and in keeping with Agenda 21 and the Barbados Programme of Action adopted at the Global Conference on the Sustainable Development of Small Island Developing States.

60. **To reduce** the level of vulnerability to natural disasters based on planning instruments such as ecological and economic land management; and **to promote** a culture of risk awareness to further their prevention and mitigation through educational processes and improved information and early warning systems while encouraging participation on the part of civil society.

61. **To strengthen** subregional and regional cooperation, including the participation of national and international financial sectors, particularly in monitoring systems and in improving the effectiveness of reconstruction works, with special emphasis on small island developing States.

62. **To call for** recognition of the high degree of vulnerability of the small island developing States of the Caribbean; and, consequently, **to devote greater attention** to the Barbados Programme of Action and **to channel** resources for its implementation, especially with respect to adaptation to climate change, the stewardship of marine and coastal resources, integrated waste management, the protection of water resources and an increase in their quantity and quality, and the development of sustainable forms of tourism.

63. **To establish** a regional strategy containing medium- and long-term actions to prevent and respond to emergencies deriving from El Niño.

64. **To promote** integrated basin management, with emphasis on cross-sectoral, decentralized management conducted from an ecosystemic vantage point, and a change in the culture and in the social perception of the value of water; and **to align** economic and market mechanisms with the increasing degree of scarcity by adopting indirect instruments to supplement direct regulation and achieve the effective management and conservation of water resources.

65. **To enhance** international cooperation schemes at the global, regional and subregional levels, particularly in shared ecosystems, and **to**

increase coordination among the many different levels and actors involved in water management.

66. **To support** international cooperation for sustainable forest management, taking related economic and commercial aspects into account; and **to promote** the implementation of the plan of action formulated by the United Nations Forum on Forests.

67. **To strengthen** schemes for cooperation with indigenous and local communities embodying relevant traditional lifestyles for the conservation and sustainable use of biodiversity with the aim of promoting programmes and financial resources to ensure their full participation.

68. **To underscore** the need to diversify the energy supply and foster energy efficiency, to assess the potential of conventional sources and to increase the share of renewable sources and the need for greater support in this area from financial agencies in order to meet the needs of each country.

69. **To establish** long-term synergies between the region's energy policies and environmental policies in order to achieve greater energy efficiency and to reduce greenhouse gas emissions and promote the use of clean technologies.

70. **To call upon** all the countries that have not yet done so expedite their ratification, taking into account their national constitutional procedures, of the Kyoto Protocol to the United Nations Framework Convention on Climate Change with a view to ensuring its entry into force prior to the World Summit on Sustainable Development.

71. **To promote and enhance** regional and international climate-change adaptation programmes that will further and complement national efforts and **to consider** undertaking efforts to reinforce adaptive capacities in the most vulnerable areas, taking into account the work and decisions of conferences held by the parties to the United Nations Framework Convention on Climate Change.

72. **To promote** policies for strengthening land management as a means of contributing to the sustainable development of biodiversity.

73. **To call upon** all countries to ratify the Convention on the Prior Informed Consent Procedure for Certain Hazardous Chemicals and Pesticides in International Trade and the Stockholm Convention on Persistent Organic Pollutants and to support the Bahia Declaration and the Priorities for Action beyond 2000 adopted by the Intergovernmental Forum on Chemical Safety in view of their significance for the solution of

problems caused by chemical contamination and its effects on human health and the environment.

74. **To underscore** the importance of a healthy population for the achievement of sustainable development because of the impact of health on quality of life and productivity levels; **to emphasize** the need to devote greater attention to strengthening the health sector, including the improvement of synergy between environment and health policies; **to call upon** the international community to assist in strengthening national capacity in this area, bearing in mind the formidable challenges in this sector, notably the increasing prevalence of HIV/AIDS.

75. **To recognize** that demographic trends in the region, including high rates of rural-urban migration, has resulted in rapid, often unplanned urbanization which increases the level of stress on natural resources, including water and energy, overburdens infrastructure for pollution control, sanitation and solid waste management, and undermines strategies for the prevention of forest destruction, soil erosion, and land degradation; and **to underscore** the need for more effective urban planning and land management as a means of improving human settlements in the region and reducing the risk of man-made disasters in the face of the dramatic natural events that have occurred.

76. **To recognize and identify** the relationship between population and the environment, to achieve greater interaction among institutions at the national and international levels that deal with population and environmental issues, and to promote access to additional financial resources for activities aimed at the analysis and development of the link between the environment and population.

77. **To further** an environmentally sustainable form of urban management linked to more rational production and consumption patterns that are associated with the reduction of emissions and the generation of less waste; and **to establish** more effective mechanisms for urban planning and for augmenting waste-water treatment facilities.

78. **To emphasize** that the achievement of sustainable development and the improvement of the quality of life will require more effective integration of environmental, social and economic components of public policies, programmes and projects at the local, national, regional and international levels.

79. **To call upon** the Economic Commission for Latin America and the Caribbean, the United Nations Development Programme and the United Nations Environment Programme to follow up on the agreements reached at this meeting and to continue to do so with respect to the global

sustainable development agenda in accordance with their mandates and capabilities.

80. **To declare** that the countries and peoples of Latin America and the Caribbean regard the World Summit on Sustainable Development as a unique opportunity to evaluate the progress made at all levels in fulfilling the commitments made at the United Nations Conference on Environment and Development and to undertake new, effective actions aimed at full compliance with those commitments and at meeting the future challenges entailed in achieving sustainable development.

81. **To propose** that the agenda of the World Summit on Sustainable Development accord high priority to, *inter alia*, the cross-sectoral issues of finance, science and technology, capacity-building and vulnerability.

82. **To call upon** the international community to reaffirm its commitment and political will so that, through a renewed form of cooperation within a spirit of solidarity, and based on the recognition of a responsible, ethical relationship between human beings and nature, effective action can be taken at the local, national, regional and global levels to ensure the full implementation of existing agreements for sustainable development, as this is the best guarantee of a more just world within a context of global peace; and, in the light of these considerations, and **to propose** the following central theme for the World Summit on Sustainable Development: "Towards a new globalization which ensures that development is sustainable, equitable and inclusive".

ECLAC
publications

ECONOMIC COMMISSION FOR LATIN AMERICA
AND THE CARIBBEAN
Casilla 179-D   Santiago, Chile

Publication may be accessed at: www.eclac.cl/publicaciones

CEPAL Review

CEPAL Review first appeared in 1976 as part of the Publications Programme of the Economic Commission for Latin America and the Caribbean, its aim being to make a contribution to the study of the economic and social development problems of the region. The views expressed in signed articles, including those by Secretariat staff members, are those of the authors and therefore do not necessarily reflect the point of view of the Organization.

CEPAL Review is published in Spanish and English versions three times a year.

Annual subscription costs for 2002 are US$ 30 for the Spanish version and US$ 35 for the English version. The price of single issues is US$ 15 in both cases.

The cost of a two-year subscription (2002-2003) is US$ 50 for Spanish-language version and US$ 60 for English.

Revista de la CEPAL, número extraordinario: CEPAL CINCUENTA AÑOS, reflexiones sobre América Latina y el Caribe, 1998, 376 p. (out of stock)

Informes periódicos institucionales

Panorama de la inserción internacional de América Latina y el Caribe, 2000-2001, 194 p.
Latin America and the Caribbean in the World Economy, *2000-2001.* 240 p.
La Inversión Extranjera en América Latina y el Caribe, 2001, 190 p.
Foreign investment of Latin America and the Caribbean, 2001 (forthcoming)
Panorama Social de América Latina, 2000-2001, 284 p.
Social Panorama of Latin America, *2000-2001,* 284 p.
Balance Preliminar de las Economías de América Latina y el Caribe, 2001, 116 p.
Preliminary Overview of the Economies of Latin America and the Caribbean, 2001, 107 p.

Síntesis estudio económico de América Latina y el Caribe, 1999-2000, 1999, 48 p.

Summary Economic Survey of Latin America and the Caribbean 1999-2000, 1999, 34 p.

Situación y perspectivas, Estudio Económico de América Latina y el Caribe 2000-2001, 2001, 44 p.

Current conditions and outlook, Economic Survey of Latin America and the Caribbean 2000-2001, 41 p.

Estudio Económico de América Latina y el Caribe		Economic Survey of Latin America and the Caribbean	
2000-2001,	314 p.	2000-2001,	292 p.
1999-2000,	352 p.	1999-2000,	352 p.
1998-1999,	359 p.	1998-1999,	326 p.
1997-1998,	386 p.	1997-1998,	360 p.

(Issues for previous years also available)

Anuario Estadístico de América Latina y el Caribe / **Statistical Yearbook for Latin America and the Caribbean** (bilingual)

2000,	857 p.	2001,	778 p.
1998,	880 p.	1999,	851 p.

(Issues for previous years also available)

Libros de la CEPAL

68 *La sostenibilidad del desarrollo en América Latina y el Caribe: desafíos y oportunidades*, 2002, 146 p

68 **The sustainability of development in Latin America and the Caribbean: challenges and opportunities**, 2002, 140 p.

67 **Growth with stability, financing for development in the new international context**, 2002, Jürgen Weller, 196 p.

66 **Economic reforms, growth and employment. Labour markets in Latin America and the Caribbean**, 2001, 205 p.

65 **The income distribution problem in Latin America and the Caribbean**, 2001, Samuel Morley, 169 p.

64 **Structural reforms, productivity and technological change in Latin America**, 2001, Jorge Katz, 143 p.

63 **Investment and economic reforms in Latin America**, 2001, Graciela Moguillansky y Ricardo Bielschowsky, 186 p.

62 **Equity, development and citizenship** (abridged edition)

61 *Apertura económica y (des)encadenamientos productivos- Reflexiones sobre el complejo lácteo en América Latina*, 2001, Martin Dirwen (compiladora), 176 p.

60 *El espacio regional. Hacia la consolidación de los asentamientos humanos en América Latina* (forthcoming)

59 *Juventud, población y desarrollo en América Latina y el Caribe. Problemas, oportunidades y desafíos*, 474 p.

58 *La dimensión ambiental en el desarrollo de América Latina, Apertura y (des)encadenamientos–Reflexiones en torno a los lácteos*, 2001, 282 p.

57 *Las mujeres chilenas en los noventa. Hablan las cifras*, 2000, 214 p.

56 *Protagonismo juvenil en proyectos locales: lecciones del cono sur*, 170 p.

55 **Financial globalization and the emerging economies**, José Antonio Ocampo, Stefano Zamagni, Ricardo Ffrench-Davis y Carlo Pietrobelli, 2000, 328 p.

54 *La CEPAL en sus 50 años. Notas de un seminario conmemorativo*, 2000, 149 p.

53 *Transformaciones recientes en el sector agropecuario brasileño*, M. Beatriz de A. David, Philippe Waniez, Violette Brustlein, Enali M. De Biaggi, Paula de Andrade Rollo y Monica dos Santos Rodrigues, 1999, 127 p.

52 *Un examen de la migración internacional en la Comunidad Andina*, 1999, 114 p.

51 *Nuevas políticas comerciales en América Latina y Asia. Algunos casos nacionales*, 1999, 584 p.

50 *Privatización portuaria: bases, alternativas y consecuencias*, 1999, 248 p.

49 *Teorías y metáforas sobre el desarrollo territorial*, Sergio Boisier, 1999, 128 p.

48 *Las dimensiones sociales de la integración regional en América Latina*, Rolando Franco y Armando Di Filippo, 1999, 238 p.

47 *El pacto fiscal. Fortalezas, debilidades, desafíos*, 1998, 280 p.

47 **The fiscal covenant. Strenghts, weaknesses, challenges**, 1998, 290 p.

45 *La grieta de las drogas. Desintegración social y políticas públicas en América Latina*, 1997, 218 p.

46 *Agroindustria y pequeña agricultura: vínculos, potencialidades y oportunidades comerciales*, 1998, 180 p.

44 *La brecha de la equidad. América Latina, el Caribe y la Cumbre Social*, 1997, 218 p.

44 **The equity Gap. Latin America, the Caribbean and the Social Summit**, 1997, 218 p.

43 *Quince años de desempeño económico. América Latina y el Caribe, 1980-1995*, 1996, 120 p.

43 **The economic experience of the last fifteen years. Latin America and the Caribbean, 1980-1995**, 1996, 206 p.

42 *Fortalecer el desarrollo. Interacciones entre macro y micro-economía*, 1996, 116 p.

42 **Strengthening development. The interplay of macro- and microeconomics**, 1996, 116 p.

41 *Las relaciones económicas entre América Latina y la Unión Europea: el papel de los servicios exteriores*, 1996, 395 p.

40 *América Latina y el Caribe: políticas para mejorar la inserción en la economía mundial*, 1995, 314 p. (out of stock)

40 **Latin America and the Caribbean: policies to improve linkages with the global economy**, 1995, 308 p.

39 *El regionalismo abierto en América Latina y el Caribe. La integración económica en servicio de la transformación tecnológica*, 1994, 120 p.

39 **Open regionalism in Latin America and the Caribbean. Economic integration as a contribution to changing productions patterns with social equity**, 1994, 103 p.

38 *Imágenes sociales de la modernización y la transformación tecnológica*, 1995, 198 p.

37 *Familia y futuro: un programa regional en América Latina y el Caribe*, 1994, 137 p.

37 **Family and future: a regional programme in Latin America and the Caribbean**, 1994, 124 p.

36 *Cambios en el perfil de las familias: la experiencia regional*, 1993, 434 p.

35 *Población, equidad y transformación productiva, 1993*, 2ª ed. 1993, 158 p.

35 **Population, social equity and changing production patterns**, 1993, 154 p.

34 *Ensayos sobre coordinación de políticas macroeconómicas, 1992*, 249 p.

33 *Educación y conocimiento: eje de la transformación productiva con equidad*, 1992, 269 p.

33 **Education and knowledge: basic pillars of changing production patterns with social equity**, 1992, 257 p.

Recent co-publications

On occassion ECLAC concludes agreements for the co-publication of texts that may be of special interest to other international organizations or to publishing houses. In the latter case, the publishing houses have exclusive sales and distribution rights.

Financial Crises in 'Successful' Emerging Economies, Ricardo Ffrench-Davis (coordinador y editor), CEPAL/Brookings Institution Press, 2001.
Capital social rural. Experiencias de México y Centroamérica, Margarita Flores y Fernando Rello, 2002.
Eqüidade, desenvolvimento e cidadania, José Antonio Ocampo, CEPAL/Editora Campus, 2002.
Crescimento, emprego e eqüidade; O Impacto das Reformas Econômicas na América Latina e Caribe, Barbara Stallings e Wilson Peres, CEPAL/Editora Campus, 2002.
Crescer com Esabilidade, José Antonio Ocampo, CEPAL/Editora Campus, 2002.
Pequeñas y medianas empresas industriales en América Latina y el Caribe, Wilson Peres y Giovanni Stumpo (coordinadores), CEPAL/Siglo XXI, México.
Aglomeraciones mineras y desarrollo local en América Latina, Rudolf M. Buitelaar (compilador), CEPAL/Alfaomega, Colombia, 2002.
Reformas, crecimiento y políticas sociales en Chile desde 1973, Ricardo Ffrench-Davis y Barbara Stallings (editores), CEPAL/LOM Ediciones, 2001.
Crecer con estabilidad. El financiamiento del desarrollo en un nuevo contexto internacional, José Antonio Ocampo (coordinador), CEPAL/Alfaomega, Colombia, 2001.
CLAROSCUROS, integración exitosa de las pequeñas y medianas empresas en México, Enrique Dussel Peters (coordinador), CEPAL/JUS, México, 2001.
Panorama de la agricultura en América Latina y el Caribe 1990-2000 / Survey of Agriculture in Latin America and the Caribbean 1990-2000, CEPAL/IICA, 2002.

Aglomeraciones mineras y desarrollo local en América Latina, Rudolf Buitelaar (compilador), CEPAL/ Alfaomega, Colombia, 2002.

Sociología del desarrollo, políticas sociales y democracia, Rolando Franco (coordinador), CEPAL/Siglo XXI, México, 2001.

Crisis financieras en países exitosos, Ricardo Ffrench-Davis (compilador), CEPAL/McGraw Hill, Santiago, 2001.

Una década de luces y sombras. América Latina y el Caribe en los noventa, CEPAL/Alfaomega, Colombia, 2001.

Desarrollo Rural en América Latina y el Caribe, Beatriz David, CEPAL/Alfaomega, Colombia, 2001.

Equidad, desarrollo y ciudadanía, Tomos I, II y III, CEPAL/Alfaomega, Colombia, 2000.

La distribución del ingreso en América Latina y el Caribe, Samuel Morley, CEPAL/Fondo de Cultura Económica, Santiago, 2000.

Inversión y reformas económicas en América Latina, Graciela Moguillansky y Ricardo Bielschowsky, CEPAL/ Fondo de Cultura Económica, Santiago, 2000.

Reformas estructurales, productividad y conducta tecnológica en América Latina, Jorge Katz, CEPAL/ Fondo de Cultura Económica, Santiago, 2000.

Reformas económicas, crecimiento y empleo. Los mercados de trabajo en América Latina y el Caribe, Jürgen Weller, CEPAL/Fondo de Cultura Económica, Santiago, 2000.

Crecimiento, empleo y equidad. El impacto de las reformas económicas en América Latina y el Caribe, Barbara Stallings y Wilson Peres, CEPAL/Fondo de Cultura Económica, Santiago, 2000.

Growth, employment, and equity. The impact of the Economic Reforms in Latin America and the Caribbean, Barbara Stallings and Wilson Peres, CEPAL/Brookings Institution Press, Washington, D.C., 2000.

Cinqüenta anos de pensamento na CEPAL, Tomos I y II, Ricardo Bielschowsky, CEPAL /RECORD/ COFECOM, Brasil, 2000.

Integración regional, desarrollo y equidad, Armando Di Filippo y Rolando Franco, CEPAL/Siglo XXI, México, 2000.

Ensayo sobre el financiamiento de la seguridad social en salud, Tomos I y II, Daniel Titelman y Andras Uthoff, CEPAL/Fondo de Cultura Económica, Chile, 2000.

Brasil uma década em transição, Renato Baumann, CEPAL/ CAMPUS, Brasil, 2000.

El gran eslabón: educación y desarrollo en el umbral del siglo XXI, Martín Hopenhayn y Ernesto Ottone, CEPAL/Fondo de Cultura Económica, Argentina, 1999.

La modernidad problemática: cuatro ensayos sobre el desarrollo Latinoamericano, Ernesto Ottone, CEPAL/JUS, México, 2000.

La inversión en Chile ¿El fin de un ciclo de expansión?, Graciela Mouguillansky, CEPAL/Fondo de Cultura Económica, Santiago, 1999.

La reforma del sistema financiero internacional: un debate en marcha, José Antonio Ocampo, CEPAL/ Fondo de Cultura Económica, Santiago, 1999.

Macroeconomía, comercio y finanzas para reformar las reformas en América Latina, Ricardo Ffrench Davis, CEPAL/Mc Graw-Hill, Santiago, 1999.

Cincuenta años de pensamiento en la CEPAL: textos seleccionados, dos volúmenes, CEPAL/Fondo de Cultura Económica, Santiago, 1998.

Grandes empresas y grupos industriales latinoamericanos, Wilson Peres (coordinador), CEPAL/Siglo XXI, Buenos Aires, 1998.

Flujos de Capital e Inversión Productiva. Lecciones para América Latina, Ricardo Ffrench-Davis-Helmut Reisen (compiladores), CEPAL/Mc Graw Hill, Santiago, 1997.

Estrategias empresariales en tiempos de cambio, Bernardo Kosacoff (editor), CEPAL/Universidad Nacional de Quilmes, Argentina, 1998.

La Igualdad de los Modernos: reflexiones acerca de la realización de los derechos económicos, sociales y culturales en América Latina, CEPAL/IIDH, Costa Rica, 1997.

La Economía Cubana. Reformas estructurales y desempeño en los noventa, Comisión Económica para América Latina y el Caribe. CEPAL/Fondo de Cultura Económica, México, 1997.

Políticas para mejorar la inserción en la economía mundial. América y El Caribe, CEPAL/Fondo de Cultura Económica, Santiago, 1997.

América Latina y el Caribe quince años después. De la década perdida a la transformación económica 1980-1995, CEPAL/Fondo de Cultura Económica, Santiago, 1996.

Tendências econômicas e sociais na América Latina e no Caribe/ Economic and social trends in Latin America and the Caribbean / *Tendencias económicas y sociales en América Latina y el Caribe*, CEPAL/IBGE/CARECON RIO, Brasil, 1996.

Hacia un nuevo modelo de organización mundial. El sector manufacturero argentino en los años noventa, Jorge Katz, Roberto Bisang, Gustavo Burachick (editores), CEPAL/IDRC/Alianza Editorial, Buenos Aires, 1996.

Las nuevas corrientes financieras hacia América Latina: Fuentes, efectos y políticas, Ricardo Ffrench-Davis y Stephany Griffith-Jones (compiladores), México, CEPAL/Fondo de Cultura Económica, primera edición, 1995.

Cuadernos de la CEPAL

86 *Industria, medio ambiente en México y Centroamérica. Un reto de supervivencia*, 2001, 182 p.

85 *Centroamérica, México y República Dominicana: maquila y transformación productiva*, 1999, 190 p.

84 *El régimen de contratación petrolera de América Latina en la década de los noventa*, 1998, 134 p.

83 *Temas y desafíos de las políticas de población en los años noventa en América Latina y el Caribe*, 1998, 268 p.

82 **A dinámica do Setor Saúde no Brasil**, 1997, 220 p.

81 *La apertura económica y el desarrollo agrícola en América Latina y el Caribe*, 1997, 136 p.

80 *Evolución del gasto público social en América Latina: 1980-1995*, 1998, 200 p.

79 *Ciudadanía y derechos humanos desde la perspectiva de las políticas públicas*, 1997, 124 p.

78 *Centroamérica y el TLC: efectos inmediatos e implicaciones futuras*, 1996, 174 p.

77 *La reforma laboral y la participación privada en los puertos del sector público*, 1996, 168 p.

77 **Labour reform and private participation in public-sector ports**, 1996, 160 p.

76 *Dinámica de la población y desarrollo económico*, 1997, 116 p.

75 *Crecimiento de la población y desarrollo*, 1995, 95 p.

74 *América Latina y el Caribe: dinámica de la población y desarrollo*, 1995, 151 p.

73 *El gasto social en América Latina: un examen cuantitativo y cualitativo*, 1995, 167 p.

72 *Productividad de los pobres rurales y urbanos*, 1995, 318 p. (out of stock)

71 *Focalización y pobreza*, 1995, 249 p. (out of stock)

70 *Canales, cadenas, corredores y competitividad: un enfoque sistémico y su aplicación a seis productos latinoamericanos de exportación*, 1993, 183 p.

69 *Las finanzas públicas de América Latina en la década de 1980*, 1993, 100 p.

69 **Public finances in Latin America in the 1980s**, 1993, 96 p.

68 *La reestructuración de empresas públicas: el caso de los puertos de América Latina y el Caribe*, 1992, 148 p.

68 *The restructuring of public-sector enterprises: the case of Latin America and Caribbean ports*, 1992, 129 p.

67 *La transferencia de recursos externos de América Latina en la posguerra*, 1991, 92 p.

67 **Postwar transfer of resources abroad by Latin America**, 1992, 90 p.

66 **The Caribbean: one and divisible**, 1994, 207 p.

65 *Cambios estructurales en los puertos y la competitividad del comercio exterior de América Latina y el Caribe*, 1991, 141 p.

65 **Structural changes in ports and the competitiveness of Latin America and Caribbean foreign trade**, 1990, 126 p.

64 *La industria de transporte regular internacional y la competitividad del comercio exterior de los países de América Latina y el Caribe*, 1989, 132 p.

64 **The international common-carrier transportation industry and the competitiveness of the foreign trade of the countries of Latin America and the Caribbean**, 1989, 116 p.

63 *Elementos para el diseño de políticas industriales y tecnológicas en América Latina*, 1990, 2ª ed. 1991, 172 p.

Cuadernos Estadísticos de la CEPAL

28 *Dirección del comercio exterior de América Latina, según la clasificación central de productos provisionales de las Naciones Unidas*, 2001, 532 p.

27 *América Latina y el Caribe: series regionales y oficiales de cuentas nacionales 1950-1998*, 2001, 136 p.

26 *América Latina y el Caribe: series estadísticas sobre comercio de servicios 1980-1997*, 1998, 124 p.

25 *Clasificaciones estadísticas internacionales incorporadas en el Banco de Datos del Comercio Exterior de América Latina y el Caribe de la CEPAL*, 1998, 287 p.

24 *Chile: comercio exterior según grupos de la Clasificación Uniforme para el Comercio Internacional, Rev. 3, y países de destino y procedencia, 1990-1995*, 1996, 480 p.

23 *América Latina y el Caribe: series regionales y oficiales de cuentas nacionales, 1950-1994*, 1996, 136 p.

22 *América Latina y el Caribe: dirección del comercio exterior de los principales productos alimenticios y agrícolas según países de destino y procedencia, 1970-1993*, 1995, 224 p.

21 *Estructura del gasto de consumo de los hogares en América Latina*, 1995, 274 p.

20 *Dirección del comercio exterior de América Latina y el Caribe según principales productos y grupos de productos, 1970-1992*, 1994, 483 p.

19 *América Latina: comercio exterior según la clasificación Industrial Internacional uniforme de todas las actividades económicas (CIIU)*

      Vol. I, Exportaciones, 1985-1991, 1993, 285 p.

      Vol. II, Importaciones, 1985-1991, 1993, 291 p.

18 *Clasificaciones estadísticas internacionales incorporadas en el Banco de Datos del Comercio Exterior de América Latina y el Caribe de la CEPAL*, 1993, 323 p.

17 *Comercio intrazonal de los países de la Asociación de Integración, según capítulos de la Clasificación Uniforme para el Comercio Internacional (CUCI), Rev. 2*, 1992, 299 p.

16 *Origen y destino del comercio exterior de los países de la Asociación Latinoamericana de Integración*, 1991, 190 p.

15 *América Latina y el Caribe: series regionales de cuentas nacionales a precios constantes de 1980*, 1991, 245 p.

Estudios e Informes de la CEPAL

Serie INFOPLAN: Temas Especiales del Desarrollo

Series de la CEPAL

Comercio internacional
Desarrollo productivo
Estudios estadísticos y prospectivos
Financiamiento del desarrollo
Gestión pública
Información y desarrollo
Manuales
Medio ambiente y desarrollo
Población y desarrollo
Política fiscal
Políticas sociales
Recursos naturales e infraestructura
Seminarios y conferencias
Temas de coyuntura
Macroeconomía del desarrollo
Estudios y perspectivas regionales
Informes y estudios especiales

Las publicaciones de la Comisión Económica para América Latina y el Caribe (CEPAL) y las del
Instituto Latinoamericano y del Caribe de Planificación Económica y Social (ILPES) se pueden
adquirir a los distribuidores locales o directamente a través de:

Publicaciones de las Naciones Unidas
Sección de Ventas - DC-2-0853
Fax (212) 963-3489
E-mail: publications@un.org
Nueva York, NY, 10017
Estados Unidos de América

Publicaciones de las Naciones Unidas
Sección de Ventas, Fax (22) 917-0027
Palais des Nations
1211 Ginebra 10, Suiza

Unidad de Distribución
CEPAL - Casilla 179 - D
Fax (562) 208-1946
E-mail: publications@eclac.cl
Santiago de Chile

Publications of the Economic Commission for Latin America and the Caribbean (ECLAC) and
those of the Latin American and Caribbean Institute for Economic and Social Planning (ILPES) can
be ordered from your local distributor or directly through:

United Nations Publications
Sales Sections DC-2-0853
Fax (212) 963-3489
E-mail: publications@un.org
New York, NY, 10017
USA

United Nations Publications
Sales Sections, Fax (22) 917-0027
Palais des Nations
1211 Geneve 10, Switzerland

Distribution Unit
CEPAL - Casilla 179 - D
Fax (562) 208-1946
E-mail: publications@eclac.cl
Santiago, Chile